Fundamentals of
Learning and Motivation

Fundamentals of Learning and Motivation

Frank A. Logan
University of New Mexico

William C. Gordon
University of New Mexico

Third Edition

ωcb
Wm. C. Brown Company Publishers
Dubuque, Iowa

Fundamentals of Psychology Series
Frank A. Logan, Consulting Editor

Contents

7   Principles of Learning: Negative Reinforcement 107

8   Response Persistence: Forgetting, Extinction, and Punishment 120

9   Generalization, Discrimination, and Differentiation 145

10   An Overview of Learning   163

11   Introduction to Motivation   166

12   Primary Motivation   179

13   Secondary Motivation   198

14   Incentive Motivation   211

15   Concluding Remarks   226

Preface

Psychology should be studied as a living subject matter; indeed, it is the most personal and intimate subject matter in the world. Nothing is quite so close to us as our own behavior, and nothing is quite so important to us as the behavior of others. In this spirit, the formal vocabulary, the technical details, and the objective procedures that form the heart of this book have been supplemented with liberal illustrations drawn from personal experiences common to most people.

Such illustrations are never so perfect as their laboratory counterparts simply because the natural environment is never so carefully controlled. The purer scientist may therefore be offended by the liberties we have taken in trying to make these principles of behavior real. While we apologize to these scholars, we nevertheless assert that there will be time enough for the serious student to sharpen the distinctions in later studies.

However, there is one danger in this approach that warrants forewarning. Students may be tempted to think that psychology is nothing more than simple, familiar common sense. Common sense as it has evolved through the generations is, admittedly, often good sense. But psychology, even in its present infancy, goes far beyond common sense—and even helps correct the misconceptions and fallacies that most people take for granted. The examples and illustrations in this book are intended to help students grasp the subject matter, to help them translate psychological concepts into personally meaningful contexts. But mastering the basic principles of behavior requires serious study and thought.

This book does not attempt to review conflicting data, ideas, and theories. Rather, it is a selective presentation meant to paint a consistent and integrated picture of the fundamental principles of learning and motivation. This is, we believe, a proper beginning—but it is only a beginning. Psychology is still a scientific infant; students should not be misled into thinking that we have yet achieved a complete understanding of behavior. On the contrary, they should be encouraged to recognize both the promise and the challenge of the study of psychology.

It is generally accepted that people are members of the animal kingdom. *Homo sapiens* is, to be sure, a unique species with a number of unusual characteristics, but at the same time, humans share some basic principles of behavior with many other animals. It is therefore not surprising that a complete understanding of human behavior must include principles that can be discovered by studying simpler organisms as well as principles that can be discovered only by studying humans. This book is therefore based predominantly on research involving such animals, and to a lesser extent, on people in very simple laboratory situations. Only under rigorously controlled conditions of deprivation and stimulation—controls usually not feasible when experimenting with humans—can the basic principles of behavior be clearly revealed. One purpose of this book is to describe some of these basic principles and to illustrate the ways in which research involving animals contributes to an understanding of human behavior.

The present edition of this book bears much in common with earlier editions; it covers the same basic topics and has the same general organization. This is as it should be because, according to their very nature, fundamental principles do not change. However, not only new principles but new perspectives on the old principles continually emerge from continuing experimental analysis, and our primary goal in this revision has been to reflect these more recent developments while retaining the enduring substance of well-established knowledge. We do not perceive the field of psychology as having changed in any dramatic, revolutionary sense, but continuing study has uncovered interesting new areas of research and developed new conceptualizations that enrich our understanding. In the process, some of the polarity that earlier characterized the field has been muted. Although the approach of this book is distinctly behavioristic in orientation, we have attempted to reflect a contemporary view.

At the end of each chapter is a list of examination questions. Each is followed by a brief analysis and explanation of the correct answer. These questions will be of greatest value to the student who thinks about the reasoning behind each question *before* reading the answer and explanation. Even the student who has carefully studied the chapter may find a few of the questions difficult; such questions are intended to approach a topic from a different angle, in order to enrich the student's understanding. In addition, many questions have been included in an attempt to correct misconceptions that some students retain. The questions do not exhaust the content of each chapter, and hence should not be relied upon exclusively for review. However, the degree to which students know and understand the answers should provide a reasonably good indication of how effectively they have studied.

We have also provided a glossary containing the technical terms used in this book. Knowing the definitions of these terms is only part of knowing their meanings. It is ultimately of greater importance to see the relationships between the terms and to recognize the situations to which they apply. Learning a theoretical subject such as this is, in large measure, learning to use the relevant vocabulary. Hence, the glossary can provide a convenient refresher as the student develops a more complete understanding.

The authors share equally the responsibility for the present edition. We have attempted to be our own critics and to reconcile our own differences before submitting the manuscript to publication. For the preparation of the manuscript itself, we are most gratefully indebted to Eleanor Orth, who worked far beyond the normal call of duty to convert our drafts into good copy. We are also indebted to our publisher for useful advice; but we are primarily indebted to students, whose encouraging comments and constructive criticisms have fostered the writing of this edition.

Frank A. Logan
William C. Gordon

Fundamentals of
Learning and Motivation

Introduction to Learning

The psychology of learning and motivation is one of the most vital and important topics of study. Certainly, knowledge about the other sciences, appreciation of the arts, and understanding of the humanities are also important aspects of a complete education, to say nothing of the great importance of the basic "three Rs." But if we want to understand behavior and individual differences in behavior, we must recognize that the most unique and critical property of living organisms is the capacity to learn.

Language is the principal feature that sets humans apart from other animals. Language, however, is *learned* in the form of talking, writing, and reading; thus, in effect, we *learn* to be human. At another level, most of our likes, dislikes, attitudes, opinions, beliefs, prejudices, superstitions, and personality characteristics are learned. In effect, then, we also *learn* to be unique individuals. Many other reasons exist for studying the phenomenon of learning. Most of our social dilemmas reflect learning. Mental illness, although sometimes resulting from neurological disorders, is often the result of learning maladaptive behaviors and failing to learn adaptive ones. Drug abuse, crime, overpopulation, and even political dishonesty, while caused by a variety of complex social factors, reflect in large measure the learning histories and the motivational conditions of the individuals involved.

But if learning about learning is the key to understanding such problems, it is also one of the keys to solving them. For example, it is now clear that Americans' heavy reliance on the private automobile, often driven at inefficiently high speeds, is rapidly depleting a limited natural resource and polluting the air we all must breathe. We have collectively learned these behaviors and must ultimately learn more sensible ones; hopefully, a better understanding of the fundamentals of learning and motivation can contribute to the solution of such problems.

In this book, we can only explore the most basic, fundamental principles of learning and motivation. These principles have been discovered mainly in the animal laboratory or by studying humans in relatively simple situations. Nevertheless, one should learn about learning not only as a formal laboratory science, but also with continual appreciation for the way these basic principles apply to the everyday behavior of people. For this reason, the technical concepts and principles in this book have been freely illustrated with typical situations to which they might apply. In short, our goal is to describe the fundamental principles of learning and motivation and to illustrate how these principles can be used in understanding (that is, in predicting and controlling) the learning and performance of personally important aspects of behavior.

In illustrating the principles of learning and motivation, we will frequently address you, the reader, in terms of experiences familiar to most college students. Our goal in doing so is to draw upon concepts you have already learned and to refine them with the knowledge gained from scientific study. For example, the last few paragraphs you have just read presume that you already know what "learning" is—as well you should, because you have been engaged in various kinds of learning activities throughout your life. Learning in the classroom has meant associating various names and facts with other names and events. For example, to the question, "Who was the first president of the United States?" you immediately associate the answer, George Washington. You probably also have learned other associations with George Washington, such as chopping down a cherry tree and crossing the Delaware. Long before you learned such associations, you learned that various combinations of letters on a page stand for certain words, and you learned to associate the answer, "six," to the question, "How many are two times three?"

Certainly your familiarity with learning is not restricted to the classroom, and the number of examples you could give of concepts you have learned would be quite impressive if it weren't for the fact that most other people your age have learned about as much during their lives. What we now need to do, as a prelude to learning more about the learning process and the factors that affect it, is to come more firmly to grips with the nature of learning itself. Although you already know, at least in a general way, what learning is, we need to bring the concept into clearer focus. The remainder of this chapter attempts to do just that.

What Is Learning?

As with many concepts that are primitive or basic to a discipline, the concept of learning is not easy to define. The reason for this is that we can never actually see "learning"; we can't point at it or even study it in isolation. The only way we can study learning is to study behavior, and we all know that behavior depends on more than learning. Learning is thus a hypothetical process, something inferred from observations of behavior.

Because we can't isolate learning directly, the most generally acceptable definition of learning is this: *Learning is a relatively permanent process resulting from experience with some task and reflected in a change in performance under appropriate circumstances.* This definition at least captures the conditions necessary to say that learning has occurred, and we would do well to reflect on the key words in it.

In this context, the word *process* implies change; an organism is somehow changed or different as a result of the learning experience. It would be valuable if we could answer the question "What is learning?" by turning to the biological bases of learning. What actually happens to an organism when learning takes place? This question is being actively researched by physiological psychologists, but at present, the knowledge is too rudimentary to be of much practical value. Still, these scientists believe that learning reflects a real biological change. Almost certainly, the nervous system—especially the brain—is involved in learning. In fact, it now appears that learning is largely a biochemical process, a modification of protein molecules within the brain. But until such knowledge has advanced considerably beyond its present stage, it is of greater practical value simply to accept learning as a hypothetical process and talk about it in behavioral terms.

Our definition restricts learning to processes resulting from *experience with some task*. Under most circumstances, "experience" involves actual practice on a task—that is, overtly or covertly engaging in the behavior to be learned—although in some situations, learning may occur as a result of observing the behavior of others. One can learn a great deal about driving a car, for example, by carefully watching an experienced driver perform the various aspects of that task; but to become truly skilled, one also needs to sit behind the wheel and practice those responses personally. Whether by observation or practice, learning requires exposure to the situation. While we can modify a person's future behavior through other means, such as surgical removal of certain parts of the body or the administration of drugs, changes in behavior resulting from such operations do not qualify as learning because they do not require experience with the task for their effects. Thus, alcohol affects one's driving ability, but the effect is obviously not of a learning nature.

We have said that learning is inferred only from a *change in performance*. This change may be a decrease or an increase in the performance of some behavior since we can learn not to respond just as we can learn to respond. Furthermore, we have stated that the change must be relatively *permanent*. Indeed, there are good reasons to believe that learning is completely permanent; at least, it can not be so temporary that it simply dissipates over a short period of time. Practicing a response may lead to reduced performance due to fatigue, or it may lead to increased performance due to improved strength and endurance, but these changes in behavior are not examples of learning because they are quickly lost through rest or disuse. Learning produces a persistent change in behavior that can not be attributed to other factors known to affect performance.

Finally, the requirement that the change in behavior occur *under appropriate circumstances* is intended to prevent us from making a logical error. It is true that we may correctly infer that learning has occurred from a relatively permanent change in behavior, but the opposite is not true: unchanged behavior does not necessarily mean that no learning has occurred. The circumstances simply may not be appropriate for the organism to display learning. As a student, you are surely familiar with the fact that even when you have learned a great deal about the material, you may miss an examination item because you can't remember the answer under the stress of taking a test. And in the laboratory, an animal may not perform because it is not properly motivated. Ultimately, therefore, we must observe a change in behavior to infer that learning has occurred, but in any particular test situation, the absence of such a change may or may not mean that learning has *not* occurred.

Hence, it is when we observe that experience with a task has produced a more or less permanent change in behavior that we may safely infer that learning has occurred. The psychology of learning is the scientific study of those situations and procedures that are known to produce such changes and the systematic analysis of the result of exposing organisms to them. Next, let's explore in greater detail the nature of what is learned.

What Is Learned?

Associations
One difficulty with understanding a psychological description of learning is revealed in the type of question often asked by beginning students: "Is yawning learned?" Of course, various students pose the same basic question in relation to other activities, ranging from stuttering to sleeping, from sighing to sexing, and from scratching to seeing. In essence, this type of question assumes that we can meaningfully divide behaviors into two types: learned and unlearned. This assumption is a hangover from earlier distinctions between nature and nurture. Does intelligence depend on heredity or environment? Is insanity inherited or acquired? Can learned characteristics be transmitted to one's children biologically?

Psychologists have learned the hard way that such questions are simply not good ones to ask. Untold time and expense have been devoted in the attempt to answer such questions and the invariable result has been that behaviors, when viewed dispassionately and objectively, *can not* be placed into two separate categories: those that are entirely innate or instinctive and those that are entirely the result of learning. The fact of the matter is that any organism's behavior is a joint product of both hereditary and environmental influences. The proper question to ask in this context, then, concerns the relative contribution of each factor to that behavior. That is, to what extent are *differences* in behavior due to genetic constitution or to experience? It is true that humans learn to talk, but it is equally true that we are the only species physically equipped for language as we know it. No amount of training will teach a rat to talk, and no human will talk a meaningful language unless taught to do so. We thus differ from other animals in part because we are equipped for language; we also differ from each other in part because of the language we have learned. Both nature (heredity) and nurture (learning) are indispensable.

Hence, one conceptual error implied by the question, "Is yawning learned?" is the notion that behaviors are either instinctive or learned. A second kind of difficulty with this question is the implication that behaviors are learned as such. The fact is that the psychologist does not mean by the term "learning" the development of the capacity for the actual muscular activity involved in a response. That is to say, although practice may be important in acquiring the ability to move the muscles of the body, such practice does not fall within the present meaning of learning. We are aware that you probably can not wiggle your ears, wrinkle your nose, or spread your toes unless you have practiced these movements. Learning in this sense is certainly important, but the psychology of learning assumes that the *ability* to perform a particular behavior is already available.

So too, the psychology of learning assumes that the organism is already capable of detecting and discriminating the relevant stimuli in the environment. The development of our sensory capacities is, in fact, very definitely dependent upon exposure in early infancy to an environment rich in sensory stimulation. It is now known that many learning difficulties in elementary school can be traced to a child's deprived environment, and that such difficulties, unless corrected through remedial instruction in the early grades, may be compounded into still greater problems later on. There thus exists a kind of pure perceptual learning that involves the development of the basic ability to detect and discriminate stimuli. But as with pure response learning, this topic is not within the scope of our interest.

We are not denying the importance of these primitive learning processes; we are simply assuming that the organisms with which we are dealing have already acquired the capacity to discriminate the requisite stimuli and to perform the requisite responses. Our topic, then, is *associative* learning, by which we mean forming a relationship between events as a result of experience. Learning can be viewed as an association between stimuli ($S - \rightarrow S$) or between a stimulus and a response ($S - \rightarrow R$), but in either case, learning is represented by the arrow, indicating a learned association between the events. If you see lightning and expect to hear thunder, learning is that expectation and not the sensory experiences themselves. If you then run indoors for protection, it is not the act of running itself that constitutes learning, but the association between the response (running) and the stimulus of being in a potentially dangerous situation. You may have learned some other response to the stimulus, such as lying flat nd, but again, learning is associating that response with the

se this distinction is often difficult to grasp initially, let's consider
familiar example. Suppose the question referred to earlier had
s talking learned?" Now, perhaps no student would ask that ques-
tio...cause it would appear that the answer is obviously "yes." But in the
sense in which we have defined the term, you do not learn to vocalize, that
is, to utter the sounds involved in talking. All infants babble and, in the
process, produce and practice all of the sounds utilized in their language-
to-be (plus additional sounds perhaps found in other languages, but not
later present in their verbal behavior). Why this is so and how practice
affects the subsequent availability of different sounds are interesting questions but are beyond the scope of study for the psychologist of learning.
Furthermore, perhaps as a result of babbling, the sounds of speech become
very distinctive from all other sounds so that, regardless of whether the
speech is intelligible, the sounds are channeled into a specialized speech
center normally located in the left hemisphere of the brain. But neither the
detection nor the production of speech sounds constitutes learning in the
sense in which the psychologist of learning uses the term.

However, we can say that talking is learned when we mean by "talking"
stringing together various vocalizations into patterns (words) and associating these words with meanings given them by the language system. The
word "cat" involves three sounds or phonemes roughly equivalent to the
letters of the word, and the ability to recognize and to produce these sounds
is assumed by the learning psychologist. Learning involves combining these
sounds (uttering the c sound is associated with uttering the a sound, which,
in turn, is associated with uttering the t sound) and associating the entire
chain of sounds with a physical stimulus—namely, a cat. Learning also
involves discriminating the word "cat" from other stimuli such as dogs and
fur coats, and associating the term with various nuances (a cat can be a
person who gossips about another). These associations illustrate the sense
in which the learning psychologist uses the term "learning."

Because this book is addressed toward the most basic, fundamental
principles, we will be concerned primarily with very simple associations.
However, it should be recognized that, in the case of complex human
learning, our simple associations become integrated into logical organiza-
tions of more complex, interrelated associations. For example, the equation
$2 \times 3 = 6$ is a simple association, as is $6 \div 2 = 3$. But we also learn
with further study that $6 \times \frac{1}{2} = 3$, that $3 \div \frac{1}{2} = 6$, and so on. The
processes involved in integrating simple associations into complex organi-
zations are poorly understood and are beyond the scope of this book. We
would be remiss if we contended that the basic principles that we will be
studying are in themselves sufficient to encompass the magnitude of your
knowledge about language or mathematics or any topic that you have

studied extensively. But in all cases, you began by learning simple associations; and learning about such associative learning is a good way to begin your study of the learning process.

Associations among Stimuli and Responses

Although most psychologists agree that learning can be viewed as an associative process, there is disagreement as to the nature of that process. The question is, "What gets associated with what?" There are a variety of subtle differences in the answers to that question, but these answers can be roughly grouped into two major alternatives.

One alternative is the S–R or *behavioristic* approach. According to this view, the association between a stimulus and a response is learned; learning represents an *acquired tendency to respond in a particular way when confronted with a particular stimulus*. You learn to step on the brakes of your car if the stoplight ahead turns red; you raise your hand if the teacher asks a question you think you can answer; you experience fear if a menacing dog appears. These illustrate motor, mental, and emotional responses that you learn to perform when exposed to particular stimuli. The behavioristic answer to the question, "What is learned?" is the associations between such stimuli and responses.

The other alternative is the S–S or *cognitive* approach. According to this view, the association between stimuli is learned; learning represents *an acquired tendency to expect the occurrence of particular subsequent events (S) whenever a particular stimulus occurs*. In the stoplight example, this approach holds that you did not learn blindly to apply the brakes when the light changes; rather you have learned the meaning of the red light, you have learned that an accident or an arrest might result from a failure to stop, and you utilize this knowledge in deciding what to do. The cognitive answer to the question, "What is learned?" is an association between such stimuli and subsequent events.

Traditionally, psychologists have adopted one or the other of these approaches and then attempted to apply it to all forms of learning. This is certainly admirable in the interests of parsimony and simplicity, but it has also led to a number of controversies that have turned out to be virtually fruitless. For example, after a rat has learned to run through a maze, the S–R theorist believes that the rat has learned a sequence of left and right turns, while the S–S theorist believes that the rat has learned a cognitive map of the maze including the location of the goal box. The flavor of the controversy can be captured if you reflect on your own behavior in going from one particular place to another. If you have to travel between two particular points frequently, you will probably realize that you unconsciously tend to take the same path every time. A man leaving his office may head for his usual parking lot even if he had to park elsewhere that day. The S–R theorist emphasizes such behavior to illustrate that learning is a sequence of responses. Yet you will also realize that, if your familiar path is blocked, you can readily chart a new path to reach your goal. The man who heads for the wrong parking lot will perhaps suffer a few moments of anguish that his car has been stolen, but he will probably soon recall that he parked in a different lot that day and take off in the appropriate direction. The S–S theorist emphasizes this kind of behavior to illustrate that learning involves knowing the spatial and temporal relationships in the environment. Each type of theorist is hard pressed to account for the behavior emphasized by the other.

For our purposes, it is not necessary to engage in the fine-grain details of this controversy, nor is there any need for the beginning student to "choose sides." This book has been written predominantly in the language of the S–R approach, but this is more a matter of convenience than conviction. In the first place, we can easily think of many familiar cognitive processes, such as attending, imagining, rehearsing, anticipating, and even thinking as being responses that we learn to make under appropriate circumstances. Furthermore, as we saw in discussing the nature of learning, we can only infer the occurrence of learning from a change in overt performance. This means that even if learning is basically an S–S association, the organism still has to do something—namely, emit learned responses.

Therein lies the crux of the difference. Behavior is not quite so automatic, so rigidly determined, if learning is of a cognitive nature. Figure 1.1 attempts to capture this difference graphically. According to the behavioristic view, the response is directly associated with the initial stimulus, and behavior reflects, more or less, precisely what is learned. According to the cognitive view, any of several responses may occur and behavior is an inadequate or, at best, imperfect reflection of what is learned. To be specific, consider again the situation where lightning has just struck nearby. This stimulus is represented by the initial S in figure 1.1. If you run inside (R_1 in figure 1.1), the behavioristic analysis would hold that running is the response you have learned to make in that situation. By contrast, the cognitive analysis would hold that you might, indeed, decide to run inside, but you also might decide to lie flat on the ground (R_2 in figure 1.1) or to stand under a tree (R_3 in figure 1.1—a very unwise choice!). According to the cognitive approach, you know that you are in a dangerous situation and make a decision based on your general knowledge about the best course of action. The behavioristic position is that you respond directly to the situation with the response you have learned to make in that particular set of circumstances.

There is really no need to favor one approach at the expense of the other. Certainly much of your everyday life is routine and largely automatic, and there are some times when you behave impetuously, impulsively, even recklessly. There are surely other times when you exercise restraint and stop to think before you act. However, a major problem with the

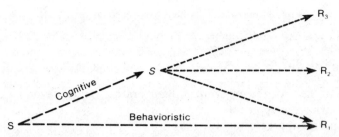

Figure 1.1 Diagram of the difference between the behavioristic and cognitive views of the nature of learned associations. The behavioristic view is a direct S-R association. The cognitive view is that the organism decides what to do based on knowledge (*S*) of the consequences of several courses of action.

cognitive approach is that no one has yet stated very clearly how you decide what to do once you have stopped to think about it. It is largely for this reason that we tend to favor the S–R terminology. The typical understanding of behavior is already largely cognitive and intuitive; we say we understand another person's behavior when it is something we ourselves would do. But it is too easy to assume that the result of engaging one's cognitive processes will be rational behavior; we must account for foolish, irrational behavior as well as for intelligent behavior, for maladaptive behavior as well as adaptive behavior, for bad behavior as well as good behavior. If you are addicted to caffeine, nicotine, alcohol, or any other drug; if you overindulge in food, sex, television, or daydreams; if you have trouble getting to bed on time, going to sleep, or getting up in the morning; if you are overly anxious about tests, dates, or speaking in front of an audience; if any of these examples are personally familiar, then you will agree that behavior is not always rational and guided by deliberate, conscious intent. One feature of the fundamental principles you will learn from this book is that they are quite indifferent as to the type of behavior under consideration. If you learn to understand them, these principles will help you when your intuitions fail.

Introduction to Learning

Multiple Choice Test Questions

1. Which of the following is *not* included in the basic definition of learning?
   a. It results from experience.
   b. It results in a change in performance.
   c. It is relatively permanent.
   d. It is directly observable.

2. The question, "What is learned?" is best answered in terms of:
   a. stimuli
   b. responses
   c. both stimuli and responses
   d. associations
3. According to the text, the experimental facts rather clearly favor:
   a. the behavioristic approach
   b. the cognitive approach
   c. neither the behavioristic or the cognitive approach
   d. either one or the other but not both

Multiple Choice Answers

1. (d) We can observe a person studying some material and then test to determine whether there has been a change in performance. But the concept of learning is hypothetical; it cannot be seen directly.
2. (d) Although stimuli and responses are involved in learning, the learning process itself is the association among stimuli and responses.
3. (c) Some experimental facts seem more amenable to a behavioristic approach, others to a cognitive approach. It is probable that some combination of the two actually takes place. But at present the facts do not clearly favor either approach.

True/False Thought Questions

1. When we say that learning is hypothetical, we mean that there is no biological basis for the process.
2. As defined in the text, learning does not imply a causal relationship between events.
3. We can infer that someone has learned only when we see an increase in that person's performance of some behavior.

True/False Answers

1. (False) Learning is hypothetical because we can only infer the process from changes in behavior. But we presume that these changes in behavior are the result of underlying biological changes that can be determined by scientific methods.
2. (True) The inference of causality is an interesting philosophical issue. In many cases, it may seem reasonable to think of a stimulus, such as the sight of a friend, as *causing* the response of extending a greeting. But learning was defined as an associative relationship; you have learned to extend a greeting to a friend, but whether and how you do so varies with the circumstances.
3. (False) Learning can be inferred from either increases or decreases in an individual's performance of some behavior. We can learn not to do something as easily as we learn to do something.

Essay/Discussion Questions

1. "We all know that behavior depends on more than learning." Identify some of the other determinants of behavior and discuss their relative importance in the context of any two specific activities.

2. "You do not learn muscular movements themselves according to the principles of learning described in this book." Describe methods that help people learn new movements, such as those involved in the hula or belly dancing. (Plan to return to this item in your final review to evaluate the relevance of the principles you have studied.)

References

What Is Learning?
*Beach, F. A. The descent of instinct. *Psychological Review*, 1955, *62*, 401–410.
*Kimble, G. A. *Conditioning and learning*. New York: Appleton-Century-Crofts, 1961. (Chapter 1)

What Is Learned?

Associations
*Kendler, H. H. What is learned? A theoretical blind alley. *Psychological Review*, 1952, *59*, 269–277.
Spence, K. W. Theoretical interpretations of learning. In S. S. Stevens (Ed.), *Handbook of experimental psychology*. New York: Wiley, 1951.

Associations among Stimuli and Responses
*Logan, F. A., and Ferraro, D. P. *Systematic analyses of learning and motivation*. New York: Wiley, 1978. (pp. 112–116)
Tolman, E. C. *Purposive behavior in animals and men*. New York: Appleton-Century-Crofts, 1932.
Watson, J. B. *Behavior, an introduction to comparative psychology*. New York: Holt, Rinehart & Winston, 1914.

---

*Suitable for additional reading by the beginning student. The others are written at a more technical level.

Elements in an Association: The Stimulus

2

Anything we notice in our environment qualifies as a stimulus. Lights, sounds, odors, even changes in one's temperature or balance are familiar stimulus events. Stated formally, we can define a stimulus as *any change in physical energy sufficient to cause an appropriate sensory receptor to respond.*

Such a definition gives the beginning student a good idea of which events are likely to function as stimuli and which are not. This definition is also consistent with the way we use the term *stimulus* in everyday conversation. We often use the term to mean some event that causes or prompts a response or action. But on closer examination, it becomes evident that this kind of definition has limited usefulness. For example, it is unclear from this definition how much of an energy change is *sufficient* to provoke a receptor response in a given situation. A dim light in a dark room may be a sufficient stimulus for a person who has been seated in the dark for a while, but it may not be sufficient for a person who has just entered the room from the bright sunshine. It is also difficult to determine in advance what an *appropriate sensory receptor* is for a given organism. Certain odors may be differentiated easily by a dog or rat, but may not be noticed at all by a human. In other words, our formal definition describes a stimulus in terms of its effects on sensory receptors. This means that to determine if an event is in fact a stimulus, we must try it out to see if it provokes a response. We are not able to determine the stimulus effectiveness of an event prior to its occurrence.

It may seem that this inability to identify an effective stimulus in advance would hamper our ability to analyze the effects of stimuli on behavior. Fortunately, this is not the case. In practice we can work within the confines of a *functional* definition: *A stimulus is any event that functions like previously identified stimuli in its effects on behavior.* This functional definition is not contradictory to the formal one; it simply states how we actually identify stimuli. If an event is indeed a stimulus, then it should have the effects on behavior that previously studied stimuli have had. If we encounter an entirely new event and are uncertain as to whether it is a stimulus for the organism being studied, we have to try it out. In doing so, we use well-established principles so that, if the event is a stimulus, we will find out that it is. Then, having once proven that the event is a stimulus for that organism, we may presume that it is a stimulus in most other situations we may wish to study. Although in the beginning this procedure is somewhat circular, it is an effective "bootstrap" procedure that enables us to determine what events qualify as stimuli for the organism we are working with.

In many cases, there are no problems with using the functional and formal definitions. We all know that the retina of the eye is the appropriate sensory receptor for changes in illumination, and we all know that the onset of a light in a dim environment is sufficient energy change for most organisms with normal vision. Those who work with rats know that they are color-blind and have relatively poor vision. Those who work with pigeons know that they have excellent color vision and remarkable distance acuity. But these facts had to be discovered first by trial and error.

Having discovered such facts, however, we can proceed to use our knowledge further in the analysis of behavior.

Events that ARE Stimuli

In this book, students are left pretty much to everyday knowledge to determine which events are stimuli. There is a simple reason for this: When dealing with fundamental principles such as those described in this book, we can stick largely to stimuli about which there is no question. However, to successfully apply these principles, some events that might not readily come to mind need also to be identified as stimuli. Some of the most important of these events are noted in this section.

Stimulus Decreases

When we speak of a stimulus, we usually think of the occurrence or onset of some event. A light shines, a tone sounds, or something touches the body. In general, then, we tend to conceive of stimuli as increases in energy.

However, it is important to recognize that decreases in energy are also effective stimulus events. The rising sun may increase the level of illumination and signal time to get up; but by the same token, the setting sun decreases the level of illumination and signals time to go to bed. Similarly, when you converse with another person, his or her words are stimuli to which you respond, but his or her cessation of talking is the cue that it is your turn to talk. The formal definition of a stimulus is stated in terms of a *change* in existing levels of energy. This serves as a reminder that decreases as well as increases in energy are effective stimuli.

Relationships

Organisms can respond not only to single, isolated events that are received by an appropriate receptor, but also to the relationships among such events. *Relationships* require the presence of two or more events for their identification; being to the left of, being brighter than, or being later in time are examples of relationships. A relationship cannot be a property of any single event. But relationships do function as behavioral stimuli.

One illustration of this fact is the "oddity" problem. A monkey, for example, is shown three objects, two of which are identical and the other different; a raisin is under the odd object. The objects themselves are changed from trial to trial, and the odd object is randomly placed in any of the three possible positions. Sometimes an object that is odd in one problem is matched in other problems, making another object the odd one. Monkeys are readily able to solve such oddity problems even though oddity is not a property of any single object. The relationship between objects defines the oddity and controls behavior in this kind of situation.

Context

Stimuli never occur in a void. Although an experimenter may be intent on presenting a single stimulus to a subject, that stimulus always occurs in the presence of background stimuli. Collectively, the background stimuli form what is called a *stimulus context*.

In analyzing the effects of stimuli on behavior, the role of the stimulus context cannot be ignored. The context in which a stimulus occurs helps to determine how we perceive that stimulus. For example, a white figure will appear to be very bright if superimposed on a black background. However, the same white figure will appear considerably less stark on a gray background. Likewise, a dog may perceive an unfamiliar person as a threat when that person enters the dog's territory. As a result, growling, snapping, and other aggressive behaviors may occur. The same encounter outside the dog's territory may well elicit playful or submissive behaviors from the dog. Thus, the effective stimulus in any situation really consists of the total stimulus complex, which consists of some combination of the primary stimulus and its context.

This principle is evident whenever we learn to perform a response within a given context. For example, assume that we have trained a rat to jump whenever a light appears and that this training always took place in one particular room. The appearance of light in a different room will normally result in little jumping. Furthermore, there will be little response if the rat is placed in the training room without any light stimulus. Usually, the learned response will occur with regularity only when the light is presented in the original training room. This suggests that neither the primary stimulus (light) nor the stimulus context (training room) is sufficient in itself to control the learned response. The jumping response is controlled by the entire stimulus complex in which learning occurred.

We can extend this fact to a variety of situations with which we are familiar. If you are to be tested over certain material in a specific classroom, it will be advantageous if at least some of your learning occurs in that classroom. The more dissimilar your study context is from the testing context, the less the likelihood that you will be able to remember what you have learned when in the test situation. Similarly, it is helpful for an athlete to practice under "game conditions" or for a musician to practice in the recital hall. All these advantages are due to the fact that context is an important stimulus in the control of learned behaviors.

One final point concerning context should be made. Stimulus context consists of *all* those background stimuli that we notice in a given situation. This includes stimuli inside an organism as well as stimuli in the external environment. Like external stimuli, internal stimuli exert some control over behavior. There is evidence to suggest that if animals are trained to respond after being given a certain drug, they will perform that response best when that same drug is readministered and, indeed, may not respond without the drug. This phenomenon is called *state-dependent learning*. Such research is often interpreted as showing that an internal stimulus context produced by a drug can exert control over a learned behavior.

Feedback

Responses produce stimuli. When you talk, you hear yourself talking; when you move your arm, you feel yourself move your arm; and if your body comes in contact with something, you feel it. Stimuli produced by responses are called *feedback stimuli* because part of the consequences of those responses are fed back into the nervous system to "tell" the organism what it is doing. Some responses produce very little in the way of distinctive feedback. For example, unless sickness or anxiety makes you salivate profusely, you may have little awareness that salivation occurs almost continuously. But there are many instances in which feedback is vital to understanding a behavior.

One rather dramatic illustration of the importance of feedback is the experimental situation in which auditory feedback from talking is delayed. In this experiment, a person talks into a microphone that records his voice on a tape recorder, and his recorded voice is replayed, after a fraction of a second delay, into earphones that effectively shield his ears from other sounds. When the person is instructed to try to read some material out loud, his reading ability is substantially affected. He stutters, reads in bursts, and talks louder and louder as if to drown out the feedback that is disturbing his performance. The fact is that we cannot talk normally without hearing ourselves talk, and if this feedback is distorted then our speech is also distorted. Similarly, walking requires that a person know where her feet are at each instant in order to make the next movement. People afflicted with tabes dorsalis, which involves a loss of sensory feedback from the muscles of the legs, are unable to walk—not because of lack of physical strength, but because they don't know when and how their legs are moving. In well-practiced skills like walking and talking, we are unaware of feedback. But even though the feedback has become automatic, its importance is inestimable.

Moreover, it is necessary to distinguish between two types of feedback effects: positive and negative. These terms refer to the *effects* of feedback and not to whether those effects are pleasant or unpleasant.

Positive feedback refers to instances in which the effect of the feedback is to increase the event itself. In effect, then, positive feedback feeds back upon itself to produce more of the same. A simple physical example of such feedback is when a microphone is placed before a loudspeaker that is connected to an amplifier. In this arrangement, any noise that gets into the system is amplified and fed back into the loudspeaker. A portion of this output is fed back into the microphone which pushes it through the amplifier and out again to the loudspeaker. This louder noise repeats the circuit, getting still louder, and so on, until the system has reached the limit of its capacity. The loud screech that occurs when performers inadvertently get their microphones on line with the loudspeaker is the familiar result.

A simple case of positive feedback in your own behavior is scratching an itch. Doing so increases the itch, leading to more scratching, leading to more itch, and so on, until you are aware that it is becoming painful and try some other form of relief. Similarly, starting to eat peanuts or popcorn increases the tendency to continue eating. In a behavioral context, when the effect of some response leads to an increase in that same response, it is called positive feedback. Mild forms of aggression may culminate in fighting because of the positive feedback that each person's behavior produces in the other person.

Negative feedback refers to situations in which the effect of the feedback is to reduce the event producing the feedback. Negative feedback thus provides a kind of error detection and correction mechanism. A familiar example in physical science is the guided missile homing in on a jet airplane. Such missiles are guided by the heat produced by their targets. Whenever the feedback indicates that the missile is off-target, the guidance system of the missile corrects the error and aims the missile back toward the target. In similar fashion, behavior is often guided by negative feedback. When you observe that your speedometer is above the speed limit, especially if you see a police car in your rearview mirror, you decelerate your car. The speedometer tells you what you are doing, and when what you are doing is in error, you respond by correcting it. At an even simpler level, when you hear yourself talking too loudly, you soften your voice; and when you feel yourself falling, you try to regain your balance.

The confusing aspect of the labels "positive" and "negative" is that, when applied to behavior, positive feedback may often be undesirable, while negative feedback may often be beneficial—quite the opposite of what the terms suggest. This confusion is compounded by an easy misinterpretation in an emotional context. For example, being told you are right is positive feedback because it increases the tendency to repeat your response and *not* because the feedback is pleasant; being told you are wrong is negative feedback because it reduces the tendency to make the response and *not* because the feedback is unpleasant. These labels, then, are neutral with respect to the desirability of the behavior or the pleasantness of the feedback itself. Positive feedback produces more of the behavior and negative feedback produces less of the behavior. In either case, one important determinant of our behavior is feedback.

Stimulus Representations

The effects of a stimulus on behavior do not necessarily end at the instant that physical stimulus terminates. Whenever a stimulus strikes an appropriate sensory receptor, the receptor transforms the physical energy of the stimulus into a nerve impulse. This nerve impulse is then relayed by way of nerve fibers to the appropriate areas of the central nervous system (that is, the brain and spinal cord). Our subsequent behaviors depend in large part on how the central nervous system interprets these impulses and on what impulses the central nervous system sends back to the muscles, glands, and organs. Thus, it is actually the nerve impulses initiated by a stimulus, and not the stimulus itself, that directly affect our behaviors.

These nerve impulses, representing stimuli within an organism, apparently continue for some time even after the stimuli they represent are terminated or gone. The representations that persist after the actual stimulus is gone are called *stimulus-memory traces*. The existence of such traces means that a stimulus need not be physically present in the immediate environment for the representation of that stimulus to remain capable of controlling behavior.

There are many familiar examples of a stimulus representation continuing to affect behavior for a time after the stimulus itself has ended. For instance, in dialing an unfamiliar telephone number, you may first look up the number in the directory and then dial. By the time the dialing response has begun, the actual stimulus (the printed number) is no longer in view. Sometimes, if you are using a pay phone or if you fumble the receiver slightly, several seconds may elapse between the termination of the visual stimulus and the dialing response. Still, in most cases you are able to dial the number correctly, since some trace of the original stimulus has persisted until the response could be made. Likewise, if someone suddenly stopped in the middle of a conversation and asked you to repeat their last sentence verbatim, you could probably comply even though you were not deliberately set to do so. Again, at the time of your response, several seconds would have elapsed since the stimulus controlling your response had ended. Apparently, however, the trace initiated by that stimulus remains long enough for a correct response to be made.

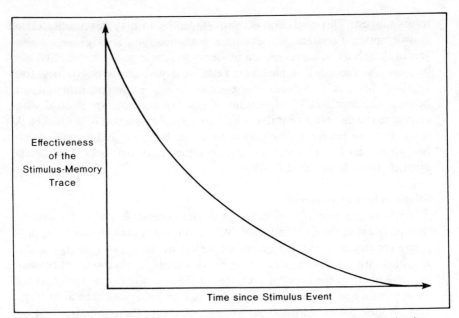

Figure 2.1 Graphic illustration of the assumption that an external stimulus event initiates a stimulus-memory trace within the organism that gradually loses its capacity for controlling behavior.

There is evidence that stimulus-memory traces also occur in animals. For example, monkeys and pigeons are quite adept at what is called a *delayed matching to sample task.* In this task, the animals are trained to observe a sample stimulus such as a red circle on a black background. They are then trained to select the sample stimulus from among a group of stimuli that includes the sample. After an adequate amount of training, animals are able to solve the problem of recognizing the sample even when several seconds elapse between the termination of the sample stimulus and the presentation of the group of stimuli that includes the sample. This suggests that some trace of the sample stimulus persists even after the visual sample is gone. Apparently, it is the trace that is present when the test stimuli are presented, and the animal matches the trace of the sample against the test stimuli to make a correct response.

We do not yet know how long these stimulus-memory traces persist. In some experimental situations, the duration appears to be only a few seconds; in other cases, traces appear to last for several minutes. However, it is commonly assumed that the ability of a trace to control behavior decreases as the time since the stimulus itself has ended increases. This assumption is represented graphically in figure 2.1. Why the effectiveness of a trace apparently decreases over time is not entirely clear. It may be that traces physically deteriorate or decay as time elapses. It may also be that traces can be disrupted or interfered with by new traces initiated by new stimuli. In other words, as time elapses, an organism is exposed to more and more stimuli and an old trace is increasingly weakened by new traces.

A variety of factors can prolong the effectiveness of a trace. Increases in the intensity or duration of the original stimulus presentation often result in longer-lasting traces. Also, humans may prolong traces by *rehearsing* the original stimuli verbally or subvocally. In any event, it is important to recognize that stimuli in the environment can be transformed into internal representations or traces that can control behavior even after the original stimuli are gone.

Events that ARE NOT Stimuli

There are numerous energy changes in our environment that do *not* qualify as stimuli. It is important to recognize these noneffective energy changes in order to explain why some events have little effect on behavior. Therefore, we will briefly discuss some of the more important situations in which energy changes do not become stimuli.

Energy Changes beyond Receptor Capabilities

The range of physical energies in nature greatly exceeds those to which our receptors are responsive. For example, our eyes can respond to light waves ranging between 360 and 750 millimicrons (nanometers) in length (a millimicron is one millionth of a millimeter), but light waves may be as short as a millionth of a millimicron and up to as long as a million miles. Similarly, our ears can hear sound waves as high as fifteen to twenty thousand cycles per second (hertz), but much higher frequencies occur and are audible to some animals. Even within the appropriate ranges, a change in energy may be too small for us to detect. Thus, we are not aware of everything that goes on in our environments.

By and large, these limitations are not of great behavioral significance. Most sources of light produce waves within the visible spectrum, and, although excessive exposure to longer or shorter waves may burn our skin or damage other organs of the body, these dangers are usually not present. The student of learning must be aware of the limitations of our sensory equipment, however, since only events that arouse a receptor can serve as stimuli in controlling behavior.

Energy Changes Undetected by Receptors

Another case when potential changes in energy may not be stimuli occurs when the receptors are not oriented toward the changes. Childish superstitions notwithstanding, parents do *not* have eyes in the back of their heads, and light energies that do not strike the eyes are not stimuli. When an organism orients its receptors so as to observe energy changes of possible relevance to behavior, we refer to it as a *receptor-orienting act.*

Receptor-orienting acts are most obvious in relation to vision, and some unlearned tendencies in this area may exist. For example, if a light flashes within our peripheral vision, we are more or less reflexively inclined to reorient our eyes to bring that light source into the center of the visual field for clarity. Receptor-orienting acts, however, may also be learned. We learn to glance into the other traffic lane before moving into it to make sure another car isn't already there. An animal learning a discrimination problem in the laboratory may have to learn to look at that portion of the stimulus containing the relevant cues before deciding what to do. In such cases, failure to learn the receptor-orienting act results in failure to solve the problem. Many children learning to read have difficulty discriminating the letters of the alphabet because they fail to orient their eyes toward the most distinguishing features of the letters.

Receptor-orienting acts apply to all sensory modalities, although they are least important in the case of hearing. You may see a dog cock his head to detect a distant sound better, but, by and large, sound energy affects us regardless of its direction. Discriminating between tastes requires that the substances be placed on the tongue. A person ironing may wet a finger and touch the iron to test its temperature; a cabinetmaker may run a finger along the wood to test its smoothness. An event is a stimulus only if an appropriate receptor is oriented toward it.

Constant Levels of Energy

Our sensory receptors respond to *changes* in energy as stimuli. However, if an energy change occurs and then the new level of energy remains constant for a period of time, we gradually become unaware of this new level of energy as an effective stimulus. This process is called *sensory adaptation.*

Familiar instances of sensory adaptation are numerous. When you first jump into an unheated swimming pool, you usually experience a noticeable decrease in temperature. This change in temperature is detected as a stimulus by the appropriate temperature receptors. However, if you remain in the pool and are continually exposed to the lower temperature of the water, you become unaware that the water is cooler than the surrounding air. Likewise, when you first enter a room you may detect a humming sound associated with an air conditioning or heating system. But, as you continue to be exposed to the same humming sound, your awareness of the sound as a stimulus decreases.

Sensory adaptation is a purely physiological affair. A receptor transmits impulses to the brain whenever there is a change in energy, and these impulses diminish over time. By and large, this is an adaptive feature. If an energy change occurs and the organism does nothing about it, the change is probably harmless or at least uncontrollable. Better, then, that the organism not be farther distracted by that energy while responding to other events in the environment. The process of sensory adaptation is of interest to the student of learning because associations are formed only with effective stimuli, and persisting energies eventually are not effective.

Attention to Selected Energy Changes

Our receptors are continually bombarded by a large number of energy changes that could qualify as stimuli. Although the process is still not well understood, it is apparent to us intuitively (and is increasingly being borne out by experimental data) that organisms selectively attend to certain aspects and ignore other aspects of a stimulus complex. You may be only vaguely aware of a conversation taking place among others at a party, but you can direct your attention to that conversation very quickly if you suddenly hear your own name mentioned.

There are unlearned tendencies to attend to certain stimuli. For example, size and intensity generally attract our attention. When looking at the evening sky, you may be attracted to the largest, brightest stars. When listening to an orchestra, you may be attracted by the loudest sounds being played. But attention is also learnable. After studying astronomy, you might be more interested in looking for constellations of stars regardless of their brightness. After studying music, you might be more interested in the counterpoint being played more softly than the melody. Attention is very much like a receptor-orienting act in that attending allows you to become aware of some stimuli while being unaware of others. But attention implies more than the overt act of orienting appropriate receptors toward a stimulus. Most of you have probably learned by now that it is quite possible to enter a classroom, train your receptors politely onto the lecturer, and yet hear or see nothing of what is said or done in class that day. In this case, you have performed a receptor-orienting act, but you have not attended to the stimuli toward which you oriented your receptors.

Since both humans and animals apparently can learn to attend to selected parts of a stimulus complex, the job of determining which stimuli actually control a given response becomes more complicated. We may say that learning is the association of a response with a stimulus. But the stimuli that gain the greatest control over a response are those to which an organism is oriented and, among those, the ones on which attention is focused. How attention presumably influences the process of learning an association will be discussed in more detail later.

The Emotional Value of Stimuli

Stimuli vary in their emotional value to the organism: some stimuli are pleasant and some are unpleasant. We can conceptualize a continuum of attractiveness. For example, you might find steak extremely attractive, chicken moderately good, hamburger more or less neutral, salmon distasteful but edible, and rattlesnake meat completely unacceptable. Clearly, we like some stimulus events, are indifferent to others, and dislike still others.

When the psychologist of learning uses the word *stimulus* (S) without a modifier, it is a stimulus he or she believes to be neutral for the organism. Lights and sounds of various kinds, for example, generally have no unlearned emotional significance to organisms. We use a number of more or less equivalent terms to describe *emotionally positive stimuli* (em+S): pleasant, satisfying, rewarding, attractive, and desirable are examples of such terms. We also use several terms to describe *emotionally negative stimuli* (em−S): for example, noxious, aversive, unpleasant, and undesirable. Examples of emotionally positive stimuli might include food, water, erotic stimulation, and the like; examples of emotionally negative stimuli include physical blows, electric shocks, and various other painful events.

Later, we will discuss the procedures used to determine whether stimuli have unlearned emotional significance for the organism. We also will show how originally neutral stimuli may acquire emotional value as a result of learning. For the time being, however, we shall rest the case on your personal familiarity with the fact that some stimulus events are desirable and some are undesirable, and with the fact that your own experiences provide a pretty good guide as to which are which.

Stimulus Satiation

Sensory adaptation is a physiological process leading to reduced sensitivity to persisting stimulus energies. A somewhat similar process can occur behaviorally. The term *stimulus satiation* is used to describe the phenomenon that repeated exposure to a stimulus temporarily reduces its attractiveness. An emotionally positive stimulus may lose some of its attractiveness as a result of overexposure, and a neutral stimulus may become somewhat aversive if it persists. These effects are only temporary but are nevertheless important to an understanding of the stimulus and its effect.

We generally do not like to listen to the same piece of music over and over again, no matter how much we like it. Although we may flatter a cook by saying we could eat the same meal every night, we actually prefer some variety. We may study a landscape for a long time, but we also like an occasional change of scenery. Whatever the nature of the stimulus, we seem to appreciate it more if we are exposed to it in moderation.

A comparable phenomenon can be demonstrated in rats. The apparatus used is a T-shaped maze (see figure 2.2) in which the lower stem is gray, and one of the arms is white while the other is black. The rats are first placed for a while in one or the other of the arms. It makes little difference whether, during this time, food is present or not; the rat is simply exposed to that arm. The rat is then placed in the gray stem of the T and allowed to run to whichever arm he prefers. Virtually all rats choose the arm opposite to that to which they have been exposed. They presumably become satiated with looking at either the black or the white during the exposure period and hence prefer the opposite arm.

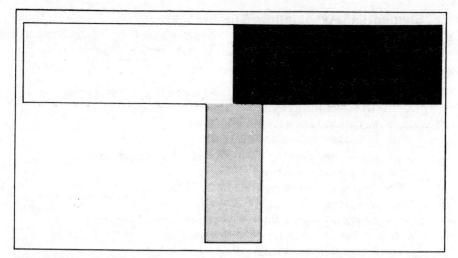

Figure 2.2 Design of a T-shaped maze used to study stimulus satiation. The left arm is white and the right arm black. Both are approached from the lower gray stem.

A number of variations of this type of experiment have been conducted, with the overall pattern of results consistently showing that organisms become *satiated* with recurring stimuli. In everyday language, we might say that the organism becomes bored. Research has not yet given a clear picture of the basis for this process, but we nevertheless need to recognize it in the study of learning. If, for example, we were trying to train a naive rat to turn to the right to get food in the maze in figure 2.2, and he happened to do so on the first trial, we might think that reward would make him more likely to turn right on the second trial. However, if we run the second trial immediately, the rat may turn left because of stimulus satiation on the right arm of the maze.

Accordingly, not only do persisting stimuli lose their effectiveness as stimuli as a result of physiological sensory adaptation, they also lose their attractiveness as a result of psychological stimulus satiation. The attention of an audience is never maintained over a long period of time by the drone of a monologue, no matter how interested the listeners may be in the subject matter. Television shows lose popularity if they habitually repeat the same format. It is well known that many children tire of school. There are certainly a number of reasons for this, but one obvious factor is that they confront the same teachers in the same rooms at the same time day after day.

This is not to say that some degree of regularity and consistency in one's environment is undesirable. Quite the contrary, an effective and efficient life requires that the environment be somewhat consistent and predictable. But we also become bored with the world if it is always invariant and perfectly repetitive. Hence the saying, "Variety is the spice of life."

Elements in Association: The Stimulus

Multiple Choice Test Questions

1. The stimulus-memory trace
   a. results from persisting reverberations in the environment
   b. decreases in strength over time
   c. has a constant strength over time
   d. increases in strength over time
2. Which of the following would provide the weakest stimulus?
   a. a decrease in energy
   b. no change in energy
   c. an increase in energy
   d. an energy level related to the sensitivity of the receptor
3. In a behavioral context, feedback may be
   a. a determinant of responding
   b. a consequence of responding
   c. both a determinant and a consequence of responding
   d. either a determinant or a consequence, but not both
4. Receptor-orienting acts and attention
   a. are fundamentally the same
   b. differ in their observability
   c. differ in their importance
   d. differ in their function
5. When we say that a stimulus has emotional value, we mean that
   a. we like it
   b. we don't like it
   c. either we like it or we don't like it
   d. in some ways we like it, in other ways we don't
6. Stimulus satiation is a
   a. physical process
   b. physiological process
   c. psychological process
   d. psychiatric process

Multiple Choice Answers

1. (b) Some energies, such as sounds, may persist a while by reflecting around the walls of a room or returning as an echo, but the stimulus-memory trace is a hypothetical process inside the organism that decreases in strength over time.
2. (b) Some receptors may indeed be more sensitive than others, but it is a change in energy (either an increase or a decrease) that constitutes a stimulus.

3. (c) Feedback is an inherent consequence of responding, but feedback stimuli may also determine subsequent responding. Hence, feedback may be viewed as a consequence of what you just did and a determinant of what you do next.
4. (b) The function of receptor-orienting acts and attention is to focus on the most relevant aspects of a complex array of stimuli. The main difference is that we can observe a person performing a receptor-orienting act, such as looking at a chalkboard, but we cannot observe whether the writing on the blackboard and the accompanying speech is holding attention.
5. (c) There are indeed stimuli about which we are ambivalent (or have feelings of both like and dislike), such as a person who is fun to dance with but who is otherwise a bore. However, ambivalence is not necessary for a stimulus to have emotional value; it is sufficient for us either to completely like it or completely dislike it.
6. (c) Stimulus satiation is perfectly normal. We tire of repetitive stimulation for no physical or physiological reason; the attractiveness of a stimulus is simply decreased by overexposure. This is one of the arguments sometimes made in favor of permitting uncontrolled display of pornographic material.

True/False Thought Questions

1. Psychologists have not been able to define stimuli to the point of being able to identify them in advance.
2. The stimulus-memory trace is hypothetical.
3. Visual stimulus-memory traces persist longer than other sensory modalities.
4. Turning off the lights is stimulating.
5. You would be more likely to remember the names of your high school friends at a class reunion than if you met them again individually.
6. Well-learned skills are performed without the need for feedback.
7. Positive feedback is desirable; negative feedback is undesirable.
8. Since we fail to detect persisting odors but continue to see persisting lights, sensory adaptation does not apply to vision.
9. Sticking your toe into a pool to test its temperature before diving in would illustrate a receptor-orienting act.
10. Attention is a learnable response.
11. An event must have positive or negative emotional value to be a stimulus.
12. Repetitive stimulation is undesirable; continual variety is essential.

True/False Answers

1. (True) Although we know that a stimulus must entail an energy change striking a suitable receptor, we have no way of identifying stimuli except by trying them out.

2. (True) Although we know that a stimulus may continue to exert control over behavior for some time after it occurs, the mechanism for this is not directly observable. Thus, the stimulus-memory trace is hypothetical.

3. (False) There is no evidence concerning the persistence of stimulus-memory traces in relation to any one modality. To date, there is no reason to believe that there are significant differences among the senses.

4. (True) Not only increases in energy but energy decreases are effective stimuli. Turning off the lights thus comprises a change in energy that constitutes a stimulus event.

5. (True) The faces of other high school friends constitute a background context for each individual friend. Learning their names was associated with this context. Hence, a reunion reestablishes more of the original context and facilitates memory.

6. (False) During the early stages in learning behavior sequences, we may have to consciously attend to the feedback in order to perform the next response; once well learned, these responses to feedback become unconscious. Nevertheless, the feedback stimuli remain essential in performing the behavior.

7. (False) In this context, the adjectives positive and negative have no bearing on the desirability of the feedback. Positive feedback leads to more of the same behavior, and negative feedback leads to less, regardless of whether the behavior is adaptive.

8. (False) Adaptation applies to all sensory modalities, including vision. The reason we are unaware of this principle in vision is that the eye, when fixed on one object, vibrates back and forth at a rate of 50 to 60 vibrations a second, constantly exposing unadapted receptors to what we are looking at. If an image is stabilized on the retina, it disappears.

9. (True) Receptor-orienting acts bring the receptors into contact with stimuli. Temperature receptors are located in the skin and must be exposed or oriented to the water.

10. (True) Attention may be reflexively attracted to particular aspects of the environment, but it is also a learnable response in that we can learn to attend to particular features of the environment.

11. (False) Stimuli may be arrayed in terms of their emotional value on a continuum from negative to positive. A large number of events are emotionally neutral, yet serve as effective stimuli with which responses may be associated.

12. (False) Although organisms become bored with repetitive stimulation, some degree of constancy and reliability is probably essential. The principle of stimulus satiation holds that some degree of variety is desirable.

Essay/Discussion Questions

1. "Everyone knows what a stimulus is." A dictionary gives two meanings for the word stimulus: (1) anything that rouses the mind or spirits; an incentive; a stimulant, and (2) any agent or form of excitation that influences the activity of an organism. Has this chapter favored one or

the other of these two meanings? Are they really two different meanings? (Plan to return to this question in your final review.)
2. "Variety is the spice of life." Might the optimal amount of variety depend on the activity or the person involved? Give some original examples of such potential differences and reflect on the ways these could affect interpersonal relations.

References

Functional Definition of Stimulus
Miller, N. E. Liberalization of basic S–R concepts: Extensions to conflict behavior, motivation, and social learning. In S. Koch (Ed.), *Psychology: A study of a science* (Study 1, Vol. 2). New York: McGraw-Hill, 1959.
*Skinner, B. F. *Science and human behavior.* New York: Macmillan, 1953.

Events that ARE Stimuli

Stimulus Decreases
*Logan, F. A., and Wagner, A. R. Direction of change in CS in eyelid conditioning. *Journal of Experimental Psychology,* 1962, *64,* 325–326.

Relationships
*Riley, D. A. *Discrimination learning.* Boston: Allyn & Bacon, 1968.

Context
*Logan, F. A. Specificity of discrimination learning to the original context. *Science,* 1961, *133,* 1355–1356.
Overton, D. A. Discriminative control of behavior by drug-states. In G. Thompson & R. Pickens (Eds.), *Stimulus properties of drugs.* New York: Appleton-Century-Crofts, 1971.

Feedback
*Mowrer, O. H. *Learning theory and behavior.* New York: Wiley, 1960.

Stimulus Representations
D'Amato, M. R. Delayed matching and short-term memory in monkeys. In G. H. Bower (Ed.), *The psychology of learning and motivation* (Vol. 7). New York: Academic Press, 1973.

---

*Suitable for additional reading by the beginning student. The others are written at a more technical level.

Events that ARE NOT Stimuli

Energy Changes Undetected by Receptors (Receptor-Orienting Acts)
Spence, K. W. *Behavior theory and learning*. Englewood Cliffs, N.J.: Prentice-Hall, 1960.
*Tolman, E. C. The determiners of behavior at a choice point. *Psychological Review*, 1938, *45*, 1–41.

Constant Levels of Energy (Sensory Adaptation)
*Blough, D. S. Animal psychophysics. *Scientific American*, 1961, *105*, 113.

Attention to Selected Energy Changes
*Mackintosh, N. J. Selective attention in animal discrimination learning. *Psychological Bulletin*, 1965, *64*, 124–150.
Wagner, A. R., Logan, F. A., Haberlandt, K., and Price, T. Stimulus selection in animal discrimination learning. *Journal of Experimental Psychology*, 1968, *76*, 171–180.

The Emotional Value of Stimuli
*Thorndike, E. L. *Animal intelligence*. New York: Macmillan, 1911.
Young, P. T. Affective processes in learning and motivation. *Psychological Review*. 1959, *66*, 104.

Stimulus Satiation
Dember, W. N., and Fowler, H. Spontaneous alternation behavior. *Psychological Bulletin*, 1958, *55*, 412–428.
Glanzer, M. The role of stimulus satiation in spontaneous alternation. *Journal of Experimental Psychology*, 1953, *45*, 387–393.

Elements in an Association: The Response

The term "response" is familiar in everyday conversation. We say that a student responds to a teacher's question, that a friend has not yet responded to our last letter, or that a race horse responds to the whip used by its rider. In each case, we use the term response to mean some action or movement. Although this is consistent with the way psychologists use the word, the formal definition used by psychologists is somewhat broader: *A response is any glandular secretion, muscle action, or other objectively identifiable aspect of an organism's behavior.* According to this definition, even minute actions occurring in isolated parts of an organism qualify as responses.

The critical component of this definition is the requirement that a response be *objectively identifiable*. In other words, there must be universal agreement that the response did or did not occur. The importance of such agreement can be seen in common experience. If two automobiles collide in an intersection that contains a traffic signal, at least one of the drivers is likely to claim that the other driver ran a red light. However, confirming that this response (running the light) did or did not occur may be difficult; the drivers will often disagree, as will different witnesses to the accident. Disagreements among the witnesses may be based on individual perspectives or views of the accident, different ideas as to what constitutes running a light, or even different interpretations of what the drivers were attempting to do at the moment the collision occurred. In any event, important decisions such as which driver will pay for damages and which driver is cited for a traffic violation may well depend on resolving the controversy concerning which driver performed a particular response.

Although such controversies are common in a court of law or in our interpersonal relationships, they cannot be tolerated in science. To avoid disagreements of this kind, the psychologist first defines precisely the type of action that will be labeled a response in a given situation. Then the experimenter establishes some criterion for how much of the defined action must occur before it qualifies as a response. Having defined the response and having set an objective criterion for the necessary degree of action, there can be no question as to when the response actually occurs. For example, to determine when an animal makes an error in running through a maze, the experimenter may put photoelectric beams at certain points in the incorrect paths. In this situation, the type of action that would be labeled an error (incorrect response) would be running into an incorrect path. The criterion for the actual occurrence of an error would be for the animal to run far enough into the incorrect path to break the photobeam.

Because such contraptions often are used to assure the careful measurement of responses, beginning students may view these experimental situations as contrived and artificial. The same students may argue that the behaviors we measure so carefully in the laboratory are unnatural and that we have sacrificed the study of real behavior to ensure reliable measurement of responses. This argument poses one of the most difficult challenges to the experimental analysis of behavior. It is true that laboratory conditions are somewhat unnatural; the very act of observing behavior may affect the behavior under observation. The dilemma confronting the behavioral scientist is illustrated clearly in the area of human sexual research. For years, our knowledge of the human sexual response was based on personal experience and the undocumented experiences of others. As a result, our knowledge in this area was often distorted and unreliable. To correct this situation, researchers began to observe and carefully measure sexual responses as they occurred in a laboratory setting. Under these conditions it became possible to measure even the most subtle behavioral and biological responses reliably. The question is, however, whether normal sexual responses can occur when a person is covered with recording electrodes and is performing under the scrutiny of a laboratory scientist. It is possible that, in an attempt to measure the sexual response objectively, we have actually altered the response we are measuring.

Although there is no perfect solution to this kind of dilemma, our choice of how to observe and measure responses must be governed by one principle: that the reliable measurement of phenomena is the cornerstone of any science. In other words, there is little value in collecting knowledge about anything unless the knowledge we collect is reliable. For this reason, most psychologists insist that responses be objectively identified and measured. The challenge to the researcher is to make these observations and measurements as unobtrusive as possible in order to preserve the integrity and naturalness of the behavior under observation. In research on learning, for example, organisms normally are familiarized with the experimenter, the apparatus, and certain unusual procedures prior to the beginning of any experiment. This familiarization minimizes the chances that the responses we measure during an experiment will be influenced by an organism's emotional reactions to these extraneous factors. Also, it is possible in most cases to record responses in such a manner that the organism is unaware that recordings are being taken. Still, psychologists recognize that behaviors that occur in the laboratory may not be identical to those that occur in a natural setting. Thus, we must always be cautious when we attempt to make statements concerning behavior in a natural setting based on conclusions we have formed in the laboratory.

The Status of Covert Behaviors

According to the definition given earlier, a behavior must be objectively identifiable to qualify as a response. This does not mean that responses must be directly observable to the naked eye. Responses such as changes in the electrical resistance of the skin or glandular secretions are hidden from view but can be objectively detected by appropriate instruments. Any behavior that can be monitored reliably fits the definition of a response.

On the other hand, it is apparent that there are a number of commonly accepted behaviors that do not qualify as responses according to our definition. We *think* when a problem is presented to us; we *attend* to important environmental changes; we *memorize* material for an exam; we *grow fearful* in the face of danger. Each of these reactions—thinking, attending, memorizing and fearing—are behaviors we are familiar with. In each case, however, these behaviors are hidden from even our most sophisticated instruments. We refer to such behaviors as *implicit* or *covert* activities to distinguish them from the explicit, overt responses that are measurable or observable. Since covert behaviors cannot be observed or measured, the occurrence of these behaviors cannot be objectively identified. It would be impossible, for example, for a group of observers to agree that a given individual is memorizing something at a given time. For this reason, covert behaviors do not qualify as responses, and must be thought of as hypothetical activities, or activities that we believe occur but which cannot be verified by objective observers. Yet nearly all of us, nonprofessionals and psychologists alike, feel that such behaviors are important in our adjustments to the environment. What, then, is the status of covert behaviors?

According to many researchers, although it is impossible to observe directly such actions as thinking or attending, it *is* possible to observe responses that indirectly reflect the occurrence of these activities. For example, if a person verbalizes a solution to a difficult problem, this measurable response (the verbalization) can be taken to indicate that thinking has occurred. Likewise, an increase in heart rate can be regarded as evidence that a fear reaction has taken place. In other words, measurable overt responses often are used as indirect measures of covert reactions. The idea is that we often make covert reactions to environmental changes and then make overt responses as a result of the covert reactions; we thus assume that the covert behaviors *intervene* between stimuli in the environment and observable responses. For this reason, covert behaviors are often labeled *intervening variables*. The act of learning, itself, is one such intervening variable, since we assess the occurrence of learning by measuring changes in overt responses.

Learnable Responses

It should be clear from our definition of a response and from the ensuing discussion which behaviors qualify as responses and which do not. However, even when a behavior qualifies as a response, it does not necessarily follow that the behavior is learnable or that it can be modified through experience.

There is presently some controversy concerning whether all responses are learnable in all situations. First, there is the question as to whether certain responses are learnable at all. For example, the pupil of the eye reflexively responds to an increase in light by contracting. It is uncertain whether, through learning, pupil contraction can become associated with stimuli other than light. Similarly, the body responds to a virus by producing antibodies. If we could learn to produce antibodies on cue, then we could prevent the spread of a virus with a minimum of medication. Yet, it is unknown whether we can learn this antibody-producing response.

Second, there is a question as to whether all learnable responses can be learned through the same procedures. Voluntary responses such as pressing a lever can usually be taught by rewarding the organism for making the response. Involuntary responses such as gland secretions, on the other hand, do not seem to be learned easily when using rewards. Although the possibility exists that different kinds of responses may be learned only through certain procedures, recent evidence suggests that this may not be the case. Some researchers, most notably Neal Miller, have had success in demonstrating that normally involuntary responses can be modified by rewarding changes in those responses. For example, the body apparently can be trained to maintain a low blood pressure through rewards for decreases in blood pressure. These recent findings suggest that earlier failures to demonstrate such learning may have been due to faulty experimental technique, not to the fact that different responses require different learning procedures.

A third question of great contemporary interest is whether all responses are equally likely to be associated with all stimuli. There is some evidence that organisms may be innately disposed to associate certain stimuli with certain responses, and may be disposed *not* to associate these same stimuli with other responses. Whether or not we can identify these kinds of innate dispositions in organisms, it does appear that particular sets of stimuli and responses are more easily associated than others. The classic example is *bait shyness* in rats. Rats that are exposed to a novel taste stimulus and that are then mildly poisoned will learn to avoid that taste stimulus. Apparently the response of becoming ill (produced by the poison) becomes associated with the taste stimulus in this situation. However, if rats are exposed to a visual or auditory stimulus before being poisoned, there is little indication that the animals later try to avoid the visual or auditory stimuli. Presumably, in this case the response of becoming ill does not become associated with the visual or auditory cues. This may seem to you to be a rather obvious finding. After all, if you have ever become ill after eating seafood in a candle-lit restaurant, it is likely that you would wish to avoid the taste or smell of seafood for a time. It is unlikely, however, that you would want to avoid future dinners in candle-lit restaurants. However obvious this finding may appear, the implications for the field of learning psychology are clear. All responses are not equally likely to become associated with a given stimulus.

These issues concerning the learnability of responses are raised as a caution to beginning students. However, as a rule, students will rarely be in error by adopting the hypothesis that *all observable responses are learnable and conform to the same principles of learning.* Certainly, such a conclusion applies to most responses we could mention. In the following section, we will identify some types of learnable responses in order to enlarge your understanding of that concept.

Not Responding as a Response

In our discussion of the stimulus, we noted that the stimulus is typically thought of as the onset of some event, but that the cessation of an event could also constitute a stimulus. A comparable reminder needs to be made with respect to responses. In short, *stopping or simply not making a response qualifies as a learnable response.*

In making that assertion, we could engage in a quarrel over definitions. Since an organism is continuously behaving, one could say that not making one response is logically equivalent to making some other response. When lost people stop calling for help because relief is in sight, they turn to other behaviors appropriate to their rescue. In the laboratory, a rat that does not run through the maze must be doing something else, such as exploring the start box, grooming, or sleeping. Nevertheless, it is convenient and informative to think of "not responding" as a learnable response.

We will encounter this notion most explicitly in the contexts of extinction and punishment. We learn not to do things for which we are punished even though we would like to do them, and we learn not to do things for which we are not rewarded even though we are freely permitted to do them. There are a variety of experimental findings that demonstrate these facts, but one particular study can serve as an illustration.

Suppose an individual rat is placed in a box that is barren except for a bar that can be pressed. Occasionally, the rat will press the bar during his meanderings. The rate at which the rat does so determines the *operant level* of the response; simply stated, an operant level is the rate at which a freely available response occurs if the consequences of that response are neutral (neither rewarding nor punishing). (Other examples of responses involving operant levels are the arbitrary movements your hands make while you're reading a book. You may make minute gestures such as clasping your hands or smoothing your hair, even though nothing is lost or gained by these responses.)

In the study with the rat, food is delivered to the rat periodically, provided he has not pressed the bar within the preceding minute. The occasional, perhaps accidental, bar presses that constitute the operant level are largely eliminated by this procedure. The rat is rewarded for keeping his paws off the bar, and he learns to do so. From another point of view, he is punished for pressing the bar by not getting the scheduled food delivery. But any way we look at it, this type of study demonstrates that not responding may be viewed as a learnable response.

Behavior Chains

Many of the responses that we have identified are actually sequences of movements strung together to accomplish a goal. We refer to an explicit sequence of responses as a *behavior chain*. A student doing homework must go to a desk or the library, locate the appropriate book, read it, take notes, and then, hopefully, study those notes and think about them; this is a long and complex behavior chain. A simpler chain is involved in throwing a baseball: The pitcher winds up, cocks his or her arm, and throws. One of the most conspicuous behavior chains is talking, whereby sequences of sounds and words are uttered in a pattern to convey an idea to a listener.

Behavior chains are important because, once fully integrated, they tend to run off as a single response. When you learn to type, for example, the early responses of typing letter by letter become hooked together into larger units; the word "reinforcement" may become so well integrated that it is difficult not to make a mistake when typing the word "reinforcing." (Similar errors happen in reading.) This integration is accomplished through feedback; the stimulus consequences of early responses in the chain elicit the later responses directly and automatically. A behavior chain constitutes a sequence of responses initiated by an external event, but the individual responses in the chain run off under the control of feedback stimuli. Once integrated, entire behavior chains may be treated as single responses.

Much of what we call learning is, in fact, the integration of little bits of behavior into longer behavior chains. Consider first a laboratory example. We wish to train a naive, hungry rat to press a bar to obtain food. This response involves a chain of simpler responses, such as approaching the bar, raising the forepaws, placing them on the bar, pressing down, releasing the bar, and going to the place where the food has been delivered. We teach a rat to do all this by a process called *shaping*, or successive approximations. This process is like the game, "you're getting warmer," and proceeds, in this case, something as follows: First, the rat is allowed to discover where the food is placed and that the click of the feeder signals another pellet of food. We repeat this until, wherever the rat is, he runs quickly to the feeder whenever he hears the click. Next, we wait until the rat happens to get near the bar; then we deliver a pellet. This causes him to run to the food cup, but then he is likely to return to the area near the bar. Next, however, we require that he be facing the bar before a pellet is given. Once he masters this, we require that he stand up, later that he place a paw on the bar, and still later that he press on the bar. In sum, the elements of the desired behavior chain are progressively built into his repertoire.

In some cases involving relatively simple responses that have a reasonably high operant level, the shaping procedure can be bypassed. A hungry rat may learn to press a bar to obtain food if he first learns the association between the sound of the feeding mechanism and the delivery of food, and then is left alone with the contingency that bar pressing produces food. Since the response will occasionally occur spontaneously, the resulting reward will lead to the acquisition of the response. In a somewhat similar manner, an inadequately trained parent quickly becomes a proficient caretaker by learning responses such as those involved in calming a distressed baby. This is called *autoshaping* because the response is acquired without any systematic training involving an experimenter or a teacher.

Shaping responses is somewhat of an art, but several guidelines can be helpful in shaping. The first and most important is that *a behavior chain is best learned in backward fashion*—in other words, the last element of the chain should be learned first. In the bar-pressing situation, we first taught the rat to approach the food cup when it clicked. The other two guidelines for shaping appear to be somewhat contradictory. On the one hand, *it is important to maintain a sufficient frequency of reward to keep the organism behaving*; if a standard is set for the next reward that the organism cannot yet achieve, the organism may stop doing the things it has already learned and will have to begin again. But on the other hand, *frequently rewarding a poor approximation of the desired response may cause the imperfect response to become so well learned that the organism fails to make progress beyond it*. Hence, the art of shaping is to give enough reward to keep the organism behaving, but not so much at any one step in the process that the organism becomes fixated there.

Now consider a parent teaching his or her child to hit a baseball. One parent spends hours pitching to the child and perhaps becomes exasperated at the child's lack of progress. Another parent ties a baseball to a string and hangs it from a reasonably high tree limb. The child first learns to hit the baseball while it is motionless—the last component of the behavior chain. Then the height of the ball is varied so that the child learns to aim the bat at the ball. Once progress is evident at this stage, the ball is swung by the parent from progressively further distances, and only after the child can hit the swinging ball does the parent begin throwing the ball, at first softly and then with increasing vigor.

In summary, many acts (such as a rat pressing a bar or a child hitting a baseball) can be broken down into a sequence of responses that must occur in a specified order. These responses may be integrated into a behavior chain through shaping and then may be treated as a single, unified response for that organism.

Response Dimensions

The old saying, "It ain't what you do, it's the way that you do it," is true of a wide range of everyday behaviors. Speaking effectively is not simply a matter of uttering meaningful words; it also involves saying those words with appropriate intonation and emphasis. The quarterback does not simply pass the football; he or she must throw the ball in the right direction and with the right force to reach the intended receiver. The fact that organisms obviously learn these things indicates that *quantitative dimensions or gradations of a response are learnable*. We will consider this fact more extensively in our discussion of correlated reinforcement, but one example here may be helpful.

Return to the situation of the rat pressing a bar to obtain food. The typical procedure requires only that the bar be pressed, but suppose we require the bar to be depressed for a particular duration to count as a response. If, for example, only responses that last between 0.2 and 0.4 seconds were rewarded, then bar presses that last less than 0.2 seconds or longer than 0.4 seconds simply do not count. Rats are remarkably adept at learning this quantitative property of a bar press and can put as many as 80 percent of their bar presses into the requisite interval. Indeed, rats are equally capable of putting their responses into another interval, say between 0.8 and 1.0 seconds. In similar fashion, rats can learn to press a bar with a particular force and to run at a particular speed.

Quantitative dimensions of a response are not only learnable when, as in the previous examples, successful performance demands it; they most probably are learned in any event. This can be shown most clearly by giving humans a simple task involving what is called paired-associates learning, in which each of several irregular patterns of light is associated with a particular number. The subject's task is to learn which number goes with which pattern; the patterns and their associated numbers are presented a number of times in different orders. The general procedure runs as follows: First, a pattern appears, then the subject responds with a number, then the correct number is shown for confirmation or correction. The subjects are divided into two groups that differ in only one respect. Both groups will hear a brief click just after the pattern is shown; the subjects are instructed to give their responses at the time of the click. For one group, this click occurs 0.75 seconds after the pattern, and for the other group, this click occurs 2.5 seconds after the pattern. In effect, one group is required to practice making their responses quickly and the other group practices responding more slowly.

After both groups have learned the associations, they can be tested in a slightly different task. Now they are instructed to respond to the patterns as fast as they can, with each response immediately producing the next pattern. This is similar to an arithmetic speed test to see how many patterns you can name in two minutes. The important result of this test is that the group that practiced fast can now respond significantly faster than the group that practiced slowly. One learns a speed of responding simply by practicing at that speed.

These and other studies collectively show that we can learn quantitative dimensions of a response when required to do so, and that, even if not required to do so, we learn the dimensions the way we practice the responses. There are many important practical implications to the fact that response dimensions are learnable responses. For example, if you practice in a slow, sloppy, or ineffectual manner, you are learning to perform in a slow, sloppy, or ineffectual manner!

Response Incompatibility

When two responses cannot be performed adequately at the same time, we call them *incompatible*. You cannot simultaneously raise and lower your arm, nor can you raise both feet off the ground while standing. The student cannot study and daydream at the same time, and, as the saying goes, you cannot have your cake and eat it too. Physical incompatibility may be only partial. For example, you can, to some extent, talk and eat at the same time, even if it is considered impolite to do so. You may find it difficult to tap on the table with each hand tapping at a slightly different beat. Less obviously, but perhaps more importantly, you probably cannot smile broadly while exercising an unhappy thought. Response incompatibility arises when the performance of one response partially or completely interferes with the performance of another response.

Some degree of response incompatibility may be learned. Although you can readily utter sounds with your mouth and make marks on a piece of paper with your hand, you will find it difficult to say "black" while repeatedly writing "white." A secretary cannot type accurately while listening to an irrelevant conversation, and you would find it difficult to count if someone else were saying random numbers aloud in your presence. When different responses have acquired different meanings for an organism, the occurrence of one may interfere with the occurrence of the other.

We will occasionally refer to response incompatibility throughout this book, but especially in the context of the elimination of responses. In general, the most effective technique for modifying behavior is to replace one response with an incompatible one. Since both cannot be performed at once, the earlier response may be precluded. One of the best examples of modifying behavior by substituting an incompatible response is the *systematic desensitization* technique used by clinical psychologists to control irrational fears. In this technique, clients are gradually trained to respond to a feared stimulus by relaxing. The idea of the treatment is that a relaxation response is incompatible with the fear reaction and should lead to the elimination of fear in that stimulus situation. The very fact that fear and relaxation are incompatible can have numerous important implications for our everyday lives. In the school setting, for example, anxiety concerning tests can prevent the relaxation necessary for efficient study and learning.

Response Satiation

We have learned that repeated presentation of the same stimulus leads to satiation or boredom with that stimulus. An analogous principle can be observed with respect to responses. Repeated performance of the same response leads to a reduced tendency to select it over other alternatives. This is called *response satiation*. As with stimulus satiation, this is a temporary state from which the organism recovers after a period of rest from the response.

You are certainly familiar with the notion of fatigue, but response satiation is more than that. Fatigue is a purely physiological process involving the muscles, just as sensory adaptation is a physiological process involving the sense organs. In contrast, response satiation is a psychological effect; organisms simply become tired of doing the same thing over and over again, even when the muscles are fully capable of continuing to perform that response.

Indeed, there is probably a close relationship between response satiation and stimulus satiation. We know that we become bored with repeated external stimuli. We also know that responses produce feedback stimuli. Response satiation could thus be viewed as a special case of stimulus satiation in which the stimuli involved are response produced. In effect, we become bored with feeling ourselves doing the same thing all the time.

The typical laboratory demonstration of response satiation involves *response alternation*. A rat might be run in a T-shaped maze, but be forced for a number of runs to turn to the right. If he is then given a choice, he is likely to turn left even if the act of turning right was rewarded. There is no reason to believe that there is any greater muscular fatigue involved in turning right than in turning left; rather, the rat is psychologically satiated with the former. The greater the number of forced turns preceding the opportunity to choose, the greater the likelihood of alternation. Also, the longer the time between the forced turns and the opportunity to choose, the lower the likelihood of alternation.

Response alternation is a very general phenomenon in situations involving choice. For example, if you try to write down a list of random numbers from zero through nine, you might be surprised to find that you simply cannot do so. In the first place, we all have favorite numbers and sequences of numbers. In generating a list of numbers rapidly so that you cannot deliberately avoid nonrandom tendencies, you may observe, for instance, that you wrote down more sevens than any other number or that you typically wrote a nine after writing a one. And you will note that you rarely repeat a number twice in succession, although, in a truly random sequence, you should repeat yourself one-tenth of the time. Organisms tend to alternate responses unless there are compelling reasons to repeat behavior.

Some psychologists have attempted to pose the question, "Which is stronger, stimulus satiation or response satiation?" This probably is not a valid question, but it does point out that both processes are present in most situations. If a rat is run in a T-maze in which one arm is black and the other white (figure 2.2), the response of turning to the right also leads to the black stimulus. If the rat alternates on the second trial, it is difficult to know whether he is alternating his response by now turning left or alternating the stimulus by now approaching white. It is possible, however, to pit the two processes against each other; for example, the arms can be reversed before the second trial so that the colors are on the opposite sides from the first run. The rat can then approach the different stimulus by making the original response (turning right), or he can make the different response, approaching the original stimulus (the black arm). In this particular context, rats are more likely to alternate the stimulus than the response; it is thus possible that stimulus satiation is the more basic process. However, we might also presume that if the stimuli were more similar and the responses more different, the opposite result might be obtained.

In any event, the psychological process of response satiation leads to alternation of behavior when repetition is not demanded. Even when repetition is desirable, we may vary our behavior simply for the sake of variety. The practical importance of this phenomenon should be apparent. Earlier we noted that students may become satiated with school because they are exposed to essentially the same stimuli day after day; now we are saying that the teacher may also become satiated with repeatedly making the same responses. A married person may become bored with a spouse whose behavior never varies; the spouse is equally bored with the same responses. The person who is bored with life is one who is obliged to keep repeating the same responses, who has developed stereotyped habits of repeating responses in spite of a basic tendency to alternate, or who has been punished for innovative behavior and who is now afraid to try new responses. In short, the bored become boring.

Elements in an Association: The Response

Multiple Choice Test Questions

1. The most critical component of the definition of a response is that a response is
   a. a glandular secretion
   b. a muscular action
   c. objectively identifiable
   d. related significantly to survival
2. The defining feature of a covert behavior is that it
   a. is some type of mental event
   b. cannot be observed directly
   c. occurs inside an organism's body
   d. is incompatible with overt behaviors
3. Systematic desensitization is based on the principle of
   a. response satiation
   b. response feedback
   c. response incompatibility
   d. shaping
4. Responses are considered incompatible when they interfere with each other
   a. physically
   b. psychologically
   c. physically and/or psychologically
   d. both physically and psychologically
5. The rate at which you cross and recross your legs during a lecture is a measure of
   a. attention
   b. operant level
   c. interest
   d. learning
6. The best strategy in shaping a complex behavior chain, such as learning to speak well, is to
   a. encourage the student by being generous in rewarding effort
   b. motivate the student by only rewarding excellence
   c. work forward from the initial components
   d. work backward from the terminal components

Multiple Choice Answers

1. (c) Many responses do not have survival value; for instance, a moth may fly into a fire. A response can be either glandular (for example, crying) or muscular (grimacing), but must be defined so that observers all agree that it did or did not occur.

2. (b) Any response that we assume occurs, but that cannot be observed reliably by others, is labeled a covert behavior.
3. (c) Systematic desensitization is an attempt to eliminate a fear response in an individual by training the person to make an incompatible response such as relaxation.
4. (c) The source of incompatibility may be physical, such as saying two different words at the same time; psychological, such as thinking about a subject and daydreaming; or a combination of both, such as uttering abusive language and concurrently thinking positive feelings.
5. (b) The rate of such a response might indeed vary with attention, interest, and learning. However, since there are no positive or negative external consequences of this behavior, its rate of occurrence is called its operant level.
6. (d) It is important to compromise between alternatives *a* and *b*, but focusing on either one alone is a poor strategy. Working backward from the terminal components of the chain is the best strategy for shaping.

True/False Thought Questions

1. The most critical component in the definition of a response is that a response must be objectively identifiable.
2. The most difficult challenge to the experimental analysis of behavior is to observe behavior without affecting it.
3. Autoshaping a response is most likely if the response has a low operant level.
4. If listening is considered a response, you may have learned how fast to listen to a lecturer.
5. When an organism learns to do something other than the behavior we are observing, we say it has learned the response of not responding.
6. The rate at which you fiddle with your pencil while sitting in a lecture would constitute that response's operant level.
7. A behavior chain becomes integrated through feedback.
8. When you reward a child for doing better than usual, even though the response is still imperfect, you are engaging in shaping.
9. A behavior chain should be shaped in backward order.
10. If you practice writing slowly, you will learn to write more quickly later.
11. Reading a book and closing your eyes are compatible responses.
12. Your tendency to alternate responses illustrates response satiation.

True/False Answers

1. (True) A response may be defined in many different ways in order to study its determinants. The only restriction is that the response be objectively identifiable.

2. (True) Any scientist runs the risk of changing the system he or she is studying simply by observing it. This is especially true of behavior since behavior is affected by the presence of others.

3. (False) Explicit shaping is required to train new responses that have low operant levels. (In other words, such responses would probably never occur without reinforcing successive approximations.) With simple responses that are already likely to occur (or have a high operant level), an organism can learn just by being exposed to the situation.

4. (True) Although you have probably not had explicit training in listening, you have practiced listening to lectures at different speeds. Still, you may find it difficult to listen if a new instructor speaks unusually fast (or slowly).

5. (True) Organisms are continually behaving, but we may safely lump together behaviors other than the one we are studying into the category of "not responding."

6. (True) Fiddling with one's pencil is a freely available response which occurs at some rate even without explicit reinforcement for doing so. This rate is the operant level.

7. (True) Each bit of behavior is always followed by another bit of behavior. It is when a sequence of these behaviors become integrated so that early ones tend to lead specifically to later ones that a chain is formed. This chain is integrated through feedback.

8. (True) Training is often best accomplished by rewarding successive approximations of a response, progressively raising the standards as performance improves.

9. (True) It is not always possible to get to the end of a behavior chain without going through earlier components. When it is possible, learning is facilitated if the terminal components are learned first and earlier components are added progressively.

10. (False) Practice does not necessarily make perfect. Indeed, practice can be detrimental if done in an imperfect manner simply because one learns what one practices.

11. (False) Responses that cannot be performed simultaneously are incompatible. Sometimes one can shift back and forth between incompatible responses without too much impairment of either, but one cannot read with closed eyes.

12. (True) We are endowed with two diametrically opposed tendencies: habit, or the tendency to repeat responses, and satiation, or the tendency to alternate responses. However, while the former is permanent, the latter is transitory. In combination, these tendencies maintain adjustment to a stable environment while ensuring some exploration for better responses.

References

The Status of Covert Behaviors
*Hill, W. F. *Learning*. New York: Harper & Row, 1977. (Chapter 1)

Learnable Responses
Garcia, J., McGowan, B. K., and Green, K. R. Biological constraints on conditioning. In A. H. Black & W. F. Prokasy (Eds.), *Classical conditioning II*. New York: Appleton-Century-Crofts, 1972.
*Miller, N. E. Learning of visceral and glandular responses. *Science*, 1969, *163*, 434–445.

Behavior Chains
Lashley, K. S. The problem of serial order in behavior. In L. A. Jeffress (Ed.), *Cerebral mechanisms in behavior*. New York: Wiley, 1951.

Response Dimensions
Notterman, J. M. Force emission during bar pressing. *Journal of Experimental Psychology*, 1959, *58*, 341–347.
Skinner, B. F. *The behavior of organisms*. New York: Appleton-Century-Crofts, 1938.

Response Incompatibility
*Wolpe, J., and Lazarus, A. A. *Behavior therapy techniques*. New York: Pergamon Press, 1966.

Response Satiation
Montgomery, K. C. "Spontaneous alternation" as a function of time between trials and amount of work. *Journal of Experimental Psychology*, 1951, *42*, 82–93.
Montgomery, K. C. A test of two explanations of spontaneous alternation. *Journal of Comparative and Physiological Psychology*, 1952, *45*, 287–293.

*Suitable for additional reading by the beginning student. The others are written at a more technical level.

Principles of Learning:
The Anticipatory Response

4

We have characterized learning as an associative process that takes place inside an organism, but that also gives rise to an observable change in behavior. Specifically, we have said that learning is reflected by a *relatively permanent change in behavior* as a result of prior experience. One of the major objectives of the psychology of learning is to formulate scientific laws or principles that govern this learning process. In other words, we attempt to derive general statements that describe the condition under which relatively permanent changes in behavior occur. In this chapter, we will begin to discuss these learning principles. As a matter of convenience, we will continue to speak as though learning involves stimulus–response associations. As we describe the learning process in more detail, however, it will become evident that many instances of learning could be viewed just as readily as resulting from a stimulus–stimulus association or some other type of association.

Probably the most fundamental rule of learning is the *principle of the anticipatory response*. This principle can be stated as follows: *Whenever a stimulus more or less regularly precedes any response in time, that stimulus will come to elicit that response sooner than it would normally occur.* Figure 4.1 illustrates the anticipatory response principle schematically. The passage of time is read from left to right, with each S–R pair in the figure indicating a separate occurrence of a stimulus and response together. The occurrence of each stimulus somewhere in time is symbolized by an S and the fact that a response occurs somewhat later in time is symbolized by the location of each R. The principle of the anticipatory response states that this temporal sequence of the stimulus followed by the response is sufficient to produce learning; in other words, there is a relatively permanent change in the time that elapses between stimulus and response. The response soon begins to occur shortly after any presentation of the stimulus. We assume that the change in response occurrence results from an association between the stimulus and response, so that the stimulus, which originally was unrelated to the response, begins to elicit the response regularly. This *learned* association is symbolized in the figure by the dashed arrow connecting the S and the R.

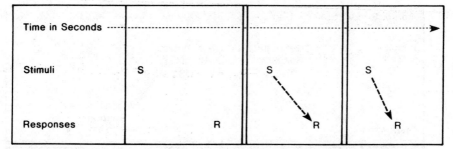

Figure 4.1 Schematic illustration of the principle of the anticipatory response. The passage of time is read from left to right, with the breaks in that line representing longer intervals. Here and subsequently, environmental stimuli are represented along one line and responses along a second line. If a response occurs following a stimulus, they become associated, as represented by the dashed arrows. This association moves the response forward so that it occurs sooner after the stimulus.

Classical Conditioning

The principle of the anticipatory response can be observed in virtually any learning situation regardless of the procedures used. Whenever we arrange for a stimulus to occur prior to a response, this arrangement will usually ultimately result in the elicitation of the response by that stimulus. This principle can be seen most clearly, however, in a *classical conditioning paradigm* (experimental procedure). Consider the following situation. A young child accidentally steps on her puppy's tail and is quickly bitten. The bite produces pain and a startled reaction on the part of the child. A few days later the child, undeterred, attempts to determine if the puppy's hair is firmly attached or removable. Again the child is bitten and again the response to the bite is pain and a startled reaction. After only a few more such episodes, the child's parents begin to notice that whenever the puppy enters the room the child is in, the child reacts as if startled or surprised. The sight of the puppy, which previously had produced no special reaction in the child, has begun to elicit a startled reaction because the sight of the puppy has regularly preceded the startled reaction in time. This situation is, in essence, an example of a classical conditioning paradigm.

In classical conditioning, we arrange for a response to occur by confronting an organism with some stimulus that naturally or reflexively produces that response. In our example, the startled response in the child was produced naturally by the dog's bite (a stimulus). The stimulus used in classical conditioning to produce a reflexive response is called the *Unconditioned Stimulus* (hereafter symbolized as the US). The response that is automatically produced by the US is called the *Unconditioned Response* (UR). These stimuli and responses are termed *unconditioned* because the connection between them is *reflexive* or *unlearned*.

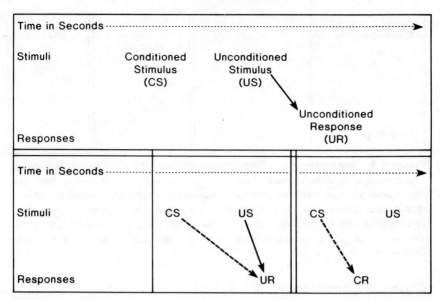

Figure 4.2 The top panel represents the arrangement of stimuli in a classical conditioning paradigm and the automatic occurrence of a response when the unconditioned stimulus is presented. The bottom panel illustrates the learned connection between the conditioned stimulus and the response that begins to occur prior to the unconditioned stimulus.

According to the anticipatory response principle, once the occurrence of a response is arranged, it should be relatively easy to get some unrelated stimulus to begin to elicit that response. All we would need to do is to arrange for the unrelated stimulus to occur prior to each occurrence of the response. This is precisely what is done in a classical conditioning procedure. A stimulus that is originally unrelated to the UR is presented regularly prior to each occurrence of the response. This is accomplished by presenting the unrelated stimulus or *Conditioned Stimulus* (CS) just prior to each occurrence of the unconditioned stimulus. (This arrangement is illustrated in the top half of figure 4.2. Note that the solid arrow connecting the US and UR in the top half of figure 4.2 indicates that the connection between the US and UR is unlearned or reflexive.)

According to the principle of the anticipatory response, this arrangement should eventually cause the CS to begin to elicit the response, and this elicitation should be reflected by the occurrence of the response prior to its regular time of occurrence. Such is the case in classical conditioning. Once the CS and US have been presented together a number of times, the UR begins to occur prior to, rather than following, the presentation of the US. Once the response begins to occur before the US, we assume that the response is being controlled by the CS due to a learned association. At this point, the response is called a *Conditioned Response* (CR) rather than a UR. This process is illustrated in the bottom half of figure 4.2. The dashed

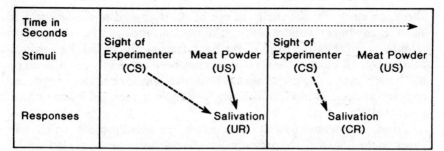

Figure 4.3 Classical conditioning within Pavlov's experimental paradigm.

line between the CS and the response in this figure indicates that the connection between the CS and the response is a *learned* connection.

Probably the best known illustration of classical conditioning comes from the work of Ivan Pavlov, who is credited with the discovery of this conditioning procedure. Actually, Pavlov's original interest was to determine the way salivation contributes to digestion; in fact, he earned a Nobel prize for his studies of the digestive process. In pursuing this interest, Pavlov developed a technique for the precise measurement of salivation in dogs. This technique involved inserting a small tube through a dog's cheek and attaching the tube to a salivary gland. Then, to produce measurable amounts of salivation, Pavlov presented the dogs with meat powder. Pavlov discovered as his experiments progressed that the dogs began to make the salivary response prior to the presentation of the meat powder. Stimuli that had always preceded the presentation of the meat powder (for example, the appearance of the experimenter) had begun to produce or elicit salivation.

In essence, Pavlov had inadvertently arranged his experimental situation so that an association could be formed between unrelated stimuli and the salivation response. In the terms we used earlier, the meat powder served as a US that regularly produced a salivation response (the UR). Stimuli that regularly preceded the occurrence of the salivation UR (such as the odor or sight of the experimenter) served as CSs. These CSs came to control the salivation response and began to elicit that response sooner than usual. Once salivation began to occur before the presentation of the US, the response became a CR rather than a UR. The concept of classical conditioning as demonstrated by Pavlov's experiment is illustrated in figure 4.3.

After this original experiment, Pavlov dedicated much of his remaining life to the study of classically conditioned associations. Pavlov's procedure is often referred to as classical *appetitive* conditioning, because the US he used to elicit a response was an emotionally positive stimulus. Most of the related research done in this country has involved classical *defense* conditioning, because the US that elicits some UR has often been a somewhat aversive event. Consider an electric shock, for example. If applied to the cheek, an electric shock elicits an eye blink. If applied to the fingertip, a shock elicits finger withdrawal. And if applied to the arm, a shock elicits minute sweating in the palm of the hand (technically called the galvanic skin response). Each of these responses has been classically conditioned in human subjects, using a wide variety of stimuli, and each of these responses appears to occur almost automatically whenever the appropriate CS is presented.

It may seem obvious that if, for instance, a signal precedes an electric shock to the fingertip, the person will withdraw his or her finger before the shock. But there are two ways to show that this anticipatory response does not represent simply a *voluntary* defense reaction. One way is to attach the shock electrodes to the fingertip itself so that the shock cannot be avoided by anticipatory responses. Even so, the subject will start to withdraw his or her finger before the shock. The second approach is simply to instruct the subject to attempt not to make an anticipatory response. Even a fully informed subject, voluntarily trying to restrain the response, cannot do so. The tendency to make anticipatory responses in the classical conditioning situation is automatic.

Variations in Classical Conditioning

There are various learning procedures that do not, for one reason or another, fit our description of classical conditioning, but that still can be viewed as simple variants of the classical conditioning paradigm. Two of these variants, temporal conditioning and higher-order conditioning, will be discussed briefly. Note that the anticipatory response principle is evident in both of these learning paradigms.

Temporal Conditioning

The major difference between classical and temporal conditioning is that in temporal conditioning the US occurs on a regular schedule *without* being preceded by an explicit CS. For example, food powder (a US) might be delivered into a dog's mouth once every ten minutes. As usual, the food powder will naturally elicit the UR of salivation. However, after several presentations of the food powder, the salivation will begin to occur prior to each food powder presentation. Thus, we could say that the dog begins to anticipate the delivery of food by salivating just before food presentation, even though no explicit CS ever precedes the salivation response. This sequence of events is illustrated in the top panel of figure 4.4.

The question that arises in temporal conditioning is how the UR begins to occur prior to each US when there is no explicit CS present to elicit this early response. Remember that according to the anticipatory response principle, a response begins to occur earlier than normal only when it has been preceded regularly by some stimulus event. To answer this question, we

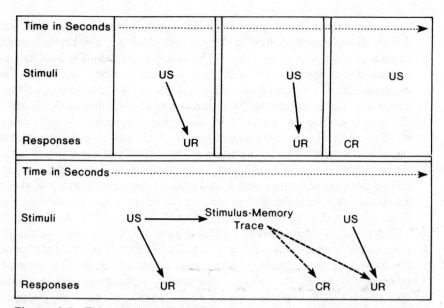

Figure 4.4 The top panel illustrates that when a US occurs at a constant interval, the UR begins to occur earlier in time until it actually precedes the US occurrence. The bottom panel illustrates one interpretation of this phenomenon in which each US results not only in a UR but also in a stimulus-memory trace. The trace serves as a CS that precedes the next US and that elicits the response prior to the next US occurrence.

must return to the concept of a stimulus-memory trace. It is assumed that any stimulus event initiates impulses within the nervous system, and that these impulses persist for some time after the event. Also, it is assumed that the strength of these impulses, or the strength of the stimulus-memory trace, decreases over time. One way to explain the occurrence of temporal conditioning is to assume that each occurrence of the US results not only in a UR, but also in a stimulus-memory trace that persists until the next US is due to occur. In essence, the stimulus-memory trace initiated by one US acts as a CS that regularly precedes the next US and UR. This interpretation is illustrated in the bottom panel of figure 4.4. We assume that the salivation response in our example begins to occur earlier than usual because its occurrence is controlled by the stimulus-memory trace of a preceding US.

Temporal conditioning occurs in the natural environment as well as in the laboratory. Normally, humans have clocks or watches to help time regular events such as the rising of the sun or the eruption of Old Faithful; but even in the absence of timepieces, we are capable of relying on the "biological clock" within each of us. For example, if we regularly retire at about the same time, we typically find that we begin to yawn and become drowsy at about that time, even without looking at a clock.

Temporal conditioning *can* also lead to maladaptive forms of behavior. An excellent laboratory illustration involves placing a monkey in a small chamber for an hour or so a day. The monkey is restrained in his chair by a chain that hangs from the ceiling and that is attached to his collar. The monkey is given an unavoidable electric shock at regular intervals, perhaps once every minute; when the shock occurs, the monkey tends to yank at his chain as if aggressing against it in his plight. The chain-pulling response is, effectively, an unconditioned response to the shock, even though the response does not affect the duration or the intensity of the shock. True to the nature of temporal conditioning, chain pulling begins to occur shortly before the next scheduled shock and usually persists through the shock. The situation is then changed so that shocks will no longer be administered if the monkey does not pull the chain but will be administered if he does. Chain pulling is thus actually *punished* by shock, but for several months the monkey will continue pulling on the chain every minute, thus producing the aversive electric shock. By temporal conditioning, he first becomes trapped into pulling the chain in anticipation of the shock and thereafter fails to learn that simply leaving the chain alone would solve his dilemma.

By and large, however, temporal conditioning is adaptive. Whenever events occur regularly in the environment, time (or better, biological processes changing over time in the form of the stimulus-memory trace) is a sufficient stimulus to enable us to learn that regular event and to begin to respond prior to its occurrence.

Higher-Order Conditioning
In the pure form of classical conditioning, the unconditioned response is reflexively or naturally elicited by the unconditioned stimulus. A dog naturally salivates when presented with food, and you naturally blink your eye in response to a puff of air or withdraw your finger from an electric shock. Classical conditioning procedures may also be used when, in the position of the unconditioned stimulus, we substitute a stimulus that automatically produces a response because of prior learning. For the anticipatory response principle to pertain, all that is necessary is that some response occur, regularly preceded by a CS. The response need not be produced reflexively, but may be produced by a stimulus which has come to elicit the response through prior conditioning. When the stimulus employed to elicit the UR is one that the subject has previously associated with that response, we call the procedure *higher-order conditioning*.

For example, in one experiment, Pavlov first trained dogs to salivate to a tone by presenting the tone before food delivery. Once salivation had been conditioned to the tone, he then presented a light before the tone and omitted the food. Since the dogs salivated to the tone because of prior conditioning, they now began to salivate in response to the light. This is called higher-order conditioning, not because any new or more complex concepts are involved, but simply because the UR occurs as the result of prior conditioning rather than as the result of a natural reflex.

This procedure as described cannot continue very far, nor do the effects last for very long. This is because, in the absence of food, the dog soon stops salivating to the tone (the original CS) and then also stops salivating to the light. The procedure described is necessary to demonstrate the phenomenon of higher-order conditioning, but we can presume that it also occurs in situations where the US is never removed. If, for example, a light precedes a tone, which in turn precedes food, the salivation first becomes conditioned to the tone, and then, while the response is maintained by the subsequent food, the response becomes further conditioned to the light. You may think of this as *higher-order conditioning* because the CS is further removed from the controlling US, and its capacity to elicit the CR depends on intermediate stimuli to bridge the gap.

There are many examples of higher-order conditioning in everyday life, but perhaps the simplest and most common involves the use of language. A child first learns, for example, that the word "good" is followed by pleasant events and hence responds to the word with emotionally positive reactions. New responses can then be taught by calling them good; the emotions conditioned to certain words can be transferred by higher-order conditioning. This provides another example of the anticipatory response principle.

Facts of Conditioning

The preceding section contained a description of various contexts in which the principle of the anticipatory response can be observed. Let's return to the particular instance of classical conditioning and illustrate some of the more detailed facts concerning this phenomenon.

The Course of Conditioning

Thus far, we have stated simply that when two stimuli are paired, the response originally elicited only by the second stimulus will eventually be elicited by the first. At this point, we should be more specific about the course of conditioning over the repeated occurrence of such sequenced events.

An idealized representation of the course of conditioning is presented in figure 4.5. Along the baseline is plotted the number of times that the stimuli have been paired. Along the ordinate, or y–axis, is plotted some measure of the strength of the conditioned response, such as its amplitude or frequency. The graph shows that, with repeated pairings, the tendency to make the CR increases gradually and steadily until it reaches an upper limit (the asymptote) at which it levels off and continues at that strength. *Conditioning is thus cumulative; each trial builds upon the strength already gained through previous experiences.*

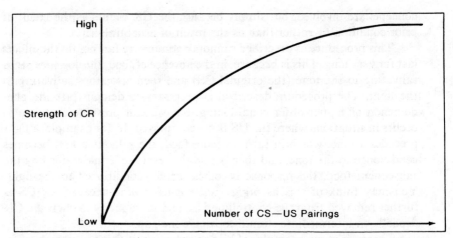

Figure 4.5 Illustration of the course of conditioning. Some measure of the strength of the CR, such as the number of drops of saliva recorded before the food is delivered, increases over repeated pairings of the CS and US.

Note that figure 4.5 does not contain any actual numbers to indicate either the number of trials or the strength of the CR. The reason for this omission is that the precise course of conditioning depends upon a number of details of the experimental arrangement. Although one can generally represent the process of learning a CR according to the course depicted in the figure, there are variables that affect both the rate of learning and the final level attained.

Let's consider a few of these factors to indicate the variety of more specific information available about classical conditioning. First, the more intense the stimuli, both CS and US, the faster the conditioning tends to proceed and the higher the level it finally reaches. The stronger the stimulus preceding the US, the more likely the occurrence of the conditioned response, and the stronger the unconditioned stimulus, the stronger the anticipatory response. Hence, *the measure of the strength of conditioning depends upon the intensity values of the CS and the US.*

A second important variable concerns the distribution of trials, or the frequency with which the CS and the US are experienced. As has been found in most forms of learning, *distributed practice produces fastest learning.* When trials are massed so that they follow each other very quickly, the number of experiences necessary for conditioning to reach its upper limit is greater than when the occurrences are distributed more widely over time.

There are a number of more specialized factors that affect conditioning; one recent discovery of interest may be mentioned. In the conditioning of the human eye blink, imagine as the conditioned stimulus a printed word flashed on a screen in front of the subject. The word "blue" is a better CS if it is presented in blue letters rather than red letters, and vice versa. The incongruity of seeing a word that means one color actually presented in another color reduces that word's effectiveness as a stimulus.

Accordingly, the course of conditioning varies according to a number of specific situational details, a large number of which have been experimentally identified and studied. For our purposes, however, the principal fact of interest is that conditioning is a cumulative process. Even under the optimal conditions, it usually takes at least several trials before maximal conditioning has been achieved.

Interstimulus Interval

One variable that affects conditioning and that is of special interest and importance is the time period separating the CS and the US. Thus far, we have simply described the conditioning procedure as one in which one stimulus precedes another, but the temporal arrangement of these stimuli is important in determining the eventual level of conditioning.

A large number of studies have investigated the effect of this factor, and the overall pattern of their findings is roughly depicted in figure 4.6. This figure refers to the limit or eventual level of conditioning after a large number of trials, as determined by the interstimulus interval between the CS and the US. There are several details to note from inspection of this figure.

First, *there is an optimal interstimulus interval,* on the order of one or a very few seconds. That is to say that conditioning will achieve the highest final level if the CS precedes the US by an interval of time in that range, while either longer or shorter intervals produce less effective conditioning. There is also an upper limit to the length of the interstimulus interval at which effective conditioning can be attained. The actual value of this upper limit is not yet fully understood; for some responses of some organisms, if the US follows the CS by more than several seconds, conditioning cannot be attained, while in other cases, separations of up to five minutes or more have been found to be effective. Since the details of this concept have not yet been fully worked out, the most we can conclude at this time is simply that conditioning is less effective when there is a separation of more than a few seconds between the CS and the US. We might also safely conclude that if the interstimulus interval becomes too long, conditioning will not occur.

When the interval between the CS and US is very short, conditioning is less effective. When the interstimulus interval is zero (meaning that the CS and the US occur simultaneously), there is *no* conditioning. Furthermore, there is no conditioning if the US precedes the CS; that is, if the stimuli are presented in reverse order. In short, conditioning only occurs if the CS precedes the US by some period of time; conditioning will be maximal if that separation is from one to a few seconds; and conditioning will be progressively poorer the longer the interstimulus interval is beyond that range.

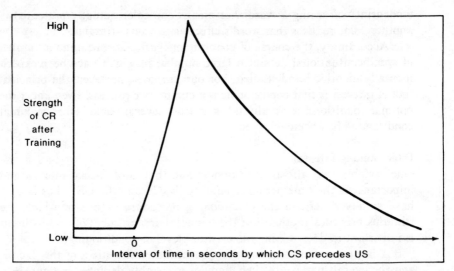

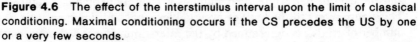

Interval of time in seconds by which CS precedes US

Figure 4.6 The effect of the interstimulus interval upon the limit of classical conditioning. Maximal conditioning occurs if the CS precedes the US by one or a very few seconds.

We will encounter various applications of these facts in later contexts; but to anticipate one, consider the parent who wishes his or her child to learn *not* to make a certain response. The mechanism of punishment the parent might use involves conditioning the child to experience certain emotional responses as a result of punishment for the undesirable behavior. This is an instance of classical conditioning, and the fact that conditioning is optimal when a very brief amount of time separates the CS and the US implies that punishment will be more effective if it is applied very quickly after the undesired response. If punishment is applied too long after the offense, punishment will be much less effective simply because the conditions fundamental to the process of classical conditioning have been weakened.

Latency of the Conditioned Response
The latency of a response is the time separating the presentation of the stimulus and the occurrence of the response. In the context of classical conditioning, latency is the time after the CS is presented and before the CR begins to occur. Thus far, we have simply stated that the CR becomes anticipatory and begins to occur before the US and hence occurs closer to the CS. The question is, when in fact does the CR tend to occur?

The answer to this depends upon the interstimulus interval. The latency of the CR can be observed to decrease progressively over the early trials of conditioning—the CR becomes anticipatory and occurs earlier and earlier. At an intermediate stage of conditioning, the CR may occur almost immediately after the occurrence of the CS. With continued practice, however, the CR gradually moves back until it is occurring just before the scheduled time for the US. For example, if the CS–US interval is one second, then a well-established CR will occur about three-quarters of a second after the CS and, hence, about a quarter of a second before the US. If the CS–US interval is longer, perhaps three seconds, then the well-established CR will occur about two and one-half seconds after the CS and about one-half second before the US. In short, *the latency of the CR adjusts to the CS–US interval so that the CR begins to occur just slightly before the US*. It may precede the US by slightly longer when the CS–US interval is longer, but a very well-established CR may actually occur almost coincidentally with the US.

With continuous responses, the CR may begin rather longer before the US and then increase in strength as the US approaches. For example, when you are forewarned of something that frightens you, such as having to perform before a group of people, you may at first begin to experience only a moderate degree of fear. However, this fear builds up as the performance draws near and reaches a maximal level as you walk upon the stage. The conditioned response tends not to occur until almost time for the US; but once started, the CR builds up progressively as the US approaches.

Generalization

When a response has been conditioned to a particular stimulus, we find that somewhat similar stimuli tend also to elicit that response. The more similar the new stimulus is to the original CS, the greater the tendency for this to occur. These facts are depicted, again in idealized form, in figure 4.7.

Along the vertical axis of figure 4.7 is plotted some measure of the strength of the CR. The baseline represents the difference between the original CS (the one initially paired with the US) and other stimuli similar to it. The strength of the original CR is represented above zero. Observe that, as other stimuli grow increasingly different, the strength of the CR decreases. In the laboratory, for example, we might condition a response to a tone of 1,000 hertz; thereafter, a tone of 2,000 hertz would also elicit a response, but a weaker response than was elicited by the original 1,000 hertz tone. Similarly, a tone of 4,000 hertz would also elicit the response, but the response would occur at a still weaker level. To take an everyday example of generalization, a child who is bitten by a dog associates fear with that dog. Similar dogs will also elicit fear; the more similar they are to the original dog, the stronger the fear response will be. If this happens early enough in the child's development, the child may even be afraid of fur coats or teddy bears. These represent generalizations of the fear response that was first conditioned to a particular dog.

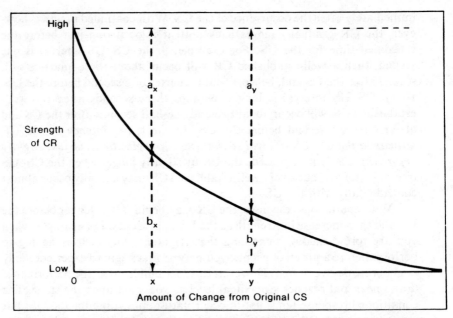

Figure 4.7 Graphic illustration of stimulus generalization. Response strength is first built up to the original CS, as shown above the zero point. This produces some generalized response strength to similar stimuli, as shown by the height of the solid curve above the baseline (generalized response to x, shown by the dashed arrow, b_x, is greater than that to y, shown by b_y). This also means that there is a loss in response strength resulting from a change in the stimulus, as shown by the difference between the generalized response strength and the response strength to the original CS (the generalization decrement to x, shown by a dashed arrow, a_x, is less than that to y, shown by a_y).

Some of the more important phenomena concerning generalization will be described in a later chapter. But first, we should recognize one confusing aspect of the way psychologists speak about generalization. On some occasions, we wish to stress the fact that a *new* stimulus will also elicit a conditioned response. The example we have given illustrates the concept of the *generalized response:* The child is afraid of a fur coat after being bitten by a dog. On other occasions, however, we are more interested in the fact that a change in the situation leads to a weakening of the response. For example, you might train a child how to behave in front of company and then be distressed because a new person is not treated properly. In this case, there is a lower response level than you would like, and we speak of this as a *stimulus generalization decrement*. The principle is the same in either case—a similar stimulus elicits a somewhat weaker response than originally obtained—but when we refer to generalization, we sometimes stress the fact that a response does occur to a different stimulus and we sometimes stress the fact that a response is not as strong to a new stimulus as to the original stimulus.

It is worthwhile to reflect for a moment on the biological significance of the principle of stimulus generalization. By and large, similar stimuli are best responded to in similar ways. Having learned how to respond to one teacher, employer, date, or friend, somewhat similar responses to similar people are usually appropriate. Were it not for this principle, we would have to relearn how to behave every time there was a slight change in any situation. Accordingly, an enormously valuable and important property of learned associations is that they generalize to similar stimuli. On occasion, however, stimulus generalization is not appropriate. Not all teachers are, in fact, alike; nor are all employers, all dates, or all friends. Discrimination learning arises simply because generalized tendencies to respond are not always adaptive.

In any event, one of the most fundamental principles of learned behavior is that of stimulus generalization. Learning to respond to one stimulus imparts a tendency to respond similarly to similar stimuli. The more similar the stimuli, the greater the tendency to generalize.

External Inhibition

Perhaps the best way to introduce the topic of external inhibition is in the context in which it was first discovered. Following his initial discovery of classical conditioning, Pavlov explained the procedure to his assistants and sent them off to different rooms to condition salivation in dogs. In time, one assistant came to Pavlov, enthusiastically claiming that he had also succeeded. Pavlov returned with him to the room where the dog was, and the assistant proudly presented the CS to the dog—who then failed to salivate! Only after this experience had occurred a number of times did Pavlov realize the problem: The dog had learned to salivate without Pavlov present; when the scientist was in the room, the situation was different, and the conditioned response did not occur.

The principle of *external inhibition* holds that if something unusual or unexpected occurs before or during the presentation of a CS, the CR is weaker or fails to occur. In the laboratory, there are many examples of external inhibition. If a heavy truck happens to pass by shortly before the presentation of a CS, the CR may be reduced. If an electric failure causes the lights to flicker unexpectedly, the next trial may be affected. One example of external inhibition may be familiar to you if you have become conditioned to going to sleep at a particular time each night. If there is an unusual news event, a severe storm, or anything out of the ordinary developing, you may look at your watch and discover that it is several hours past your normal bedtime before you feel sleepy.

The principles necessary to understand external inhibition have already been introduced. First, the *context* of a stimulus is part of the stimulus to which a response is learned; second, a *generalized response* is weaker to a changed stimulus than to the original one. External inhibition is a reflection of both of these principles; an unusual event changes the context of the

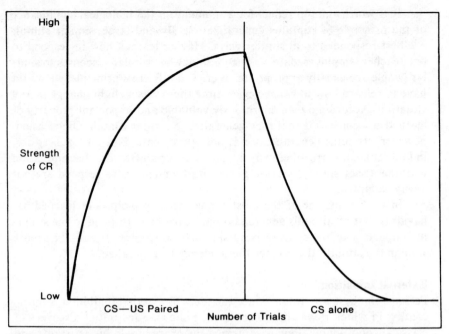

Figure 4.8 Graphic illustration of experimental extinction. In the left portion is the course of conditioning resulting from pairing a CS with a US. When the CS is presented alone for a number of trials, the CR grows progressively weaker, as shown in the right portion of the diagram.

stimulus, hence changing the stimulus situation and leading to a lower response strength. In short, external inhibition is a special case of stimulus generalization decrement.

Experimental Extinction

In the laboratory, when the conditions are changed so that a CS that initially preceded a US is now presented alone, we refer to it as *experimental extinction*. A specific example can be drawn from the experiment in which a dog is conditioned to salivate. If a bell is rung just before the delivery of food for a number of trials and, thereafter, the food (the US) is omitted and the bell (the CS) presented alone, the dog will eventually cease to salivate to the stimulus of the bell. The results of such a procedure are shown in figure 4.8.

In figure 4.8, the original acquisition curve shows the increase in the conditioned response when the CS and US are repeatedly paired. The right portion of the figure shows the results of then presenting the CS alone (without the US). A gradual decrease in the strength of the conditioned response occurs over repeated presentations of the CS alone.

Continued occurrence of the CR in response to the CS is thus dependent upon the continued presentation of the US following the CS. If the conditions change, the organism gradually learns this fact and eventually stops responding. When the organism no longer responds, we say that the CR is *extinguished*. This phenomenon will be discussed in detail in a later chapter.

A related principle holds that if an interval of time is allowed to elapse after the experimental extinction of a CR, the CR will regain some of the strength lost. This is called *spontaneous recovery*. In effect, then, extinction is partly temporary. The conceptual significance of this fact will be discussed in the next chapter.

Summary

Although there are many more detailed principles concerning the concept of conditioning, the most important facts for the beginning student to know are those that have been described. These facts may be summarized as follows:

1. Pairing a CS with a US causes the CR to gradually increase in strength to the CS.
2. This strength reaches an upper limit with repeated trials; the limit is greater for more intense stimuli.
3. The rate of conditioning is faster when trials are distributed broadly over time.
4. The effectiveness of pairing a CS with a US is greatest if the US follows the CS by no more than a few seconds. There is no conditioning if the stimuli are presented at the same time or in the reverse order, and there is poorer conditioning if the US occurs very long after the CS.
5. The conditioned response, after extended training, tends to occur shortly before the US. The longer the CS–US interval, the longer the latency before the CR occurs.
6. Responses conditioned to one stimulus generalize to similar stimuli, but as the change from the original CS becomes greater, the response weakens.
7. The occurrence of an unusual event just before or during the presentation of a CS leads to external inhibition, producing a weaker CR.
8. Presenting the CS alone after a CR has been established results in experimental extinction, or a progressive weakening of the CR.
9. An extinguished CR spontaneously recovers some strength over time.

Conditioning Failures

We have stated flatly that whenever an unrelated stimulus (CS) regularly precedes a US, the CS will come to elicit the response that originally was produced only by the US. This statement holds under an extremely wide range of conditions. There are, however, a few important exceptions to the anticipatory response principle. Recognizing them should improve your understanding of the basic principle itself.

Latent Inhibition

Suppose that before using a CS in a classical conditioning paradigm, we simply present the CS to a subject a number of times *without* any US. Later, when this CS regularly precedes a US, there may be little, if any, association formed between the CS and the response. For example, if we first present a certain tone to a dog several times and then present the same tone followed by food powder, the tone may not come to elicit a salivation CR. Note that the tone and food powder have been presented in such a way as to cause conditioning. This failure in conditioning due to prior exposure to the CS is called *latent inhibition*.

Such conditioning failures, though rare in the lab, may be quite familiar in everyday life. For example, if a young child is repeatedly threatened but never actually punished, it will be difficult later to condition the child to fear serious threats. More generally, it is hard to learn to trust others if your early experiences have been with untrustworthy people.

To understand why latent inhibition occurs, we need only recall our earlier description of what constitutes an *effective* stimulus. We said that for a stimulus to control behavior, the organism must attend to that stimulus. Apparently, when a CS is presented to a subject a number of times without resulting in anything of consequence, the subject learns *not* to pay any attention to it. Then, when the CS is later paired with a US, the subject will respond as if the US has been presented alone, ignoring the CS. Under these conditions, it is not surprising that the CS is never associated with the response.

Overshadowing

Until now, whenever we have talked about a CS, we have always spoken of a single stimulus presented prior to a US. It is possible, however, to combine two stimuli into what is called a *compound CS*. For example, instead of presenting either a light or a tone as a CS, we can present the light and tone together and follow this compound with the presentation of the US.

When a compound CS is used in classical conditioning, each of the individual stimuli in the compound may become associated with the response, but this is not always the case. When the stimuli are presented separately, often only one of the stimuli in the compound produces a CR; the other stimulus is ineffective. This is the case even when each of the stimuli is known to be effective as a CS when presented alone prior to the US and even though both of the stimuli in the compound regularly preceded the occurrence of the US. When one stimulus in a compound becomes associated with the response and the other does not, we call the result *overshadowing*. One stimulus overshadows the other and more effectively elicits the response.

There are a number of conditions under which overshadowing is likely to occur. For example, if one stimulus in the compound CS is more conspicuous or more intense than the other, this stimulus often will elicit a CR, while the less conspicuous stimulus will not. Overshadowing also occurs if one stimulus in a compound CS already has come to elicit the CR through prior conditioning. For example, suppose we present a bell to a dog several times and follow each presentation of the bell with food powder. After a while, the bell will begin to elicit the salivation CR. Now suppose that we present a compound CS several times, and that this compound CS consists of the same bell along with a light, while the US that follows is food powder. In this situation, the light will often fail to elicit the salivation response, even though the light has regularly preceded the presentation of the food powder. The bell, because of its prior association with salivation, overshadows the light when they are presented in compound.

Overshadowing is also common in everyday life. For example, if you especially enjoyed a particular movie, you might become a fan of the star in the movie, even though the supporting cast was also a part of the total stimulus complex that you enjoyed. And once you had developed a positively conditioned attitude toward that movie star, it would be even more difficult for performers who joined the star in other movies to develop separate positive associations in your thinking.

The reason for overshadowing is still unclear. According to one view, the stimuli that gain control over responses are the parts of the compound to which the subject attends. This view contends that the stimuli that are overshadowed were ignored or not attended to during conditioning. This explanation is similar to the interpretation of latent inhibition. Whether this or some other explanation of overshadowing turns out to be correct, the mere occurrence of overshadowing is important. Phenomena such as overshadowing and latent inhibition demonstrate that not all stimuli that regularly precede a response will necessarily come to elicit that response through association. One of the interesting challenges to present-day researchers is to discover the conditions under which exceptions to the anticipatory response principle occur.

Principles of Learning: The Anticipatory Response

Multiple Choice Test Questions

1. Which of the following associations describes the anticipatory response principle?
   a. CS–CR
   b. CS–UR
   c. US–CR
   d. US–UR

2. In temporal conditioning, we find that
   a. there is a preceding conditioned stimulus
   b. there is not a preceding conditioned stimulus
   c. irregularity in time exists
   d. there is no way to understand the phenomenon
3. Higher-order conditioning requires
   a. higher cognitive processes, such as language
   b. an emotionally positive US
   c. more than one CS
   d. new principles to explain its occurrence
4. Which of the following is *not* a fact concerning conditioning?
   a. The strength of the response usually increases gradually.
   b. The response strength limit is greater for strong stimuli.
   c. The rate of conditioning is slower with rapidly paced trials.
   d. The optimal situation for conditioning is when the CS and the US occur simultaneously.
5. The latency of the CR is shorter for
   a. short CS–US intervals
   b. long CS–US intervals
   c. weak stimuli
   d. strong stimuli
6. If a CS is presented several times alone before being paired with a US, conditioning may fail to occur. This failure in conditioning is called
   a. latent inhibition
   b. overshadowing
   c. external inhibition
   d. extinction

Multiple Choice Answers

1. (a) The CS is the originally ineffective stimulus. When there is a response to it before the US occurs, there is evidence of a learned association.
2. (b) Temporal conditioning can be understood by recognizing that, if the occurrence of the US is regular in time, the trace of each one can effectively serve as a CS for the next CR.
3. (c) Higher-order conditioning occurs when a CR is first associated with one CS and then transferred to a second CS. Our use of language provides examples, but language is not necessary for this type of conditioning. Any type of US can be used, and the basic principle of the anticipatory response is sufficient to explain the existence of higher-order conditioning.
4. (d) The CS must precede the US for conditioning to occur. The other answers are all correct.
5. (a) No mention was made of the effect of stimulus intensity on latency; actually, there is little or no effect. The principal controlling factor is the CS–US interval; the latency of the CR corresponds in length to the inter-stimulus interval.

6. (a) A difficulty in conditioning due to prior exposure to the CS alone is termed latent inhibition.

True/False Thought Questions

1. The anticipatory response represents a conscious response in anticipation of an impending event.
2. In classical conditioning, the conditioned stimulus is the one that already produces the response, and the unconditioned stimulus is the one that does not produce the response before conditioning.
3. A US may function as a CS.
4. Higher-order conditioning refers to higher mental processes such as thinking and problem solving.
5. The principle of the anticipatory response may lead to maladaptive behavior.
6. Conditioning is accomplished by a single pairing of a US with a CS.
7. The best conditioning is achieved by presenting the CS and the US at the same time.
8. The well-established CR does not occur immediately after the occurrence of the CS.
9. The greater the change from an original CS, the less the generalized response and the greater the generalization decrement.
10. External inhibition occurs if the subject is told not to respond.
11. Prolonged presentations of the CS and US result in experimental extinction.
12. It is possible for a weak stimulus to overshadow a strong one.

True/False Answers

1. (False) It is true that in many situations, humans learn that a stimulus signals an impending event and they are able to plan and prepare for it. However, the principle of the anticipatory response does not presume any such conscious process. The tendency to respond ahead of time is automatic.
2. (False) This description is reversed, even though it may sound correct. Think of the term *conditioned* as meaning "learned in this situation." The association between the CS and CR is the one conditioned in the situation; the association between the US and UR is reflexive and unlearned.
3. (True) A stimulus may elicit a response reflexively and hence be a US; it also initiates a stimulus-memory trace that can come to elicit another response if regularly paired with another US. This is illustrated explicitly in the case of temporal conditioning. For example, the US of food not only elicits salivation when eating, but also elicits subsequent salivation before the next food delivery.
4. (False) In higher-order conditioning, a previously conditioned CS–CR association is used to condition the response to other stimuli. This type of conditioning does not require any new processes or principles.

5. (True) Sometimes, making a response early means making it *too* soon, with the result that the reward is denied or delayed. The principle applies in any event, even if the behavior is maladaptive.

6. (False) There are extreme situations in which full conditioning may be accomplished in a single experience; you might have to survive but one plane wreck to be intensely afraid of flying, even though the probability of a repeat event is very remote. Under typical conditions, b'oth in the laboratory and in everyday life, at least several experiences are necessary to produce a strong CR.

7. (False) Simultaneous presentation of the two stimuli leads to *no* conditioning. Only if the US follows the CS (preferably by a short interval of time) does a CR develop.

8. (True) The CR tends to occur immediately preceding the US. If there is a reasonable interval of time between the CS and the US, there will be a reasonable interval of time after the CS before the CR occurs.

9. (True) A weaker response occurs if the stimulus is changed. We can describe this in terms of the amount of response that does occur (generalized response strength) or in terms of the amount of response strength lost as a result of the change (generalization decrement). These are, however, opposite sides of the same coin—the more that remains, the less that is lost.

10. (False) People can, to some extent, voluntarily suppress a CR, although they cannot do so perfectly. However, external inhibition is no more voluntary than conditioning itself; adding an unusual stimulus changes the total situation and leads to a weaker CR.

11. (False) As long as the US is continued in the classical conditioning process, the CR persists. The CR grows weaker when the US is omitted; this constitutes experimental extinction.

12. (True) If the organism attends to the weak stimulus, perhaps as a result of prior conditioning, it may prevent the organism from learning about a physically stronger stimulus.

Essay/Discussion Questions

1. "The most basic, fundamental principle of learning is that of the anticipatory response." Think of original personal examples of each of the types of conditioning described in the text—classical conditioning, temporal conditioning, higher-order conditioning, and anticipatory instrumental responses.

2. Many students learn to dislike certain subjects. It is commonly presumed that attitudes result from classical conditioning. How might teachers make use of the facts of conditioning to decrease the incidence of such negative attitudes?

References

Classical Conditioning

Hilgard, E. R., and Humphreys, L. G. The effect of supporting and antagonistic voluntary instructions on conditioned discrimination. *Journal of Experimental Psychology*, 1938, *22*, 291–304.

Pavlov, I. P. *Conditioned reflexes*. London: Oxford University Press, 1927

Variations in Classical Conditioning

Rizley, R. C., & Rescorla, R. A. Associations in second-order conditioning and sensory preconditioning. *Journal of Comparative and Physiological Psychology*, 1972, *81*, 1–11.

Facts of Conditioning

*Beecroft, R. S. *Classical conditioning*. Goleta, Calif: Psychonomic Press, 1966.

Spence, K. W. *Behavior theory and conditioning*. New Haven: Yale University Press, 1956.

Conditioning Failures

*Grant, D. A. Adding communication to the signalling property of the CS in classical conditioning. *Journal of General Psychology*, 1968, *79*, 147–175.

*Kamin, L. J. Predictability, surprise, attention and conditioning. In B. A. Campbell and R. M. Church (Eds.), *Punishment and aversive behavior*. New York: Appleton-Century-Crofts, 1969.

*Suitable for additional reading by the beginning student. The others are written at a more technical level.

A Scientific Theory of Classical Conditioning

5

Many scientists are not content simply to describe the outcome of their experiments in empirical terms. In addition, they are inclined to speculate about the underlying reasons for the results they obtain; to attempt to answer the question, "Why?" In point of fact, scientists cannot really answer that question in any ultimate sense, but they do construct scientific theories that help them better understand their field. *A scientific theory is a set of hypotheses about the inner workings of a system.* In this book, we are interested in the hypothetical processes that change inside the organism when learning occurs. As we indicated in the first chapter, scientists may someday be able to tell us more about the physiological bases of learning; meanwhile, theorists develop hunches based on their observations.

Naturally, different people are likely to have different hypotheses and ideas, and hence there is no single, universally accepted learning theory today. But several very basic ideas are so common that we can use them to illustrate a scientific theory of classical conditioning.

Primary Associations in Conditioning: Habit

The most fundamental principle of classical conditioning is that, if we regularly present an initially neutral conditioned stimulus (such as a bell) prior to an unconditioned stimulus (such as food), an anticipatory conditioned response (salivation) will begin to occur to the CS alone. From this fact, we can infer that simply presenting the two stimuli, one before the other, leads to an associative process inside the organism. Some theorists believe that the association is formed between the CS and the unconditioned *stimulus* while others believe that the association is formed between the CS and the unconditioned *response*. For our purposes, it really makes no difference whether the association is of a cognitive (S–S) nature or a behavioristic (S–R) nature; all we need to recognize is that some kind of association is formed as a result of the occurrence of the two stimuli reasonably close together in time. We call this internal associative process *habit*.

Habit is a familiar term in everyday language, but there is a distinction between the scientific usage and the familiar one. The word "habit" is usually used to refer to some behavior of doubtful social value: the drinking habit, the smoking habit, the nailbiting habit, or whatever. In addition, the everyday meaning of the word usually applies to some specific class of behavior and to the fact that this behavior occurs frequently. The theoretical term "habit" is more general, since it takes into account *all* learned associations, desirable and undesirable. For example, your verbal habits probably include both correct and incorrect spellings. Furthermore, as we have defined the term, cognitive habits come into play when a stimulus makes you think about something—even when you don't engage in any overt behavior as a result. Accordingly, the theoretical sense of the term "habit" refers to simple associations formed within the organism—without regard to their merits and including mental as well as motor associations.

In the early days of learning theory, it was common to conceptualize the brain as being something like a telephone switchboard. There are potential neural connections between all brain cells, sensory as well as motor, and one could imagine that these connections somehow become strengthened or bonded together as a result of classical conditioning. It is now generally recognized that such a view is much too simplistic and mechanistic, and our habit construct is therefore purely hypothetical. Whatever its nature, habit is a structural change within the nervous system that increases in strength on each trial. Its eventual strength after a number of trials depends on various details of the conditioning situation, particularly on the intensity of the unconditioned stimulus. The stronger the US, the stronger the habit association that is developed.

Since habit is a structural change, it is very durable and possibly even permanent. This may appear contrary to common sense because we all have the capacity to forget. Nevertheless, a few examples may help make the possibility that habit is permanent seem more reasonable. First, isn't it true that when you say you have forgotten something, you often mean that you simply cannot think of it at the moment? Frequently, you may feel quite confident that you would recognize it if given a hint, or that it will "come to you" in a few minutes. In such situations, forgetting, not learning, is temporary. If you were to return home after several years' absence, you would probably find your memories of home to be essentially complete; in fact, you might even be disturbed by small changes that had occurred. If you try to skate, play jacks, or ride a bicycle after years without practice, those skills will return almost immediately. And you have probably at least heard of the remarkably detailed memories that can be obtained under hypnosis. For these and a variety of other reasons, it appears to be fruitful to think of habits as essentially permanent and to account for the weakening of responses by other processes. One such process is described in the next section.

Secondary Associations in Extinction: Inhibition

Consider another empirical phenomenon introduced in the preceding chapter: experimental extinction. We noted that the process of classical conditioning is reversible; that the CR develops over a series of trials in which a CS is followed by a US, but that the CR gradually disappears over a subsequent series of trials if the CS is not followed by the US. The most obvious theoretical explanation for experimental extinction would be that habit is lost as a result of presenting the CS alone.

This is *not,* however, the assumption we will make. If, after the extinction of a conditioned response, a period of time elapses during which the CS is not presented, the CR is likely to reappear after a subsequent presentation of the CS. This is called *spontaneous recovery.* A conditioned response may be experimentally extinguished, but it will spontaneously recover some of its lost strength over the period of time during which the CS does not occur. Spontaneous recovery is not complete; the amount of recovery depends on how completely extinction was effected and on the amount of recovery time permitted. Under typical laboratory conditions, a reasonable rule of thumb is that an extinguished CR will recover about half of the strength it had before extinction.

Before discussing the theoretical significance of this finding, let's think for a moment about its practical significance. Suppose, for example, that you have decided to take up horseback riding and, during your first session, you are thrown from the horse. As a result of the pain and humiliation experienced, you may find that you are now afraid of that horse (and probably of other horses, too, as a result of stimulus generalization). You may feel that this fear is unwarranted and undertake to "get over it." Even without formally studying psychology, you might believe that the best way to handle the fear would be to arrange a session in which you could ride a number of horses with little likelihood of any aversive experience. In effect, the horse is a CS, the fall was a US that conditioned you to fear, and experiencing the CS without the US will result in experimental extinction of that fear. However, although your contrived session may be so successful that you are riding fearlessly by the end of the day, you'll find that some of your fear will spontaneously recover. The next time you go to the stables, your fear may, to some extent, return.

The effort, however, was still to some avail. Because you extinguished your fear, the recovered fear will be less intense. And if that recovered fear is extinguished during your next riding experience, still less recovery will occur on the following occasion. The practical significance of spontaneous recovery is simply that an undesirable response can not be completely extinguished in a single session; a series of extinction sessions is typically necessary, each one followed by progressively less spontaneous recovery.

The theoretical significance of spontaneous recovery may seem obvious. Were one to assume that habit is lost as a result of experimental extinction, then the organism should, following extinction, be restored to the condition that prevailed prior to conditioning; for the habit to be restored, new conditioning trials would be necessary. Stated another way, although the organism is not responding after the extinction, there still must be some habit remaining because the conditioned response will eventually reappear without any additional conditioning trials.

Accordingly, we can now introduce the other major construct within the theory: inhibition. Rather than assuming that extinction results from the loss of a habit, we assume that it reflects the accumulation of a secondary process, *inhibition,* that opposes habit and suppresses the tendency to respond. In this context, we refer to inhibition as being *secondary* because it is the second process acquired; normally, inhibition does not develop until after habit has been acquired. As with habit, inhibition can be conceived of as either a cognitive or behavioristic association. In the former case, inhibition might be described as learning to no longer expect the unconditioned stimulus because it has not occurred during the nonreinforced trials of extinction. The organism may well remember that the US did occur during original conditioning, and this memory represents the persistence of habit; but the organism also learns during extinction to inhibit the expectation that the US will occur. In behavioristic terms, on the other hand, inhibition simply weakens the tendency to make the conditioned response. In either case, this secondary associative process must have somewhat different properties from the primary process to account for spontaneous recovery. One of these properties seems to be that inhibition can, at least in part, dissipate over time. The reason the organism does not respond after extinction is not because habit has been lost, but rather because that habit is inhibited.

Disinhibition

There is another reason for believing that extinction results from the buildup of a secondary associative process (inhibition) that opposes the primary associative process (habit), and for believing that inhibition is more fragile than habit. This reason can be demonstrated through the following study, conducted by Pavlov. First a response is conditioned and then extinguished repeatedly so that little or no spontaneous recovery occurs. Then a novel or unusual event occurs prior to presentation of the CS. This is the same operation, in which an unusual stimulus is introduced into the situation, that we described in the context of external inhibition. However, in this case, the new stimulus occurs after extinction rather than during the original conditioning process.

Our natural expectation is that the conditioned response would be even weaker than it would be in the absence of the unusual stimulus. What Pavlov observed, however, was that the CR was actually stronger than expected. *Disinhibition* is the phenomenon that an extinguished conditioned response may reappear if the CS occurs in an unusual context.

Let's pause to reflect on the practical significance of this phenomenon. Perhaps there is no more dramatic proof that habits are persistent and that they are simply suppressed by inhibition. For example, consider again the example concerning fear of horses. You may have completely lost your fear under normal circumstances, but if something unusual or unexpected happens before you go to the stables to ride, your fear is likely to return. This event need not even have any particular relation to horses; if, for example, you narrowly miss having an accident on the way to the stables, you are likely to find yourself more fearful of the horses when you arrive. Even if you were to go to a different stable, some fear might return.

The point we are making is that once a person has learned a conditioned response, he or she will never be the same as the person who never learned it in the first place—even though the former may have successfully extinguished the response. Thus, a child who is permitted to learn to fear the dark may overcome that fear as an adult, but will still be different from an adult who never learned that particular fear. If something changes the normal routine of life, the learned-but-extinguished-response person will experience a return of fear, while the person who never learned the fear can take such an event in stride. The person who, for example, has unusual difficulty adjusting to the death of a loved one is perhaps the person who has extinguished a number of fears and anxieties—which are then disinhibited by this trauma.

To account for disinhibition through habit-inhibition theory, we must make several specific assumptions. First, we assume that the occurrence of an unusual event changes the stimulus context, which, as we pointed out in chapter 2, is an important part of the total stimulus complex. This means that there should be a stimulus generalization decrement in *both* habit and inhibition. By assuming further that the decrement in inhibition is greater than the decrement in habit, the *net* effect is an increase in habit.

Perhaps a physical example will help make this idea clear. Imagine that you are pressing one foot on the accelerator pedal of a car while your other foot presses firmly on the brake pedal so that the car's motor is running fast but the car is standing still. If you take your foot off the brake, the car will move forward—even if, at the same time, you let up slightly on the accelerator. In this illustration, the brake has been "inhibiting" the movement of the car, and releasing the brake is analogous to "disinhibition."

As we have presented the facts to this point, habit is a durable, persisting process, whereas inhibition is temporary and more subject to generalization decrement; this is, in fact, usually the case. But the point must be made that the *first* associative process acquired has the greater durability and generality. If conditions are arranged so that nothing new or unusual happens during the initial exposures to a conditioned stimulus, the resulting inhibitory associations will be the primary dominant associations. It is then more difficult to form habits as secondary associations, and any such associations will tend to be temporary and subject to greater generalization decrement.

To illustrate, let's return for the last time to the fear-of-horses example. If a person is thrown for the first time after riding a number of horses many times without any unpleasant happening, the pain and humiliation may be great, but the conditioned fear resulting from the event will be weaker and less persistent than it would be for a novice rider. Certainly you can think of someone who has taken a tumble skiing, roller skating, or bike riding but bounced back almost as if nothing had happened. In this case, the primary association (inhibition of fear) dominates over the secondary association (fear).

This is one reason why great attention should be paid to early experiences. The first associations we develop with anything—animals of various kinds, swimming, camping, dates, parties, and even going to school—will tend to be highly persistent. If those associations are appropriate and adaptive ones, we are much better able to cope with occasional unfortunate experiences. If, on the other hand, those first associations are inappropriate and maladaptive, then we are at a disadvantage when trying to develop more desirable attitudes and behaviors. The important point is that new experiences do not irradicate the associations developed from previous experiences; instead, they lead to new associations that may supplant the old ones but are less durable.

Differential Classical Conditioning

Differential classical conditioning is a procedure involving two somewhat similar stimuli used as CS. For convenience, let's return to the Pavlovian laboratory and use a moderately high-pitched tone as one CS and a somewhat lower tone as a second CS in an experiment involving dogs, food, and salivation. On some occasions, the high-pitched tone is presented and followed by the delivery of the US (food). We'll call this high-pitched tone CS+. On other occasions, interspersed irregularly and unpredictably with the CS+ are occasions on which the low-pitched tone is presented and *not* followed by the US of food. We'll call this tone CS−. The empirical outcome of this procedure is that, with training, the dog will tend to salivate when CS+ occurs, and not to salivate when CS− occurs. The dog learns to discriminate between the tones, responding only when the appropriate signal occurs.

We can understand the development of such a discrimination in terms of habit–inhibition theory. In the first place, a primary association (habit) will develop to CS+ because that stimulus is paired with food. This habit will generalize to similar stimuli, including CS−; hence, initially, the dog will also salivate when CS− occurs. However, the trials involving CS−

eventually lead to extinction because the US does not occur after the CS−tone. A secondary association (inhibition) will develop to CS−. (This takes considerable training because habit is repeatedly being strengthened to CS+ and generalizing to CS−.) Habit-inhibition theory implies, correctly, that the major difficulty encountered in differential classical conditioning is the occurrence of errors of commission; that is, the dog salivates when CS− occurs and food is not to be delivered. Rarely are there errors of omission, or the failure to salivate when CS+ occurs, because the habit strength to that stimulus is opposed by only a small amount of inhibition generalized from CS−. And, of course, the more similar the stimuli, the greater the generalization of habit and inhibition between CS+ and CS− (and the more difficult the discrimination).

Even so, Pavlov used the procedure of differential classical conditioning to attempt to determine how fine a discrimination an animal can make. Human subjects can simply state whether two tones sound alike or different, but animals must make some nonverbal response to communicate to the experimenter. Clearly, if an animal can learn to respond differentially to two stimuli, the stimuli must be distinguishable to that animal.

To determine whether animals can distinguish between stimuli, Pavlov first employed differential conditioning with stimuli that were quite dissimilar, for example, a very high-pitched tone versus a very low-pitched tone. This made the initial discrimination easy because there was little generalization of habit and inhibition between CS+ and CS−. Then, after that discrimination was well learned, Pavlov gradually made the stimuli progressively more similar to find out at what point the discrimination would break down. Interestingly enough, he found that when the stimuli became very similar, not only did the discrimination break down, so did the dogs! The dogs showed obvious signs of fear and anxiety about the experimental situation so that, rather than standing quietly in the stock and salivating when appropriate, they resisted the situation. This behavior even carried over to other situations. Some of the dogs would huddle in a corner of the living cage, cower at the sight of their familiar handlers, refuse to eat regularly, and overreact to the slightest sound or distraction. Pavlov called this result an *experimental neurosis,* because of its apparent similarity to many human neurotic behaviors, and he usually had to send the affected dogs away from the laboratory for a rest cure of tender care in the country.

Perhaps this extrapolation to human neuroses is exaggerated, but there is evidence that many maladjustments do in fact, stem from the stress of being confronted with very difficult decisions in which there are strong tendencies both to make a response (habit) and not to make the response (inhibition). Not infrequently, the latter tendency is due to punishment rather than a lack of reinforcement, but the conflict between strong tendencies certainly is a conspicuous part of neurotic behavior. While the story of human neuroses is undoubtedly more complicated, research with animals strongly suggests the following dictum: If you are concerned about the general well-being of another person, avoid causing a severe conflict between habit and inhibition. If a child is strongly tempted to engage in some behavior as a result of peer pressure but is strongly inhibited by threats of parental displeasure, the seeds of maladjustment may have been planted. As an all too common example, if a person's natural sexual urges are continually thwarted by fears that masturbation is harmful and intercourse fraught with dangers, that person is unlikely to enjoy a full, well-adjusted life. There is nothing unkind about differential conditioning, provided the stimuli are so clearly different that the person can readily learn the discrimination. But when the stimuli are very similar, as when a child cannot be sure whether a parental statement is a request or a command, conflict often results.

The concepts of habit and inhibition, as developed here, are certainly rudimentary and, at best, suggestive. Nevertheless, the range of phenomena to which they apply strongly suggests that some such mechanism is a useful way to conceptualize learning. Performance is a two-way street; traffic flows in one direction to produce responding and in the opposite direction to resist responding. In some form or other, this image derived from habit–inhibition theory has many important and largely true implications for the understanding of behavior.

A Scientific Theory of Classical Conditioning

Multiple Choice Test Questions

1. According to the theory of classical conditioning described in the text, learning (habit) is conceptualized as
   a. an S–S association
   b. an S–R association
   c. either an S–S or S–R association
   d. something other than an associative process
2. Spontaneous recovery refers to the fact that
   a. illnesses may disappear after a while
   b. illnesses may reappear after a while
   c. extinguished responses may disappear after a while
   d. extinguished responses may reappear after a while
3. The major difference between habit and inhibition is
   a. habit grows gradually and inhibition occurs suddenly
   b. habit generalizes to similar stimuli and inhibition does not
   c. habit is permanent and inhibition is not
   d. habit is directly observable and inhibition is not

4. Theoretically, disinhibition is a result of a
   a. decrease in habit
   b. decrease in inhibition
   c. greater decrease in habit than in inhibition
   d. greater decrease in inhibition than in habit
5. In differential classical conditioning, it is assumed that
   a. habit is more important than inhibition
   b. habit is less important than inhibition
   c. habit and inhibition are equally important
   d. the relative importance of habit and inhibition depends on the response strength of each
6. Experimental neuroses may result from very strong
   a. habits
   b. inhibitions
   c. habits or inhibitions separately
   d. habits and inhibitions combined

Multiple Choice Answers

1. (c) The critical assumption in the theory of classical conditioning is that some learning process results from pairing a CS with a US. This learning could be S-S or S-R, but it is explicitly associative.
2. (d) Some psychosomatic illnesses may be treated by procedures involving extinction of underlying fears and hence are subject to spontaneous recovery. However, the more appropriate answer in the context of this chapter is that spontaneous recovery involves the reappearance of extinguished responses.
3. (c) Both habit and inhibition are hypothetical and thus are not directly observable. Both grow gradually (although not necessarily at the same rate) and generalize to similar stimuli (although not to the same degree). The major difference involves their durability.
4. (d) Disinhibition could be accounted for simply by a decrease in inhibition, but we know that habit must also decrease in order to account for generalization decrements. The theory of classical conditioning assumes a relatively greater decrease in inhibition than habit, producing a net increase in response strength.
5. (c) It is true that the measurement of inhibition depends upon the prior development of habit. It is also true that the response level at any point in time depends on the strength of each. But to effect differential conditioning, it is equally important that habit be developed to the positive stimulus and inhibition be developed to the negative stimulus.
6. (d) A person may have either very strong habits or inhibitions and either type of association may prevail. It is when both are very strong that the person is in severe conflict and may suffer an emotional disturbance.

True/False Thought Questions

1. The value of a behavioral theory depends primarily on how well the theory describes what is really going on inside the subject.
2. Habit, in the theoretical sense, refers to excessive indulgence in a behavior that is considered socially undesirable.
3. Good habits spontaneously recover more often than bad habits do.
4. The term "inhibition," as used by behaviorists, refers to an inability to behave naturally because of fear or anxiety.
5. The fact that reconditioning (following extinction) proceeds faster than original conditioning implies that habits are quickly regained.
6. If you want to overcome a habit "once and for all," it is best to include some unusual experiences in the context of that habit.
7. Disinhibition indicates that extinguished habits fail to generalize.
8. Conditioning should occur more slowly when the US is occasionally omitted than when the US occurs each time the CS occurs.
9. External inhibition will result from an unusual event no matter how long the event occurs before the next trial.
10. Generalization should be more pervasive if the CS is changed from trial to trial during conditioning.
11. Differential conditioning cannot occur if both stimuli are first followed by the US for several trials and then only one of them is followed by the US for several more.
12. If we are to prevent mental illness, we must avoid inhibitions.

True/False Answers

1. (False) The value of any scientific theory depends on how correctly the theory describes data—in this case, behavioral data. It is not necessary that there really be a "habit" and an "inhibition" localized in the subject for the habit-inhibition theory to be of value.
2. (False) Although the term "habit" is often used in this manner in everyday language, habit in the theoretical sense refers to an association between a stimulus and a response.
3. (False) The principle of spontaneous recovery is indifferent to the desirability of an extinguished response.
4. (False) Again, in everyday language, we often speak of an "inhibited" person as one who seems overly fearful or anxious. However, inhibition in the sense that we have used it refers to a process that results from nonreinforcement and opposes habit.
5. (False) Extinguished responses are, indeed, regained rapidly. Recall, however, that habit is not lost during extinction; rather, inhibition is built up. Hence, reconditioning involves the removal of inhibition, and this fact indicates that inhibition is removed more quickly than habit is gained.

6. (True) Even if you repeatedly extinguish a response in a single context, it will be subject to disinhibition if any unusual experiences happen. Better, then, to include some unusual experiences during the extinction process so they will no longer be unusual and produce disinhibition.
7. (False) When a conditioned response is extinguished, the result is inhibition of the habit. When the situation changes, both processes suffer a generalization decrement, but habit generalizes more than inhibition, producing a net increase in response tendency.
8. (True) Each time the US is omitted, habit fails to increase while inhibition increases. Thus, the CR would gain strength more slowly if only part of the trials inlcude the US.
9. (False) External inhibition will occur only if an unusual event happens soon enough before a trial that the stimulus trace of that event persists and changes the context.
10. (True) Although varying the CS from trial to trial would lead to slower learning, the wider the variety of stimuli to which the CR has become conditioned, the wider the range of generalization.
11. (False) If both stimuli are followed by the US, both will gain equally in habit strength. But, if the US is subsequently omitted for one of them, inhibition begins to accrue to it and results in differential conditioning to the two stimuli.
12. (False) Conflict arises only when a strong inhibition *opposes* a strong habit. If a response is completely inhibited, as when extinguished, no experimental neurosis is found. In fact, inhibition of undesirable responses is adaptive.

Essay/Discussion Questions

1. Habit is a familiar term in everyday language. Discuss the ways in which the term is used differently in scientific theory and the possible practical significance of the difference.
2. Inhibition is a familiar term in everyday language. Describe the contexts in which the term is conventionally used and relate these contexts to the meaning of the term in scientific theory.

References

Primary Associations in Conditioning: Habit
Hull, C. L. *Principles of behavior.* New York: Appleton-Century-Crofts, 1943.
Logan, F. A. Hybrid theory of classical conditioning. In G. H. Bower (Ed.), *Psychology of learning and motivation.* New York: Academic Press, 1977.

Secondary Associations in Extinction: Inhibition

*Hearst, E. Summation of excitation and inhibition. *Science,* 1963, *162,* 303.

Pavlov, I. P. *Conditioned reflexes.* (Anrep translation) Oxford: Oxford University Press, 1927.

Disinhibition

*Mednick, S. A., and Wild, C. Reciprocal augmentation of generalization and anxiety. *Journal of Experimental Psychology,* 1962, *63,* 621–626.

*Rescorla, R. A. Pavlovian excitation and inhibition. In W. K. Estes (Ed.), *Handbook of learning and cognitive processes.* Hillsdale, N.J.: Lawrence Erlbaum Associates, 1975.

Differential Classical Conditioning

*Miller, N. E. Learning theory and psychopathology. *Proceedings of the International Congress of Psychology,* 1969, *18,* 146.

Pavlov, I P. *Conditioned reflexes and psychiatry.* New York: International Publishers, 1941.

---

*Suitable for additional reading by the beginning student. The others are written at a more technical level.

Principles of Learning: Positive Reinforcement

6

In the previous chapters, we dealt mainly with the learning of responses that could be produced automatically by some stimulus event. Obviously, however, many of the responses we learn to perform cannot be produced reliably by any particular stimulus. An infant may babble spontaneously, but, as any parent knows, there is no stimulus that will elicit speech sounds automatically. Likewise, students may learn to smile politely when an instructor tells a joke. However, given the jokes made by many instructors, most of these smiles are not produced automatically by any stimulus in the situation. We do know that if a response is to be learned, that response must first occur (at least on a covert level). The problem of response occurrence is relatively minor when the response in question can be elicited naturally by some stimulus. However, when a response is not the automatic consequence of some stimulus, how can we ensure that the response will occur with enough regularity to be learned? In many cases, we ensure the regular occurrence of a response by following the *principle of positive reinforcement*.

Humankind certainly did not wait for the advent of scientific psychology to discover the principle of positive reinforcement. From the time they began to domesticate animals (and train children), they surely recognized that behavior can be controlled by the administration of rewards. Accordingly, although it is still difficult to provide a completely adequate statement of the principle of positive reinforcement, most people already know that *whenever a response is closely followed in time by a reward, the tendency for that response to occur in the future is increased.*

Don't be misled by the apparent simplicity of this principle. In later sections of this chapter, we will explore some of the details surrounding its application. First, however, let's discuss two popular misconceptions about the principle of positive reinforcement.

The reward does not have to be an effect of (that is, produced by) the response to be effective. The principle of positive reinforcement simply states that the temporal contiguity of the reward and the response is sufficient to increase the likelihood of that response. This fact was demonstrated most clearly in a study done by B. F. Skinner. Skinner placed a pigeon in an apparatus containing a food receptacle that could be presented to the pigeon automatically. He set the apparatus so that the food receptacle was presented periodically; say, for three seconds every thirty seconds. The pigeon was not required to make any response for the food to be presented. Nevertheless, Skinner observed that the pigeon demonstrated an increasing tendency to engage in some type of consistent behavior such as strutting around the cage with its neck stretched upward. Skinner could not predict *what* the pigeon would learn to do, and, in fact, the same pigeon might change behaviors occasionally. But the fact that the pigeon would learn to perform some response regularly was predictable from the principle of positive reinforcement.

The reason this phenomenon occurred is as follows. Whenever the food reward was delivered, the pigeon was, by necessity, doing *something*. If, for example, the pigeon was exploring the top of the box when the reward was presented, it would be more likely to resume that type of behavior afterwards. Thus, the pigeon would likely be engaging in the same behavior the next time a reward was given, and so on. The pigeon, in effect, becomes trapped into making a response as if that response had produced the reward when, in fact, the reward was actually completely independent of the pigeon's behavior.

Skinner called this type of behavior in the pigeon *superstitious behavior* because such behaviors apparently arise in the same way as many human superstitions. A softball coach may wear the same hat to every game as long as his or her team continues to win. Probably the response of wearing the hat has nothing to do with producing the reward (a win). However, the response continues to occur because it is followed consistently with reward. Whenever something good happens to us, we tend to review our recent behaviors to identify what we "did" to deserve the reward. The behaviors we identify in this way will continue to occur regardless of their true relationship to the reward.

The second disclaimer concerning the principle of positive reinforcement is that *a person need not recognize the relationship between a response and a reward for the principle to work*. According to the principle of positive reinforcement, the effect of a reward on response is automatic; an organism need not "see" or understand the relationship between them. Although the area called *learning without awareness* is still somewhat controversial, the evidence favors the interpretation that reward effects are automatic. All of us, for example, have various mannerisms we are unaware of, usually because we were unaware of these mannerisms when they were rewarded and learned. A teacher may develop the habit of pacing during a lecture because students have, in the past, been more attentive when the teacher stepped away from the lectern. A mother may learn to raise her voice when she speaks to her children because, in the past, raising her voice has produced attentiveness on the part of her children. In both cases, the individuals involved would probably be surprised to discover that they were making these responses. Almost certainly, neither would be able to explain how these responses were learned.

This is not to say that awareness of response-reward relationships cannot affect learning. When we are aware that our behavior does not affect the reward, we may try to talk ourselves out of developing a superstition about it. And when we see that our behavior does produce a reward, we can rehearse that sequence of events to foster learning. But the important point remains: *Awareness of a response-reward relationship is not necessary for learning to occur.*

These qualifications are important for effective application of the principle of positive reinforcement. Consider, for example, the parent who feeds a baby on a carefully timed schedule. The baby is fed by the clock, whether hungry or not. Holding the baby provides the strong reward of physical contact, and feeding is also a reward if the baby is hungry. If, therefore, the baby is crying at the time the clock signals feeding time, holding and feeding the infant increases the likelihood that he or she will cry in the future! The parent may not intend to reward such behavior, and the baby may not be aware of what is going on, but the principle of positive reinforcement works relentlessly on behavior, desirable or undesirable, intentional or adventitious.

The principle of positive reinforcement is studied experimentally in two types of situations, involving either operant or instrumental conditioning. In *operant conditioning*, a response is freely available to the organism, at least for some period of time. In the laboratory, for example, a rat may be in an apparatus containing a bar that it can press at any time; similarly, studying is a freely available response to students. In studying operant conditioning, we will be principally concerned with how the principle of positive reinforcement determines the rate at which the freely available response occurs. In *instrumental conditioning*, a response is periodically enabled by the environment so that its occurrence is restricted to discrete trials. In the laboratory, for example, a rat may be released from a start box, enabling the rat to run through a maze, but the rat cannot do so unless the start door is opened. Similarly, a student has the periodic opportunity to attend lectures but can only attend lectures when they are actually given. In studying instrumental conditioning, we will be principally concerned with how the principle of positive reinforcement determines the likelihood and speed with which the organism responds when an opportunity arises. The principle of positive reinforcement is the same in both cases but the conditions under which the principle operates differ.

Before describing some of the details of these two types of conditioning, it is necessary to discuss the problem of identifying rewarding events. How can we determine which events will serve as effective rewards, leading to an increase in the tendency to make certain responses?

Events that ARE Rewarding

The principle of positive reinforcement affects a wide range of behaviors and is thus of great practical significance. In applying this principle, however, one inevitably faces the problem of identifying events that actually are rewarding. Our intuition tells us that food will reward a hungry organism, but we really do not know in advance what commodities constitute food for a particular species. Pigeons reject raisins while monkeys devour them eagerly, even when reasonably satiated. One child may spend hours to earn praise or a good grade from a teacher while another child is largely indifferent to such events. Surely it would be advantageous to know in advance whether a particular event would serve as a reward.

There is, to date, no agreed-upon solution to this problem. However, psychologists have taken several approaches to identifying rewards; these approaches deserve some discussion.

Functional Identification

We have already noted that the basic technique for determining whether an event is a stimulus is a functional approach: Events that can be shown to function as stimuli according to behavioral laws are stimuli. In practice, the most common method for determining whether a stimulus is emotionally positive is also functional. That is to say, *a reward is a stimulus that has been shown to function as a reward according to the principle of positive reinforcement.*

The basic procedure for testing an event as a reward involves the following steps: The organism is placed in a learning situation in which prior knowledge ensures that the response is readily learnable when followed by known rewards. The stimulus event in question is then presented following that response, and if some appropriate response measure indicates learning, the event is classified as a reward. The circularity of this procedure is reduced by the further assumption that the event will function as a reward for that organism and similar organisms in learning other responses.

Often, this procedure can lead to the discovery of unexpected rewarding events. For example, shock can be administered to a rat through small electrodes lowered into the rat's brain. It is well known that when an electric shock is applied to the paws or other exterior surface of a rat, the stimulus is aversive. It would thus seem reasonable to expect that a shock applied internally would also be aversive. Surprisingly, stimulation of certain regions of the brain (notably the septum) are actually rewarding rather than aversive.

Rats quickly learn to press a bar to produce brain stimulation. Although a rat may require several preliminary brain shocks to "prime" its behavior before it begins to respond by itself each day, the power of this reward is apparently considerable. If the rat is left alone with two bars, one that produces food and one that produces brain stimulation, the rat, unless rescued, is likely to starve to death because of its preference for brain stimulation!

The full impact of this discovery has by no means yet been realized. Our understanding of the underlying biological mechanisms of reward will undoubtedly be significantly advanced by further experimental analysis. In the meantime, we can say that electrically stimulating certain regions of the brain qualifies as a reward simply because this stimulus has been shown experimentally to function as a reward.

The Drive Reduction Hypothesis

Although it is possible to identify rewarding events after seeing how they function, psychologists have long attempted to identify characteristics shared by all rewards so that rewards could be identified in advance. To date, the most influential hypothesis concerning the critical characteristics of reward was formalized and integrated into a general behavior theory by Clark Hull. Hull viewed learning as an adaptive process. According to his view, all organisms are confronted regularly with a variety of biological needs: the need for nutrients, the need for water, the need for sexual contact. Each of these biological needs has a psychological counterpart which is termed a *drive*. Thus, the need for nutrients results in a hunger drive, and the need for water gives rise to a thirst drive. Hull suggested that learning is, in essence, a mechanism that enables organisms to make responses that fulfill their biological needs, thereby reducing or eliminating their drives. Thus, Hull's idea holds that all rewards share at least one important characteristic: *All rewards are stimuli that reduce drives.*

The popularity of this hypothesis stems in part from its general applicability. Most of the stimuli actually used as rewards can readily be identified according to this rule. The response of eating reduces hunger, the response of drinking reduces thirst, the response of copulating reduces sex drive. An even more important aspect of Hull's theory is the biological significance of such a rule. As we will see, most (if not all) drives are based upon the survival needs of the organism: We must eat and drink to live. Imagine an organism that was not rewarded (in a learning sense) by the deliverance of food. Each time the organism became hungry, it would have to engage in random, trial-and-error behavior until it chanced to find and consume food. Such an organism would obviously be at a disadvantage in competition with an organism that could learn to make food-gathering and eating responses quickly and efficiently. The data are consistent with this compelling argument, and it is now generally accepted that at least part of the drive reduction hypothesis is true: *Any event that leads to drive reduction functions as a reward.*

You should recognize, however, that the drive reduction hypothesis goes beyond the statement that all drive reducers function as rewards. The hypothesis states that for something to serve as a reward it *must* reduce some drive. The question is whether there are rewards that *do not* reduce drives. Unfortunately for the drive reduction hypothesis, the answer to this question is, apparently, yes. We have already stated that certain types of electrical brain stimulation can function as rewards. Yet, it would be difficult at present to identify any biological need for such stimulation or to point to any drive that electrical stimulation reduces.

There are numerous other examples of rewards that apparently have no drive-reducing function. It is well known, for example, that rats will learn to run through a maze if the only reward is a saccharine solution. Although saccharine provides a sweet taste, it is a non-nutritive substance that is nondigestible and that is eliminated from the body chemically unchanged. Thus, although saccharine acts as a reward, it fills no biological need and reduces no known drive. Similarly, organisms will learn responses that are rewarded by simple changes in the environment. Rats will learn to press a bar if rewarded with a change in illumination. They will learn to negotiate a maze if they are rewarded by an opportunity to explore a new chamber. Monkeys will learn to open a latched door if they are rewarded by the sight of other monkeys. In all these instances, the environmental changes that act as rewards reduce no drive that we can readily identify.

One of the best examples of a reward that apparently is not drive reducing comes from a study in which male rats learned to run through a maze to a specific goal box where they were rewarded by the opportunity to copulate with a female rat. This reward, however, did not include the opportunity for the males to ejaculate because they were removed from the females after only a short time. Although few would deny that erotic stimulation is, in itself, pleasurable, it is reasonably clear that the sex drive is reduced by orgasm, not by the prior sexual stimulation. Such stimulation can, however, function as a reward.

Thus, there is no fully adequate solution to the problem of identifying common characteristics of rewards. The drive reduction hypothesis provides a general guide to reward identification: Stimuli that reduce drives are rewards. It is clear, however, that many stimuli that do not reduce drives also serve as rewards. Many of these stimuli can be identified only by trial and error to determine if they function as rewards according to the principle of positive reinforcement.

Secondary Reinforcement

The term *primary reinforcement* refers to an event that functions as a reward without any special training. Food to a hungry organism and water to a thirsty one are familiar primary reinforcers. But obviously, little everyday human behavior is actually controlled by such primary events. Perhaps of greater practical importance, therefore, is the concept of *secondary reinforcement*. Stimuli that are initially neutral in their effects on response may acquire reinforcing properties as a result of being paired with primary reinforcers. The basic procedure for establishing a secondary reinforcer is the process of classical conditioning; the positive emotional responses elicited by a primary reward become associated with a neutral stimulus according to the principle of the anticipatory response.

There are several laboratory demonstrations of this phenomenon. In an early one, rats were trained to press a bar to obtain food, and the food was delivered with a distinctive click of the feeding mechanism. During extinction, some rats continued to receive the click (but no food) while others got nothing for continuing to press the bar. The rats that heard the click persisted longer in pressing, presumably because the click had regularly preceded food delivery and had acquired secondary reinforcing power that maintained the response longer.

A stronger demonstration is when a new response is learned to obtain stimuli whose reinforcing value has been acquired. One way to do this is to run rats down a short, straight alley, sometimes terminating in a white goal box and sometimes in a black goal box. The white box contains food, the black box is empty. After a number of runs to each goal box, the boxes are placed at the ends of a T-maze—but now, both are empty. Nevertheless, the rats develop a temporary preference for going in the direction of the white goal box (which had previously contained food), thus learning a new maze to obtain a stimulus previously associated with food.

Still more comparable to learned rewards for human behavior are studies using token rewards. Chimpanzees will work for grapes for a while but then become satiated and quit. One way to overcome this problem is to use a vending machine that delivers grapes when a poker chip is inserted; this pairing effectively establishes the chips as secondary reinforcers. The chimps will then work consistently to accumulate a supply of poker chips that they later can turn in for grapes.

The obvious analogy to this last procedure is the way humans handle money. The pieces of paper we call dollars have little or no intrinsic value, but they may acquire reinforcing value by being paired with a wide variety of rewards and pleasures. While virtually everyone has learned the value of money, other events that have secondary reinforcing value usually vary from person to person. It's true, for example, that many students accept praise and good grades from teachers as secondary reinforcers, but not all do. Most people are rewarded if you will simply listen while they talk; others require verbal approval. Some people are strongly competitive and enjoy displaying their ability and versatility; others find cooperation more satisfying. These are but a few of the countless array of events that have acquired reinforcing value for different people.

The basic mechanism is always the same: *Events that have been associated with rewarding experiences acquire reinforcing power*—the sight of another person, a stamp collection, news that one's favorite team won its game—any of these might serve as rewards. We differ as to secondary reinforcers because we differ in past learning experiences, but all of the principles of classical conditioning apply to the learning of secondary reinforcers. One way to identify rewards for an individual is to study that person's past history. And one way to misidentify rewards is to assume that everyone else has had the same experiences you have had and hence is rewarded by the same events that reward you. A flashy sports car may be a symbol of success for one person; a patched-up heap of a car the ultimate for another.

Summary

The principle of positive reinforcement says that responses become more likely to occur if they are followed by rewarding events. The following two sections describe these effects in greater detail. But the first problem is to identify rewarding events. There have been a variety of attempts, including the ones described here, to solve this problem; but so far, none has gained wide acceptance. We can summarize the current knowledge briefly: A stimulus is a reward if it will reduce a drive or if it has previously been associated with a known reward. Otherwise, you know you have a reward only if you have previously found that it serves as one. These guidelines, although not providing a satisfactory scientific theory of reward, do provide enough information to employ the principle of positive reinforcement with great effectiveness.

Operant Conditioning

When the opportunity to make a response is continually present, at least during a certain period of time, it is referred to as an operant response and the experimental analysis of it is called an operant conditioning situation. Examples of such responses can be found both in the laboratory and in everyday life. If a rat is placed in a chamber containing a bar or lever, the rat can press the bar as often as it wishes until it is removed from the chamber. Likewise, during a conversation with a friend, you are free to make a smiling or nodding response as often as you like until the conversation is ended. Both the rat's bar press and your smiling response are operant responses because you and the rat are free to make these responses as often as and whenever you like during a given period of time. In studying such responses, the experimental variable of primary interest is the *schedule of reinforcement* that is applied to these responses. A schedule of reinforcement is a rule that governs how often and under what circumstances a response will be rewarded. Specifically, in an operant conditioning situation, our goal is to describe how different schedules of reinforcement affect the rate at which an operant response occurs.

Consider, for example, the babbling response of an infant. This is an operant response since the infant may perform the response at any time or not at all. However, the evidence clearly shows that the rate at which babbling occurs depends in great part on how often and under what circumstances the parents reward the babbling with smiles, physical affection, or babbles of their own.

There are two basic types of reinforcement schedules, each of which has two primary variations. The first basic type of schedule is called a *ratio schedule* since the occurrence of each reward depends on the occurrence of a certain number of responses. In essence, a specified number of responses is required for each reward. If a *fixed-ratio* schedule is used, we require the same number of responses for each reward. If a *variable-ratio* schedule is used, we vary the number of responses required for each reward.

The second basic type of reinforcement schedule is called an *interval schedule* because the presentation of a reward depends on the time that has passed since the last reward was given. When an interval schedule is applied, we require that a certain period of time pass after one reward before another response can be rewarded. If a *fixed-interval* schedule is employed, the time we require after each reward is the same. With a *variable-interval* schedule, the time required after each reward is varied.

These four types of reinforcement schedules do not exhaust the list of possible schedules that can be applied to operant behaviors. They are, however, the primary schedules studied in operant conditioning situations. For this reason, we will illustrate each of these schedules in more detail and describe the response pattern produced by each.

Fixed-Ratio Schedule Behavior

On a fixed-ratio schedule, an organism must make a certain number of responses for each reward and the number of responses required does not vary. For example, if a pigeon is placed on a fixed-ratio–5 schedule (FR–5) for pecking a key, we would require that the pigeon peck the key 5 times for each reward. Likewise, a person working in a political campaign might be given $1.00 for each 100 circulars that he or she folds and places in an envelope. This worker would be performing on a fixed-ratio schedule (FR–100), since 100 responses are required for each reward. Under this reward schedule, response has two distinct features. First, the organism pauses, and then it maintains a rapid and steady response rate until the required number of responses for the next reward is complete. In effect, the organism seems to feel that once the chain of responses is begun, there is no better approach than to run through the entire ratio as rapidly as possible; however, after obtaining the reward, the organism is likely to take a break before starting again. Naturally, the duration of the pause depends on the number of responses required for each reward; the greater the number of responses required, the longer the pause before response begins again. But once the response is under way, there is an essentially uninterrupted sequence of responses. This type of behavior is illustrated graphically in figure 6.1.

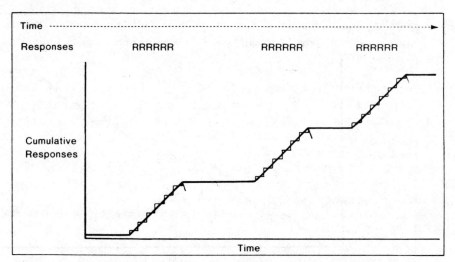

Figure 6.1 Performance under a fixed-ratio schedule of reinforcement. The line in the graph represents the total number of responses that has occurred up until a given point in time. Each response (signified by an *R* at the top of the graph) causes the line to move vertically in the graph. Periods of time in which no responses occur are represented by the horizontal movement of the line. The diagonal slash mark at the end of each group of responses signifies the administration of reward. Thus, in this illustration, reward is always available but requires six responses. There is a pause after each reinforcement and then a rapid run of responses sufficient to obtain another reward.

Variable-Ratio Schedule Behavior

Like the fixed-ratio schedule, a variable-ratio schedule requires that a given number of responses be made for each reward. However, in this schedule, the number of responses required for each reward varies and is thus unpredictable for the responder. A pigeon, for example, may have to make five key pecks to gain the first reward and fifteen key pecks to receive the second reward. Similarly, a slot machine player is reinforced on a variable-ratio schedule. The slot machine may pay off the first time after only one pull of the lever, but the next payoff may require ninety-five lever pulls. As with the fixed ratio, once an organism begins to respond, there seems to be no better approach than to complete the required number of responses (whatever that number happens to be). But there is generally less tendency to pause after a reward because the next response requirement might be a very easy one. There may be some tendency to pause after the reward, especially if the average number of required responses increases, but the general tendency is to respond rapidly and steadily. This type of behavior is graphed in figure 6.2.

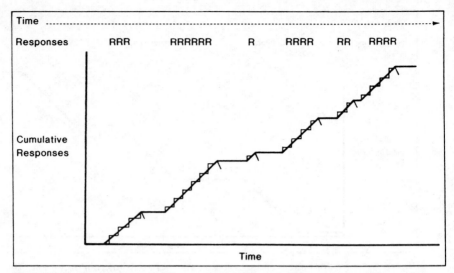

Figure 6.2 Performance under a variable-ratio schedule of reinforcement. The number of responses required to obtain reward varies from occasion to occasion. A brief pause after reward is followed by a high rate of response until the next reward is obtained.

Fixed-Interval Schedule Behavior

When a fixed-interval schedule is employed, each reward is followed by a period of time in which no responses are rewarded. The length of this period of time is the same after each reward. One example of such a reinforcement schedule is when individuals check for a mail delivery that always occurs at the same time each day. Receiving mail on one day constitutes a reward. Since the next delivery will not be made until twenty-four hours later, checking the mailbox during that twenty-four hour period will not be rewarded. However, the first response following that twenty-four hour period will be rewarded with a new delivery.

The optimal behavior in a fixed-interval schedule is easy to surmise: The organism should wait precisely the length of the interval, make a single response, receive the reward, and wait again. This would ensure the receipt of all available rewards with the least possible effort. However, most organisms do not adjust this well to a fixed-interval schedule. There are two closely related reasons for this.

The first is simply that the natural timing capacity of the organism is not perfect. All mammals contain what may be called an "internal clock," or the ability to judge the passage of time, presumably on the basis of rhythmic processes within the body. But this judgment is only approximate. A person with a watch, or a rat given a comparable timing stimulus, could handle a fixed-interval schedule more accurately. In the absence of such timing instruments, they can only approximate a fixed interval.

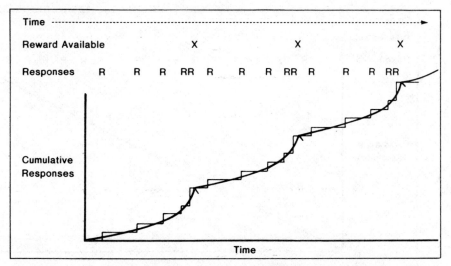

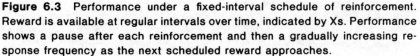

Figure 6.3 Performance under a fixed-interval schedule of reinforcement. Reward is available at regular intervals over time, indicated by Xs. Performance shows a pause after each reinforcement and then a gradually increasing response frequency as the next scheduled reward approaches.

The second reason for the failure to adjust optimally to a fixed-interval schedule is the principle of the anticipatory response. If a rewarded response occurs at the end of an interval of time, this response is regularly preceded by earlier temporal cues that tend to elicit the response before its regularly scheduled time. Even if the organism's measure of timing were perfect, there would be a tendency to begin responding before the appointed time. For example, you may know that the mail is not delivered until noon each day and you may also know that it's now only 11:30 A.M., but unless there are stronger competing alternatives, you are likely to begin checking the mailbox in order to be there when the mail is delivered.

Thus, the typical behavior of an organism under a fixed-interval schedule of reinforcement might be summarized as follows. For a while after a reward is received, the organism does not respond at all. Even if the organism is dependent on only its internal clock, it knows that it is not yet time to respond. As time passes and the appropriate moment approaches, the anticipatory tendency increases, the temporal cues become similar to the reinforced ones, and responding begins—at first slowly and then progressively more rapidly so that the organism is almost certain to make a response at the time a reward is next available. This behavior is often referred to as a "fixed-interval scallop," indicating that an organism under such a schedule first exhibits a very low response rate and then a continuously increasing rate as reinforcement approaches. This behavior is shown graphically in figure 6.3.

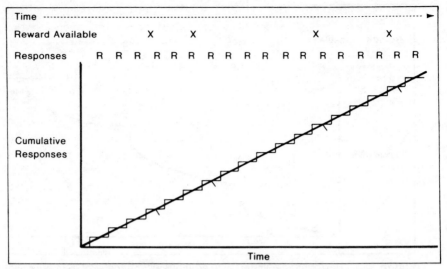

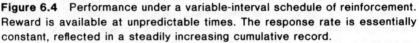

Figure 6.4 Performance under a variable-interval schedule of reinforcement. Reward is available at unpredictable times. The response rate is essentially constant, reflected in a steadily increasing cumulative record.

Variable-Interval Schedule Behavior

The variable-interval schedule is like the fixed-interval schedule except that the length of time between reward opportunities varies unpredictably. This makes it impossible for an organism to judge the amount of time it should wait before making another response. Examples of this type of schedule in everyday situations are difficult to find, but they do exist. For example, if you are attempting to telephone a list of people, some dialing responses are rewarded when people answer their phones. Sometimes, however, a dialing response is met with either no answer or a busy signal. In these cases, if you continue to respond, you may get an answer immediately or it may take an hour of dialing before your response is rewarded. This situation represents a variable-interval schedule since there is an unpredictable period of time between completed calls. The behavior of organisms under such a schedule shows a kind of compromise between responding very fast in order to be sure to get every possible reward and responding very slowly in order not to make many unnecessary responses. The result, as shown in figure 6.4, is a relatively low but steady rate of responding.

Complex Schedules

An enormous number of more complex schedules can be designed by various combinations of these four basic schedules. For example, a *mixed* schedule can be obtained by combining two different schedules so that one is in effect sometimes and the other is in effect at other times. If some external stimulus signals to the organism which schedule is in force, the reinforcement schedule is referred to as a *multiple* schedule. Several schedules may be in force for different responses at the same time. The organism may be given a choice between schedules, or they may be run in sequence so that first one and then the other must be satisfied in order to obtain reward. By and large, the behavior observed under these more complex schedules is some reasonable combination of the performance generated by the simple schedules that comprise them. Suppose, for example, that a fixed-interval schedule is combined with a fixed-ratio schedule so that reward is available at regular intervals but a number of responses is required to obtain it when available. This causes the organism first to wait out most of the interval, as characteristic of a fixed-interval schedule, but then to respond at a high, steady rate as characteristic of a fixed-ratio schedule. This behavior, if graphed, would look very much like figure 6.1, except that the pause after each reward is now controlled by the length of the fixed-interval schedule.

Summary and Applications

The rate at which freely available responses occur over time is controlled to a large degree by the schedule for rewarding such responses. When reward is confined to regular or fixed intervals, responding tends to be confined to those intervals. On the other hand, when reward is confined to irregular or unpredictable intervals, responding tends to be steady but relatively slow. When reward is always available but several responses are required to get it, response, once it begins, is rapid; but there is a pause after each reward before the response starts again. This pause can be reduced or eliminated by varying the number of responses required. And various combinations of all these behaviors can be obtained by various combinations of the different schedules.

There are at least two reasons why these facts are important in controlling behavior. The first reason involves the ability to control the behavior of another organism—to do so, it is important to schedule rewards to produce the desired response rate. For example, to maintain order in a first grade classroom, a teacher may decide to reward well-behaved children by rewarding them with gold stars or stickers. If these rewards are given out on a regular, predictable time schedule, for example at the beginning of each hour, the teacher is not scheduling rewards optimally. Such a fixed-interval schedule will produce good behavior around the beginning of each hour, but will lead to a weaker tendency for good behavior at other times. Better the rewards be made at variable intervals to maintain a steady rate of expectation.

The second reason why these facts are important concerns the scheduling of one's own rewards. We are all in a position to administer rewards to ourselves, whether the reward is a trip to the movies, a splurge on food or clothing, or simply some free time to daydream for a while. We can thus control our own behavior, at least in part, by the way we schedule these rewards. This is of special value when the schedule imposed by the external world is not one that generates optimal behavior. For example, a worker should normally maintain a steady rate of production, even though "pay-day" constitutes a fixed-interval schedule that tends to produce a pause and then an acceleration in response rate. Probably the most familiar context for scheduled rewards is studying. Studying is an operant response because you are free to study at any time. If your exams have been scheduled at regular intervals, you will surely have observed the tendency for your studying behavior to follow the fixed-interval scallop; you probably take a break from studying after each exam, then gradually increase your rate of studying, culminating in cramming. Even as simple a procedure as waiting to get a drink of water until you have finished a designated task can have a large effect upon your productive capacity.

Instrumental Conditioning

In the operant conditioning situation, we were interested in the factors that determine the response rate when an organism is free to respond at any time. However, there are numerous situations in which an organism's opportunities for response are limited by environmental constraints to only certain occasions. For example, a student having grade problems might resolve to improve the situation by attending classes on a more regular basis. If this decision is made at 3 A.M., the student might experience a strong desire to begin performing this response (going to class) immediately, but the opportunity to respond would not exist since no classes are held at that time. The opportunity to make the response in this case is limited to particular occasions by environmental constraints. Similarly, assume that a rat has learned to press a lever and that following each response we remove the lever from the experimental chamber for a period of time. The opportunity to make bar press responses in this situation is not freely available, but is confined to times when the bar is present.

Responses that are periodically enabled by some controlling event in the environment are referred to as *instrumental responses,* and the experimental analysis of such responses takes place in an *instrumental conditioning situation.* Obviously, in studying instrumental responses, we have little interest in the rate at which the responses occur since the rate is partially controlled by external events. The major experimental variable of interest in instrumental conditioning is the *condition of reinforcement.* This condition involves the strength of an instrumental response as determined by the properties of the reward (such as amount, delay, or probability).

Recall that a *schedule* of reinforcement in operant conditioning determines when a particular reward is available; availability may depend on time or on the number of responses the organism makes. The *condition* of reinforcement refers to the descriptive properties of the reward itself—how big it is, how good it is, how quickly it is received. The purpose of this section is to consider the properties of a reward that are known to affect the tendency to make instrumental responses.

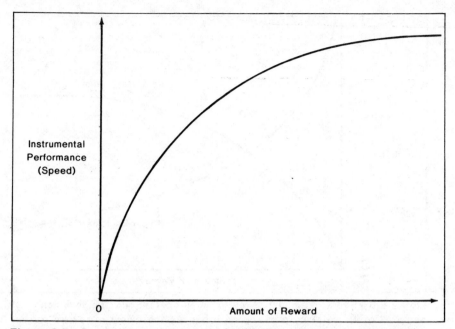

Figure 6.5 Summary of experimental findings showing that instrumental response as measured, for example, by the speed of making a response once it is enabled increases as the amount of reward increases.

Amount of Reward

Perhaps the most obvious property of a reward concerns its amount or quantity. The effects of amount of reward have been studied in a variety of instrumental contexts, the simplest of which is a rat running down a short, straight alley toward a reward of food. Combining the results of various studies, we can represent the effect of the amount variable according to the graph in figure 6.5. Two properties of this graph deserve special attention: First, as would be intuitively expected, *performance generally increases as the amount of the reward increases.* However, and this is the second important point, the curve shows "diminishing returns." In other words, adding a unit of reward to a small amount increases performance more than adding that same unit to a larger amount of reward. In the language of the economist, the "marginal utility" of reward is a decreasing function; increasing salary by ten cents an hour means more to a person with low income than to a person with higher income.

At this point, we can illustrate the difference between the effects of a variable such as amount of reward on instrumental, as opposed to operant, responses. Consider a rat living in a situation in which it earns all of its water by pressing on a bar that is freely available. In this operant context, we can study the effects of rewards of different sizes for pressing the bar. The results of such a study are depicted in figure 6.6. The larger the drop of water the rat receives for bar pressing, the more water it consumes on

Principles of Learning: Positive Reinforcement   **95**

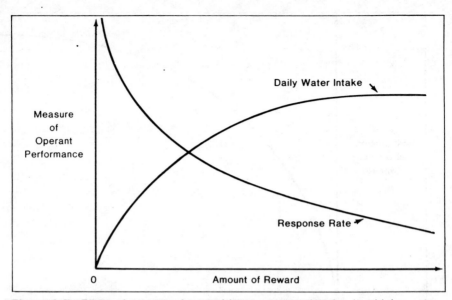

Figure 6.6 Effect of amount of reward in an operant situation in which a rat earns all of its water by pressing on a bar. As the amout of reward for bar pressing increases, so does the animal's daily water intake. However, its response rate decreases, presumably because the rat can obtain all the water it wants by making fewer responses.

a daily basis; but, at the same time, the fewer responses it actually makes per day. The presumed reason is perhaps obvious: The rat's thirst is reduced more quickly by the larger drop of water it receives for bar pressing; hence, it needs fewer drops to maintain equilibrium. If we measure the operant response in this case by its rate of occurrence, we would conclude that response strength grows weaker as the reward grows larger. It is this interaction of reward with drive motivation that makes the operant situation a complicated one in which to determine the effects of conditions of reinforcement.

It should be noted that, if the trials occur very frequently, a comparable complication can arise in the instrumental situation because, again, the subject's motivation may be reduced. However, we can arrange to control motivation by distributing the instrumental conditioning trials at widely spaced intervals, and when we do so, we find that response strength, measured in such ways as response speed, becomes greater as the reward becomes larger.

One additional question should be considered in this context, namely, the effect of changing to a new amount of reward after performance has stabilized on one amount. Reward can be either increased or decreased; in either case, the result is clear: *A change in the amount of reward leads to a rapid alteration in the performance level, which changes in the same direction as the change in amount.* In other words, increasing the reward leads to increased performance, and decreasing the reward leads to decreased performance. Thus, the level of performance that occurs under a given amount of reward is not fixed permanently, but varies in accordance with changes in the amount of the reward.

Delay of Reward
Up until this point, we have talked about rewards as if they always followed a response immediately. Of course, it is possible for rewards to be delayed and to occur some period of time after the response in question. This condition of reinforcement has also received extensive experimental study.

It is probably not surprising to learn that *the longer the reward is delayed, the poorer the performance of an instrumental response.* This basic fact is illustrated graphically in figure 6.7. Note that the optimal condition of reinforcement involves no delay, but that some performance can be maintained by rewards that occur some time after the response. This graph also shows the "diminishing returns" characteristic of reward delay: The detrimental effects of an added unit of delay decrease as the length of the entire delay increases.

It isn't possible to put specific numbers along the baseline of the delay graph to show how long after a response a reward still has an effect. The entire range of time we are dealing with is only a matter of seconds; even a delayed reward must occur rather soon after the response to be effective at all.

One reason for difficulty in placing actual units of time along the baseline of the graph can be seen by considering the differential effect of delayed reward in instrumental and operant contexts. In operant conditioning, the response is freely available and may be made repeatedly. Suppose, then, that a response initiates a delayed reward that will occur without further response at some later time. During that delay, however, the organism may engage in more of the same behavior—so that the actual time of delay cannot be rigidly controlled. For example, a rat's bar press may not produce a reward for several seconds, but since the rat may continue to press the bar during the delay, the reward might well occur immediately following a later press. For this reason, delay can best be studied in an instrumental context, where the response can be disabled during the delay interval.

But even in an instrumental situation, an organism is always doing *something* during a delay period. It now appears that *the major factor determining the detrimental effects of delayed reward is the behavior that occurs during the delay interval.* If, during the delay period, the organism engages in responses that are incompatible with the instrumental response, the later responses are more strongly reinforced than the intended response and are likely to compete with it. Conversely, if the organism engages in

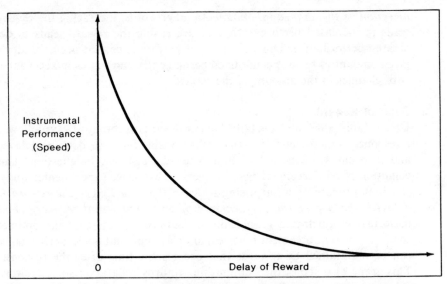

Figure 6.7 Summary of experimental findings showing that instrumental performance as measured, for example, by the speed of a response grows weaker as the delay of the reward increases.

little overt behavior but quietly waits for the deserved reward, the detrimental effects of delay are less evident.

Delayed reward is very common in everyday life; indeed, one of the important factors in human maturity is the ability to sustain what is often called "delayed gratification." Rather than demanding immediate satisfaction for their responses, mature individuals learn to tolerate delay, especially when this increases the payoff. One common illustration of this type of behavior involves the study habits of most good students. Studying regularly throughout a course is not rewarded immediately (since exams and grades are scheduled at intervals), but good students know that their diligence in studying will eventually be rewarded.

There are two ways that language can help humans offset the detrimental effects of delayed reward. Humans can be told (or can tell themselves) that a particular response will be rewarded sometime later; these words provide immediate secondary reinforcement to help bridge the delay before the reward. The second way language helps humans offset the effects of delayed reward is by giving them the ability to verbally relate the reward to the appropriate response just before the delayed reward occurs. Thus, when a parent says, "I'm giving you this reward because you behaved so well at the party," the parent ensures that the intended response, rather than a more recent one, is reinforced. However, neither of these human abilities is perfect, and the optimal condition of reinforcement, even for humans, is still achieved when the reward occurs as quickly as possible after the response.

Partial Reinforcement and the Goal Gradient

An instrumental response is not necessarily reinforced every time it occurs. Not every lecture, concert, or movie that you attend is enjoyable. Similarly, a rat may not find food at the end of a maze every time it runs there. When reward occurs for only part of the trials for an instrumental response, we refer to it as *partial reinforcement*. We are not saying that only part of the reward is received; rather, we are talking about the frequency with which reward occurs following a response.

One result of partial reinforcement is nearly universal: Performance improves more gradually than if every trial is reinforced. You may think of partial reinforcement as a combination of acquisition and extinction of the response, with the decremental effects of the nonreinforced experiences retarding the incremental effects of the reinforced experiences. Accordingly, although performance can be maintained (and is perhaps best maintained) with partial reinforcement, original acquisition is faster with continuous reinforcement.

Before describing the performance resulting from partial reinforcement, it is necessary to introduce the concept of the *goal gradient*. Whenever reward occurs at the end of a sequence of responses—such as running through a maze, taking an examination, or writing a theme—changes in behavior occur as the goal is approached. The term *goal gradient* refers to these changes in performance.

The effects of continuous and partial reinforcement on the goal gradient are depicted graphically in figure 6.8. When reward is received every time, response chain performance steadily increases until very near the goal, when performance decreases somewhat. This last minute decrease presumably reflects the fact that the end of a response chain signals the beginning of new behavior; these other responses become anticipatory and tend to interfere with completion of the behavior chain itself.

When the completion of the behavior chain is followed by reward only part of the time, performance again increases over the early portions of the chain; in fact, as figure 6.8 shows, performance actually reaches a higher level than that produced by continuous reinforcement. Thus, at least some portions of the response may be performed with greater vigor if the response is only occasionally rewarded. However, as the chain continues, the performance produced by partial reinforcement begins to decrease sooner and decreases more rapidly, terminating at a lower level than if reward is regularly received. In short, partial reinforcement leads organisms to start faster and perform harder. This may mean that, with long response chains, they actually complete the response sooner, but they also taper off more

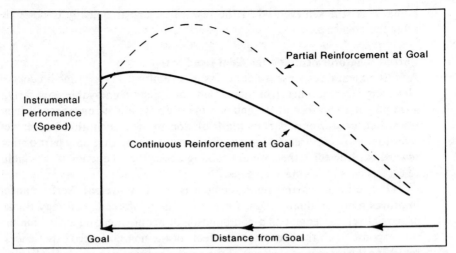

Figure 6.8 The goal gradients for continuous and partial reinforcement. The goal is approached from the right toward the vertical axis. In the case of continuous reinforcement, speed increases as the goal is approached until very near the goal, where the organism must stop. In the case of partial reinforcement, speed is generally faster than with continuous reinforcement, but the organism begins to slow down sooner and is performing slower when the goal is reached than if reward occurred every time.

quickly and end up at a slower speed than when the response is continuously reinforced.

We can understand part of this effect from theoretical constructs already introduced: Habit and inhibition. Recall our assumptions that reinforcement produces habit while nonreinforcement produces inhibition and that habit generalizes more extensively than inhibition. The reason that the partially reinforced organism begins to slow down as the goal is approached and eventually reaches a lower level very near the goal is because of the presence of inhibition, resulting from occasional nonreinforcement. We may informally describe this analysis as follows: When an organism receives only occasional reward, it begins each trial optimistically, as it expects a reward. As the organism gets closer to the goal, however, the inhibition resulting from occasional nonreinforcement begins to appear, changing the attitude of the organism to one of pessimism.

You are undoubtedly familiar with this phenomenon. A student may start out on a project or paper with enthusiasm, confident that his or her work will lead to a good grade; but as the completion of the paper nears, the student feels an increasing concern that the paper will not do as well as he or she initially thought. Similarly, an author may begin each new book or article thinking that this work will surely have an impact, but enthusiasm tends to taper off as the end comes into sight. This tendency

Chapter 6

may be so strong that the inhibition near the goal actually exceeds the habit; if so, the response is never finished. Instead, the organism stops short of the goal and begins another response, about which, because the new response is a long distance from its goal, the organism can be enthusiastic. Many garages are filled with unfinished inventions!

To summarize the effects of partial reinforcement, several experimental results may be reviewed. As might be expected, performance under partial reinforcement improves more gradually, but is nevertheless maintained effectively. Furthermore, performance generated by partial reinforcement may come to exceed that produced by continuous reinforcement, especially during the early portions of a behavior chain. As the goal is approached, however, the occasional nonreinforcement produces a rapid decrease in the vigor of the response, so that performance terminates at a level below that produced by continuous reward. We shall also observe in a later chapter that partial reinforcement has important effects on the persistence of a response and the generality of learning.

The Power of Positive Control

We, the authors of this book, may have committed a crime. If you have read this chapter muttering to yourself, "I knew all that," we have wasted your time. Perhaps it's true that if you deliberately set about to teach your dog a new trick, the facts and principles described in this chapter can help you understand only a little better why your natural techniques work reasonably well. But the power of positive control has enormous potential that is too little used and too much misused. A few examples may help convince you.

Mail

A letter from a child who is away at school is a great reward to parents. Conversely, a letter from home is equally a reward to the child, especially if the child is somewhat homesick. But we are likely to schedule our lives so that letters are written and mailed with such regularity that they arrive on a fixed-interval schedule. The parents' response of expecting a letter wanes after receiving one, but then increases progressively to a high pitch just before the scheduled time arrives. Small wonder they become frantic if the letter is not there.

On the other hand, perhaps the student at school feels a little more lonely than usual on mail day, stays late in bed, cuts a class, and waits for a letter to arrive. If the student does this, he or she is, at best, wasting a unit of reward; at worst, the student is rewarding behaviors quite the opposite of those the parents had hoped to train. Better that the child place the letter unopened on the desk, find a friend who did attend the class, copy the lecture notes, do some extra study to make up, and *then* devour the unit of reward.

Listening

Listening is a powerful reward to most people. We all have troubles and like to bend a sympathetic ear with them. The person who realizes this and who has a little skill in the art of shaping can, for example, induce the stranger sitting in the next seat on an airplane to talk about his or her problems within the time it takes the plane to leave the gate and get into the air. Perhaps you do not want to listen to a stranger's problems (unless he or she will return the favor and listen to yours!), but sometimes listening can be useful. Consider the waitress confronting what seems to her an endless flow of largely nondescript faces, grunting their way through life. If you pause to say, "Hello again, how are things today?" you will soon become recognized as a person deserving special treatment. A similar effect could take place in the context of an employer's relationship with employees.

We are more likely to misuse than make use of the reward of listening. The amateur psychologist may think it helps people to listen to their troubles and respond sympathetically. But, most likely, this type of listening just rewards people for feeling sorry for themselves! You will never be the most popular listener if you respond critically, helping people see how they have contributed to their own misery and how they might do something about it. But you will be a respected listener when people are really in trouble.

And don't forget yourself. If you seek out only listeners who will "understand," you are contributing to your own self-pity. Indeed, even listening to yourself can be misused. In sum, every time you listen, you reward the behavior being uttered.

Principles of Learning: Positive Reinforcement

Multiple Choice Test Questions

1. For rewards to be effective, they must
   a. be an effect of the response
   b. be apparent to the organism receiving them
   c. occur shortly after the response
   d. result in drive reduction
2. Which of the following means of determining rewards requires prior learning?
   a. functional identification
   b. drive reduction
   c. secondary reinforcement
   d. high-probability behaviors

3. A pause followed by a high, steady response rate is characteristic of
   a. fixed-interval and fixed-ratio schedules
   b. variable-interval and variable-ratio schedules
   c. fixed-interval and variable-interval schedules
   d. fixed-ratio and variable-ratio schedules
4. The rate at which reinforcement is received is *more* dependent on
   a. the person in ratio schedules and the environment in interval schedules
   b. the person in interval schedules and the environment in ratio schedules
   c. the person in the day and the environment in the night
   d. the person in the night and the environment in the day
5. To predict whether a larger amount of reward will lead to higher instrumental performance, you need to know the
   a. nature of the reward
   b. amounts of reward involved
   c. nature of the response
   d. amount of response required
6. Partial reinforcement refers to the procedure of
   a. giving only part of the reward
   b. giving reward on only part of the trials
   c. requiring only part of the response
   d. requiring the response on only part of the trials

Multiple Choice Answers

1. (c) A reward may very well be the effect of the response; it may also be apparent to the organism, and it may result in drive reduction. But the necessary feature of an effective reward is that it occur shortly after the response.
2. (c) The other means may lead to the identification of rewards based on prior learning, but prior learning is a necessary feature of secondary reinforcement.
3. (d) There is a tendency to pause in both types of ratio schedules. Interval schedules typically do not produce a high, steady response rate.
4. (a) A reinforcement schedule is the same both day and night. The rate of reinforcement in a ratio schedule will, to some extent, be determined by the length of the ratio as set by the environment, but the person can work toward reinforcement at any time. The person must respond to obtain reinforcement on interval schedules, but the maximum rate of reinforcement depends on the program set by the environment.
5. (b) The amount of reward affects all instrumental responses and applies to all kinds of rewards. But if the total amount of reward is already very large, giving a slightly larger one won't increase performance—perhaps because the organism is already responding as vigorously as possible.

6. (b) As previously stated, all of the response is required on every trial under partial reinforcement, and all of the reward is given on schedule. Partial reinforcement refers to giving reward on only part of the trials.

True/False Thought Questions

1. A superstition is a response that was originally learned because it produced positive reinforcement but that no longer does so.
2. Adolescents with poor vocabularies may learn to interject the words "you know" because their listeners agree with them when they say these words.
3. Awareness of reinforcement is unnecessary and unimportant.
4. We can determine whether grades and teacher approval are rewards for a student through functional identification.
5. If all drive reductions are rewards, then all rewards are drive reductions.
6. Young people really don't like to pet unless they can "go all the way."
7. Someone who occasionally and unexpectedly buys flowers or presents for his or her spouse is providing the spouse with variable-interval reinforcement.
8. A person who sometimes accepts and sometimes declines another's requests for dates may be placing the other person on a variable-ratio schedule.
9. People can control their own behavior by scheduling rewards that they themselves control.
10. The rate of operant responding depends on the schedule and not the condition of reinforcement.
11. It is usually best to delay rewards because most people want rewards more after a delay.
12. Organisms may perform more vigorously if they don't receive a reward after every trial.

True/False Answers

1. (False) A response that no longer produces reinforcement undergoes experimental extinction. Human superstitions are everyday examples of the laboratory findings that responses may be learned simply because they happen to occur before a reward, even though they do not actually produce the reward.
2. (True) Agreement is a form of secondary reinforcement for humans and will increase the frequency of response even when both parties are unaware of what is going on.
3. (False) When human beings are aware of whether or not a response will produce a reward, they can rehearse their behavior verbally and use their knowledge to bring their behavior under control.

4. (True) Whether grades and teacher approval constitute rewards depends on whether they have acquired secondary reinforcing value during the student's past history. Students differ in this regard, but functional identification can help determine whether grades and approval are rewards for any particular student.

5. (False) The logic is fallacious. Most psychologists agree that all drive reductions are rewarding, but many contend that there are also other sources of reward.

6. (False) Various forms of sensory pleasures, including erotic stimulation, appear to be reinforcing, even when they do not culminate in the reduction of a primary drive.

7. (True) Assuming that the spouse is not the suspicious type, the flowers and presents should constitute a type of reward. Although birthdays, Christmas, and similar occasions may occur at irregular intervals, they are predictable and hence do not generate the steady behavior characteristic of a variable-interval schedule.

8. (True) If the acceptances depend on other commitments, this might be more nearly an interval schedule. If, however, the person varies the number of times he or she must be asked out before accepting, the situation is a variable-ratio schedule and generates a high, steady rate of responding.

9. (True) Rewards affect behavior with equal force whether administered by oneself or by an outside agent. Few people have learned to use the principle of positive reinforcement to control their own behavior. For example, a student may go to the movies before rather than after finishing his or her homework.

10. (False) The condition of reinforcement is defined as the momentary properties, such as amount, of the conditioning situation. Although the schedule of reinforcement is studied in the operant conditioning context, the rate of a freely available response depends on the reinforcement condition as well as on the schedule.

11. (False) Although there may be special circumstances in which delaying a reward makes the reward more valuable, the greatest effect on instrumental performance is typically obtained by giving rewards immediately.

12. (True) If reward is too infrequent, the organism may be reluctant to complete a response lest it go unrewarded again. However, occasional reward produces a higher level of overall performance than consistent reward.

Essay/Discussion Questions

1. Think of several familiar superstitions, and speculate on how these superstitious beliefs might have been acquired by adventitious reinforcement. Further discuss how they might continue to receive some schedule of reinforcement.

2. Think of several examples of events or objects that you find rewarding. In light of this chapter, discuss how the occurrence of these rewards affects your behavior.

References

Events that ARE Rewarding

*Butler, R. A. Discrimination learning by rhesus monkeys to visual-exploration motivation. *Journal of Comparative and Physiological Psychology*, 1953, *46*, 95–99.

Cowles, J. T. Food tokens as incentives for learning by chimpanzees. *Comparative Psychology Monographs*, 1937, *14*, No. 5.

Greenspoon, J. The reinforcing effect of two spoken sounds on the frequency of two responses. *American Journal of Psychology*, 1955, *68*, 409–416.

*Harlow, H. F. Learning and satiation of responses in intrinsically motivated complex puzzle performance by monkeys. *Journal of Comparative and Physiological Psychology*, 1950, *43*, 289–294.

Hull, C. L. The conflicting psychologies of learning—a way out. *Psychological Review*, 1935, *42*, 491–516.

Olds, J., and Milner, P. Positive reinforcement produced by electrical stimulation of septal area and other region of rat brain. *Journal of Comparative and Physiological Psychology*, 1954, *47*, 419–427.

Premack, D. Toward empirical behavior laws. I. Positive reinforcement. *Psychological Review*, 1959, *66*, 219–233.

Sheffield, F. D., and Roby, T. B. Reward value of a non-nutritive sweet taste. *Journal of Comparative and Physiological Psychology*, 1950, *43*, 471–481.

Sheffield, F. D.; Wulff, J. J.; and Backer, R. Reward value of copulation without sex drive reduction. *Journal of Comparative and Physiological Psychology*, 1951, *44*, 3–8.

Operant Conditioning

Ferster, C. S., and Skinner, B. F. *Schedules of reinforcement*. New York: Appleton-Century-Crofts, 1957.

*Skinner, B. F. "Superstition" in the pigeon. *Journal of Experimental Psychology*, 1948, *38*, 168–172.

Instrumental Conditioning

*Black, R. W. Reward in instrumental conditioning. In G. H. Bower (Ed.), *Psychology of learning and motivation*. New York: Academic Press, 1976.

Hull, C. L. The goal gradient hypothesis and maze learning. *Psychological Review*, 1932, *39*, 25–43.

Spence, K. W. *Behavior theory and conditioning*. New Haven: Yale University Press, 1956.

The Power of Positive Control

*Logan, F. A. The experimental psychology of animal learning and now. *American Psychologist*, 1972, *27*, 1055–1062.

*Suitable for additional reading by the beginning student. The others are written at a more technical level.

Principles of Learning: Negative Reinforcement

Organisms not only attempt to maximize their contact with pleasant events, they also attempt to minimize their contact with unpleasant events. Indeed, the so-called instinct for self-preservation suggests that we will do more to avoid physical harm than to obtain physical pleasure. Some people may occasionally endure pain or take risks in the interest of personal gain; but, more often than not, we behave as if we strongly dislike discomfort. Accordingly, to accompany the principle of positive reinforcement, there is also a principle of negative reinforcement: *Whenever a response if closely followed by a reduction in an aversive state, the tendency for that response to occur in the future is increased.* Reducing or, preferably, terminating an unpleasant situation is reinforcing and makes the preceding behavior more likely to recur.

The same disclaimers made previously concerning positive reinforcement apply equally to negative reinforcement, although little experimental evidence has been obtained with respect to them. Negative reinforcement need not be actually produced by the response for the response to be learned, nor need the person be aware of any causal connection between the behavior and the event for the reinforcement to be effective. Negative reinforcement is as automatic as positive reinforcement.

Some psychologists have used the term *negative reinforcement* as another way of saying "punishment"; however, the present usage is more common and appropriate. The concept of reinforcement is always one of *strengthening* a response; this type of reinforcement is called negative only because it is occasioned by reducing or terminating stimulus conditions rather than by presenting them. For example, a coach might strengthen team performance by removing a discordant or ineffective player, even if no replacement is available. Thus, although the basic principles of positive and negative reinforcement are very much the same, there is nevertheless justification for the distinction between them.

In part, this distinction is necessary because some of the procedures described with respect to positive reinforcement are difficult or impossible to employ in the process of negative reinforcement. For example, we could use the expression, "variable-interval negative reinforcement," but it is not

7

at all clear how such a schedule could be realized. An organism would have to be left in an aversive state with an available response that would occasionally permit reduction of that state. But, at the same time, the aversive state would have to be reinstated on some schedule.

The principal reason for discriminating between positive and negative reinforcement concerns the other effects of those events in addition to the reinforcing effect itself. Consider two rats that have been trained to press a bar in a small box. One rat learned the response when hungry in order to obtain food, and the other learned the response to turn off a mildly painful electric shock that sometimes occurred. Insofar as their bar-pressing behavior is concerned, the two rats may perform equally well. But the rat controlled by positive reinforcement (food) displays distinct eagerness when the experimenter approaches to take the rat from its home cage to the apparatus; by contrast, the rat controlled by negative reinforcement (shock termination) may make distinct efforts to avoid the situation, such as biting the experimenter.

The same principle can be seen in everyday life. Some children learn to play the piano through support, praise, and encouragement, and some learn to play under threat and denial to force them to practice. Both procedures may produce equally good piano players. But in the future, the child trained with positive reinforcement will approach the piano voluntarily, while the child trained with negative reinforcement will have to be persuaded to perform. The next time you see an animal act, try to figure out whether the animals were trained under threat of physical violence. Do they really seem to enjoy performing? An organism's attitudes toward the environment are greatly affected by the type of reinforcement, positive or negative, that has been used to promote learning.

It may therefore seem strange (and is perhaps unfortunate) that most human behavior is under "aversive control," including punishment, as will be discussed in a later chapter. For example, many religions threaten punishment rather than offering attractive inducements for moral behavior. Our legal system, geared as it is to fines and imprisonment, capitalizes on the power of negative reinforcement. And many parents, although proclaiming love and affection, control the behavior of their children through threats and punishments.

But whether we like it or not, behavior is controlled to a significant extent by the principle of negative reinforcement, and the experimental analysis concerning this principle is therefore a proper topic for psychology. In the next few sections, we will review two basic procedures in which the principle of negative reinforcement is revealed: escape learning and avoidance learning.

Events that ARE Aversive

Before exploring the topics of escape and avoidance learning, it is necessary to discuss the way in which aversive events are identified. By now, you should be prepared for an approach involving a functional definition. An *aversive event* is an event that, when terminated, leads to an increase in the occurrence of the preceding responses. Aversive events are unpleasant and noxious, events that the organism seeks to remove. They are emotionally negative and their termination is reinforcing.

There are three characteristics of aversive events that will be important to the subsequent study of negative reinforcement. The first characteristic is that aversive events elicit some unlearned motor responses. If a shock is applied to the paws of a rat, it squeals and prances around the cage; a child who touches a hot stove reflexively withdraws. A second characteristic is that aversive events elicit an internal, implicit fear response. We will have more to say about the nature of this response later, under the topic of secondary motivation. The third and final characteristic of aversive stimuli is that these stimuli not only have emotional consequences but are stimuli in the sense that new responses can be associated with them.

Primary Negative Reinforcement: Escape Learning

When an organism is in a primary (unlearned) aversive state and a response is required to reduce or eliminate it, we refer to the conditioning situation as *escape learning*. A wide variety of conditions are painful or unpleasant by their very nature, and we dislike such events instinctively. Physical blows, intense heat or cold, bright lights, loud sounds, and extreme pressures are a few of the countless familiar examples of aversive events. Electric shock has been the most commonly used aversive condition in the laboratory because of the ease with which it can be controlled. An organism experiencing a shock naturally tries to terminate it (escape from it) and will learn responses that accomplish this goal.

You have learned to put on a coat when you're cold. You may have learned to fight when attacked by another person or animal. You have learned to take an aspirin if you have a headache. You have learned a variety of techniques for reducing or terminating itches, burns, and painful objects, such as a cinder in your eye. These are a few everyday illustrations of escape learning. The paradigm for this type of learning is shown in figure 7.1.

In escape learning, there is nothing the organism can do to prevent the onset of the aversive event. Only after the event occurs can anything be done about it. Normally, aversive stimuli produce vigorous responding that, in many cases, successfully removes the painful event. When this is the

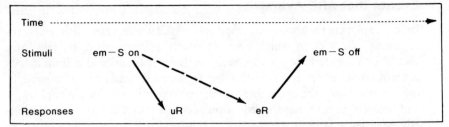

Figure 7.1 Schematic description of escape learning. An aversive event (em — S) may elicit a variety of unlearned reflexive responses (uR) but remains on until a particular escape response (eR) is made.

case, no learning is required. It is when our natural responses to the aversive stimulus do not remove the stimulus that we are motivated to try other responses and to learn the one that works most effectively. Hence, *escape learning* means more than simple escape; it means that a new response is associated with the aversive event. This fact is indicated by the dashed arrow in figure 7.1.

When the natural responses to an aversive stimulus are incompatible with the escape response, the natural responses become the major impediment to escape learning. When subjected to a painful event, the organism engages vigorously in many reflexive activities. If these activities reduce the likelihood that the organism will ever even try the response that is actually effective in escaping the pain, then it is unlikely that the organism will receive the negative reinforcement necessary for learning. A response must be made to be reinforced; sometimes shaping may be necessary to produce the desired escape response.

Consider, for example, trying to train a rat to stand immobile on a grid floor hot with electric shock in order to turn the shock off. The rat's natural response is to jump and prance around, and maybe even to roll onto its back so that its fur will insulate its skin from the painful shock. Repeatedly engaging in these behaviors simply precludes a stationary stance. Training the response would be difficult, but it might be accomplished by requiring at first only a very brief moment of immobility and then progressively lengthening the requirement as the rat begins to learn.

Such difficulties with escape learning may also be observed in humans. Our natural tendency, when irritated by an itch, is to scratch. Only by experience and with difficulty have we learned that this response is incompatible with the effective treatment. When sunburned, we are tempted to take a cold bath for temporary relief, but actually a mildly uncomfortable hot bath is more likely to reduce the persisting pain. The asthmatic encounters an even more trying problem. Difficult breathing leads to gasping and increasing anxiety, responses that are the opposite of those most appropriate to an asthmatic attack. The asthmatic person must learn to overcome these natural tendencies, to relax and breathe slowly to gain relief.

By way of summary, escape learning is based on negative reinforcement, or the reduction or termination of an aversive state. When reflexive responses are inadequate, new responses will be learned; but learning will be difficult if the required and natural responses are incompatible.

Secondary Negative Reinforcement: Avoidance Learning

Although we have not yet discussed in detail the principle of secondary motivation, the basic ideas are familiar enough that a brief explanation should enable us to discuss avoidance learning. The important point to remember is that originally neutral stimuli may acquire learned aversive properties by being paired with aversive events. The fundamental procedure in secondary motivation is that of classical conditioning: A stimulus that precedes an aversive unconditioned stimulus will itself acquire motivating properties. This is referred to as secondary motivation not because it is weaker or of lesser importance but because it is learned. This learned motivation often takes the form of fear.

When we speak of *secondary negative reinforcement,* we are referring to the termination of a stimulus that has acquired aversive (fear-inducing) properties as a result of past experience. The context in which this principle is studied is called *avoidance learning.* Avoidance learning occurs when an organism can learn to respond to a warning signal in order to prevent an aversive event. The paradigm for this type of learning is depicted in figure 7.2.

The avoidance response (aR) in Figure 7.2 may be the same as the unconditioned response (uR) or the escape response (eR), or it may be totally different. If it is the same as the uR, we are dealing with *classical* avoidance conditioning, since the aR will occur as a conditioned response according to the anticipatory response principle. Otherwise, we are dealing with *instrumental* avoidance learning. However, when the aR is the same as the eR, the latter (although a learned instrumental response) also occurs shortly after the CS and will tend to become anticipatory. This means that learning is faster if the aR is the same as the eR, and that, like escape learning, avoidance learning will be slowest if the aR is incompatible with either the uR or the eR. In interpersonal conflicts, for example, the avoidance response typically involves compromising actions, while the escape response, if aggression occurs, is to fight. People (and nations) may have difficulty learning to avoid conflict because of this incompatibility between avoidance and escape responses.

Basically, the difference between the escape learning and avoidance learning situations is this: In escape learning, there is nothing the organism

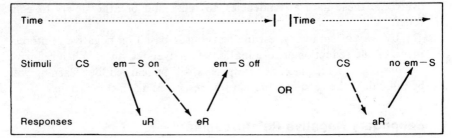

Figure 7.2 Schematic description of avoidance learning. A warning signal (CS) precedes the occurrence of an aversive event (em−S), which elicits unconditioned responses as well as a learned escape response (eR). If, however, an avoidance response (aR) occurs before the em−S, the em−S is prevented.

can do to prevent the occurrence of the aversive event; the best it can do is to terminate the event quickly once it occurs. In avoidance learning, by contrast, a warning signal takes place, and if the organism responds in time, the aversive event is prevented. Thus, in avoidance learning, the organism has greater control over the environment.

Our analysis of avoidance learning assumes first that the warning signal (CS), since it precedes an aversive event (em−S), will itself acquire secondary aversive properties as a result of classical conditioning. Fear, originally elicited by the em−S, becomes conditioned to the CS. When an avoidance response occurs, the CS is terminated, leading to secondary negative reinforcement for making the response. In effect, avoidance responses are learned because they get the organism out of situations it has learned to fear.

Everyday examples of avoidance responses are numerous and hardly need identification. We mentioned that you may put on a coat to *escape* the cold, but you may also put on your coat before leaving the house to *avoid* the cold. Similarly, a small child may learn to avoid being attacked by a bully by staying away from places where an encounter is likely to occur.

Although we cannot review all of the variants of avoidance procedures, one procedure deserves particular mention. This procedure is called *non-discriminated avoidance learning* because there is no explicit warning signal preceding the em−S; rather, the em−S simply occurs at regularly scheduled times. The procedure is analogous to temporal conditioning, except that now the US is aversive and can be avoided by an anticipatory response. In other words, organisms can learn to avoid regularly scheduled aversive events, presumably on the basis of the decaying stimulus-memory trace produced by the preceding aversive event (or the response that prevented it from occurring). Closing the windows of your house before leaving in case of a summer afternoon shower, seeing a doctor at regular intervals, and even winding your watch each morning may be thought of as avoidance responses performed to prevent unsignaled aversive events.

Many avoidance responses are adaptive, but not all of them are. Avoiding the dentist for fear of pain may lead to later dental problems. Avoiding a class because you find the lecturer dull may lead to a poor grade. Accordingly, as with positive reinforcement, it is important to understand the principles of negative reinforcement in order to try to counter the possibly undesirable consequences.

Avoidance responses are extremely persistent. This is simply because the response removes the organism from the feared situation and hence prevents the organism from determining whether the aversive stimulus will actually occur. This is true even when the response is no longer adaptive. The child who becomes afraid of a bully may continue to avoid a confrontation even after they both have matured so that a fight might not occur or so that, if it did, the match would be more even. Laboratory studies have shown that the "enforced reality testing" procedure is not as effective as might be presumed. For example, a dog that continues to run away from a compartment in which it used to receive shock may be forced to sit in the compartment by putting up a barrier.Once the barrier is removed, however, the dog is likely to resume avoidance responding. In effect, the dog learns that the situation is safe when the barrier is in place, but that is a different situation from the one in which shock occurred. Similarly, parents may lead their child by the hand to confront the bully and thereafter say, "See, you really didn't get hurt, did you?" This confirms that the child is safe when the parents are around, but it hardly reduces the child's fear of confronting the bully alone.

Learning NOT to Learn

We noted earlier that aversive control may not be as desirable as positive control because of the emotional consequences. Organisms will learn to escape or avoid aversive situations but their enthusiasm for doing so is minimal. There is also the possibility that aversive events not only affect the organism's behavior in that particular situation but also the ability to adjust to future situations.

Helplessness

R. L. Solomon has trained dogs to make an avoidance response in a shuttle box. Two compartments are separated by a hurdle that the dog can jump over, and electric shock can be administered on either side. A light comes on in the compartment in which the dog is located, signaling an impending shock ten seconds later. If the dog jumps in time, the light goes out and no shock takes place; if the dog fails to jump before the shock, it must then jump over the hurdle to escape it. As could be predicted from our earlier discussion, normal dogs readily learn not only to escape but to avoid shock by jumping when the warning light comes on.

Solomon placed dogs in slings and gave them a series of unavoidable and inescapable electric shocks. Although the dogs were capable of struggling against the slings and the restraining ropes that held their paws, they could do nothing that effectively reduced or terminated the shock. The shock occurred, ran its course, and terminated; all the dogs could do was lie in the sling and endure it.

The day after this admittedly aversive experience (actually, the shock used in these studies was not so intense as to be traumatic), the dogs were for the first time placed in the shuttle apparatus where they could either avoid or escape the shock. The result was that many of these dogs did not learn either response. The dogs did not learn to jump when the light came on, but not because they failed to detect the significance of the light—they soon began to cower and whimper whenever the light came on. Even more surprisingly, the dogs did not even learn to escape from the shock; instead, they stood on the hot grids and endured it. Even if they ocasionally happened to move across the barrier, or if they were pulled across the barrier by the experimenter, the resulting negative reinforcement was largely ineffectual. On the next trial, the dogs were likely to remain in the shock compartment until the experimenter, out of kindness, turned the shock off.

Apparently, an organism that is required to endure an aversive state about which nothing can be done not only learns to submit to it but also to act helpless in a new, controllable situation. To extrapolate this generalization to a human situation, consider the student who finds a classroom aversive because his performance is poor there. He may try in a variety of ways to improve his performance, but the teacher, who has decided that the student is a dunce, continues to give him the same bad grades. The student may learn that he is helpless in that class and may give up trying; he may continue to feel and act helpless in later classes, even when the teacher is more responsive to his efforts. The important practical implication is this: If one uses aversive control over another, it is important to be responsive to the other person's efforts to reduce it. Otherwise, you may be teaching a persistent sense of helplessness.

Elicited Aggression
One limitation of the principle of secondary negative reinforcement has been indicated by putting two organisms together in the same aversive situation. N. H. Azrin and R. E. Ulrich have shown that shocking two rats at the same time in the same apparatus induces them to aggress against each other. Even though neither is responsible for their mutual discomfort, they fight.

What is more important is that the two rats might first be trained to avoid an electric shock by turning a wheel when a warning light comes on five seconds before the shock. This training is given individually until both are avoiding almost all of the threatened shocks. If, however, they are then placed together in the aversive situation, their avoidance behavior is virtually eliminated. They may continue to escape the shock effectively once it comes on, but even then, this escape is followed by aggression against each other. And finally, if they are returned to the situation individually, it is likely that the rats will not resume avoidance responding.

Essentially the same result occurs if neither rat is first trained on the avoidance response, or even if one is trained and the other is not. The presence of another oganism in an aversive situation provides a new stimulus that may interfere with adjustment. This is particularly true when a single avoidance response is required to prevent the shock for both of them; if both must respond, as by, for example, jumping over a hurdle, little impairment results. It has been said that misery loves company; but perhaps if there were no company, the person in misery would learn how to cope more effectively with the environment.

Principles of Learning:
Negative Reinforcement

Multiple Choice Test Questions

1. Negative reinforcement refers to the procedure of
   a. administering a pleasant event
   b. administering an unpleasant event
   c. terminating a pleasant event
   d. terminating an unpleasant event
2. Negative reinforcement differs most from positive reinforcement in the
   a. stimulus that is learned
   b. response that is learned
   c. attitude that is engendered
   d. physical symptoms that are engendered
3. Escape learning is most rapid if the reflexive response to the aversive stimulus
   a. terminates the stimulus
   b. does not terminate the stimulus
   c. is incompatible with the escape response
   d. is compatible with the escape response
4. Avoidance responses are
   a. adaptive
   b. maladaptive
   c. sometimes adaptive and sometimes maladaptive
   d. unrelated to adaptation

5. According to the text, avoidance responses are the result of
   a. pain
   b. fear
   c. intuition
   d. premonition
6. Inescapable and unavoidable aversive events may
   a. improve later adjustment to aversive control
   b. impair later adjustment to aversive control
   c. improve later resistance to neuroses
   d. impair later resistance to neuroses

Multiple Choice Answers

1. (d) Negative reinforcement does not involve the administration or termination of pleasant events. Administering an unpleasant event is called punishment. Terminating an unpleasant event in order to strengthen a response is called negative reinforcement.
2. (c) The same stimuli and responses can be learned using either positive or negative reinforcement. It is possible for physical symptoms to develop from prolonged exposure to aversive situations, but the most prevalent difference between the two types of reinforcement is in the resulting attitudes about the situation.
3. (d) No learning is required if the reflexive response terminates the stimulus; if the response does not, it merely defines the situation but doesn't affect the rate of learning. Learning will be most rapid when the reflexive response is compatible with the escape response and, hence, does not retard its occurrence.
4. (c) We believe that all fundamental principles of behavior evolve because they are generally adaptive. But it is obvious that they can sometimes lead to maladaptive behavior.
5. (b) People may make responses as the result of intuition and/or premonitions, but these factors were not related to avoidance responses in the text's discussion. Pain is involved avoidance learning, but the avoidance responses *result* from fear and *prevent* pain.
6. (b) We do not know the effects of inescapable and unavoidable aversive stimuli on later emotional adjustment, but we do know that later adjustment and adaptation to aversive control may be impaired.

True/False Thought Questions

1. A positive reinforcer strengthens responses, and a negative reinforcer weakens responses.
2. Superstitions can be formed on the basis of negative reinforcement.
3. The total pattern of behavior is the same following positive and negative reinforcement.
4. Aversive events elicit responses reflexively and hence cannot be treated as stimuli to which new responses can become associated.

5. The act of dropping out of school illustrates escape learning.
6. It is easier to learn some escape responses than others.
7. The difference between escape learning and avoidance learning is that the latter requires a warning signal.
8. Termination of a warning signal constitutes secondary negative reinforcement.
9. It is easier to learn some avoidance responses than others.
10. Preventing the avoidance response (so as to force the organism to confront the feared situation and find that it is not now dangerous) is not very successful because of stimulus generalization decrement.
11. One can learn to give up when faced with aversive control.
12. Parents may inadvertently train their children to squabble with each other by assigning a single chore to several children.

True/False Answers

1. (False) Reinforcers always strengthen responses; the distinction between positive and negative reinforcers rests on whether the stimulus event is pleasant or unpleasant.
2. (True) Negative reinforcement is effective even if the aversive event is not actually produced by a response but simply follows it. Many "old wives" remedies for sickness are superstitions based on negative reinforcement.
3. (False) A specified response may be controlled equally well with either type of reinforcement, but negative reinforcement requires that the organism first be placed in an aversive state. This can lead the organism to form unpleasant associations with the situation.
4. (False) Aversive events do elicit a variety of reflexive behaviors that may or may not be adaptive in removing the source of irritation. When the response is not adaptive, the organism must learn new responses to cope with aversive events.
5. (True) If a student is doing poorly in school, that situation becomes aversive. Each day she does not go to school, she receives negative reinforcement. Eventually, she may drop out completely.
6. (True) It is difficult to learn an escape response that is incompatible with the responses produced reflexively by the aversive event. Hence, if several escape responses are possible, the organism is more likely to try and learn the responses most compatible with its reflex behavior.
7. (False) Avoidance learning usually does entail a warning signal preceding the aversive event. However, avoidance learning also requires that some response be possible to prevent or avoid the occurrence of that event. Telling a boy that his father or mother will spank him for his misbehavior when they get home doesn't foster avoidance learning unless the boy can do something to avoid the licking.
8. (True) It is assumed that the warning signal takes on learned aversive properties through classical conditioning. Its termination is therefore a form of reinforcement; the reinforcement is secondary because the association is learned.

9. (True) Learning to respond before an aversive event is difficult if the response is incompatible with either the natural response or an escape response to the aversive event. This is true because the reflexive and escape responses tend to become anticipatory.
10. (True) The situation must be changed to force an organism to confront a feared stimulus. Hence, extinction takes place in a different situation than when the avoidance response is possible. If the original situation recurs, the organism is likely to revert to the avoidance response.
11. (True) If the early environment is not responsive to an organism's efforts to control aversive events, the organism may generalize this experience and give up in later situations, where such events *can* be controlled.
12. (True) Doing chores around the home may be viewed as an avoidance response to prevent parental displeasure. If a single chore is assigned to several children, none may perform the avoidance response; after being reprimanded by the parent, (an aversive event) the children may fight.

Essay/Discussion Questions

1. Discuss the distinction between escape in general and escape learning. Discuss the distinction in the context of drug addiction.
2. Elaborate on the analysis of avoidance learning given in the text. Discuss this analysis in the context of venereal disease.

References

Events that ARE Aversive
Bower, G. H. and Miller, N. E. Rewarding and punishing effects from stimulating the same place in the rat's brain. *Journal of Comparative and Physiological Psychology*, 1958, *51*, 669–674.

Primary Negative Reinforcement:
Escape Learning
Bower, G. H. Partial and correlated reward in escape learning. *Journal of Experimental Psychology*, 1960, *59*, 126–130.

Secondary Negative Reinforcement:
Avoidance Learning
*Mowrer, O. H. A stimulus-response analysis of anxiety and its role as a reinforcing agent. *Psychological Review*, 1939, *46*, 553–565.
Sidman, M. The temporal parameters of the maintenance of avoidance behavior by the white rat. *Journal of Comparative and Physiological Psychology*, 1953, *46*, 253–261.

*Suitable for additional reading by the beginning student. The others are written at a more technical level.

Learning NOT to Learn

*Maier, S. F., Seligman, M. E. P., and Solomon, R. L. Pavlovian fear conditioning and learned helplessness. In B. A. Campbell and R. M. Church (Eds.), *Punishment and aversive control*. New York: Appleton-Century-Crofts, 1969.

Solomon, R. L., and Wynne, L. C. Traumatic avoidance learning: The principles of anxiety conservation and partial irreversibility. *Psychological Review*, 1954, *61*, 353–385.

Response Persistence: Forgetting, Extinction, and Punishment

8

The most important practical consideration when we attempt to apply learning principles probably concerns response persistence. How long and under what conditions will a learned response continue to occur? In some instances, we're concerned with response persistence because we want a response to occur regularly once it has been acquired. Obviously, paper training a new puppy is of little use if the response ceases to occur after an hour, or if the response stops as soon as we stop rewarding it. In other situations, the persistence of a learned response presents a problem. If a child has learned to cry whenever the doorbell rings (perhaps because, in the past, the sound of the doorbell was followed by the appearance of fear-provoking strangers), the persistence of such behavior may become irritating to the child's parents. In such cases, we are concerned with the persistence of learned behaviors because we want to find some way to eliminate or suppress an undesirable response.

In this chapter, we will deal with two aspects of response persistence. First, we will examine the question of how well learned responses persist over time. We will discuss the phenomenon of *forgetting* and will point out some of the factors that determine the rate or amount of forgetting that occurs after learning. The second aspect we will discuss involves techniques such as *extinction* and *punishment* that are used to eliminate learned responses. Here, we will identify some of the conditions under which learned responses persist in the face of such techniques.

Forgetting

We train children to look both ways before crossing the street not only so they perform the response while we are there but so they will respond appropriately in the future when no adults are nearby. Likewise, we practice a tennis stroke or learn the name of an acquaintance to have these responses ready at some future time. Because of the importance of the future applications of a response, it is necessary to consider what happens to responses after a learning experience is over. In other words, under what conditions are learned responses remembered and under what conditions does forgetting occur?

It is safe to say that any organism that has learned has also forgotten. To most of us, forgetting simply means the inability to remember. But to study forgetting experimentally, we need a more formal definition. We define forgetting as *a decrease in the performance of a learned response since the time of learning that is not due to any sensory, motor, or motivational change in the organism.*

There are two important aspects of this definition. First, forgetting is the difference between performance at the end of learning and performance at a later time. The difference between what you learn and what you remember defines what you forget. Accordingly, one cannot forget unless one has learned something. This point may appear obvious, but it eliminates many of the instances we casually label as examples of forgetting. If you glance through a large set of class notes just before an exam and then do poorly, you may contend that you "forgot" the material. In reality, you probably never learned much of the material; thus, we would not properly use the term forgetting to describe your test performance. An even more common example is the person who complains about having difficulty remembering names. Actually, such people typically do not pay attention when being introduced to someone and hence never really learn the name in the first place. So, we repeat: You can't forget what you never learned.

A second important aspect of our definition is that we use the term forgetting *only* when we have excluded sensory, motor, or motivational changes as the causes of poor performance. The poor performance of a learned response can result from numerous factors other than forgetting. For example, assume that you have trained your dog to jump through a hoop when you blow a whistle, and you plan to have the dog perform the trick at a party. If the dog is struck deaf (or is run over by a truck) just before the party, the likelihood of its giving a good performance for your friends will be limited. Only your pickiest friends will claim that the dog has forgotten its trick. Most will assume that the animal's poor performance is due to physical defects that preclude the dog from performing. Similarly, an athlete may spend hours preparing for a crucial game. However, if just prior to the game, the athlete's team is eliminated from consideration for the championship trophy, the athlete may perform poorly despite the hours of practice. Is this poor performance due to forgetting? Probably not. Most likely the poor performance results from a lack of motivation to perform the correct responses, even though these responses have been well learned and remembered.

Even with these qualifications in mind, we should recognize that there remain numerous instances of forgetting that are familiar to each of us. Because of this we need to examine the circumstances under which forgetting is most likely to occur.

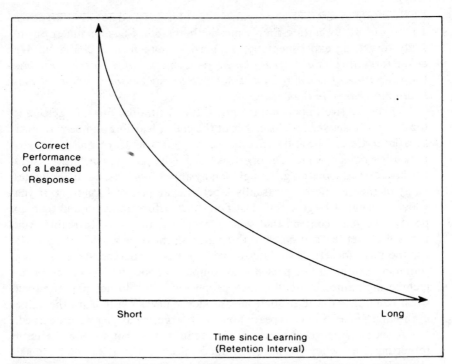

Figure 8.1 The effect of increasing the retention interval after learning on the probability of performing a learned response correctly.

Long Retention Intervals

A *retention interval* is simply the time between the end of learning and the occasion of a retention test to determine whether the response can be performed. It should not be surprising that, *in general, the longer a retention interval is, the more forgetting occurs.* This fact is illustrated in figure 8.1. Note that in this figure, although the amount of forgetting increases steadily as the retention interval is lengthened, the *rate* of forgetting usually is greater just after learning and decreases as the retention interval grows longer. For example, assume that you have learned a set of formulas for a math exam. In most cases, you will remember the formulas better one day after learning than seven days after learning. However, you will normally forget more during the first twenty-four hours after learning than you will during any subsequent twenty-four-hour period. The total *amount* of forgetting increases as the retention interval lengthens, but the *rate* of forgetting decreases as the retention interval grows longer.

One other aspect of figure 8.1 should be mentioned. This figure includes no mention of specific retention interval durations. This is because even though forgetting normally follows the general pattern illustrated in the figure, the actual length of time it takes for a response to be forgotten depends on numerous factors. Some responses are forgotten very slowly,

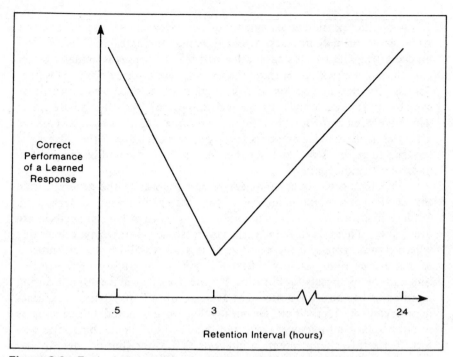

Figure 8.2 Typical "forgetting curve" when learning involves exposure to an aversive stimulus.

while others tend to be forgotten almost as soon as they are learned. For example, most of us who were old enough at the time remember precisely what responses we were making when the first moon landing occurred several years ago. But we are not so sure of exactly what our behaviors were at dinner two weeks ago. Identifying the factors that account for such great differences in forgetting is one of the major challenges to researchers presently interested in memory phenomena.

We have stated that the time it takes for forgetting to occur may vary widely but that, in general, the longer the retention interval, the greater the amount of forgetting. As with most general statements, there are some notable exceptions. For example, when learning involves negative reinforcement (as in escape or avoidance learning), the subsequent performance of the learned response often *does not* decrease steadily as the retention interval increases. Performance of such responses is normally excellent immediately after learning, poor one to six hours after learning, and then progressively better as the retention interval approaches twenty-four hours. Only after the first twenty-four hours does forgetting begin to increase as the retention interval increases. This type of "forgetting curve" is illustrated in figure 8.2.

Response Persistence: Forgetting, Extinction, and Punishment

A similar phenomenon sometimes occurs when we use an aversive stimulus as the US in classical conditioning. In some instances, performance of the CR (in this case, a learned fear response) is actually better twenty-four hours after learning than it was just after learning. This phenomenon, called *incubation of fear,* suggests that once we learn to fear something, the fear grows stronger as time passes. We often advise riders who have been thrown from a horse to resume riding as soon as possible after the incident. This advice is based on our belief that if the rider waits too long to get back on her horse, her fear of the horse will be too great to allow her to ride again.

Obviously such findings appear to run counter to the generalization that the longer a retention interval is, the greater the amount of forgetting. In all such instances, performance seems to improve rather than deteriorate over time. There is presently, however, some controversy concerning whether these apparent increases in an organism's ability to remember a response over time actually reflect changes in the ability to remember. Since many of these situations involve the use of aversive stimuli during learning, it has been suggested that aversive stimuli may trigger increases in an organism's motivation. The idea is that, once initiated, these increases in motivation continue over time, and this is why animals sometimes perform better after long retention intervals than after shorter ones. In any event, such phenomena serve to caution us that the performance of a learned response cannot always be predicted simply by looking at the time that has passed since the response was learned.

Proactive and Retroactive Interference

You have probably noticed that when you prepare for an exam, it is not always the last material you study that you remember best. In many cases, the last material you study is forgotten more readily than some of the earlier material. This phenomenon is called *proactive interference.* We define proactive interference as follows: *If two or more responses are learned in a similar context, the more recently learned response will be forgotten more rapidly than if it had been learned alone.* In other words, prior learning may interfere with your ability to remember a recently learned response.

To illustrate this phenomenon, consider the following situation. One group of rats is trained to jump from a white to a black chamber when a tone is sounded. Then the rats are tested for performance of this response either one or sixty minutes later. A second group of rats is trained identically to the first group—except that before being trained to jump from the white to the black chamber, they are trained to remain in the white chamber when a light is on. Like the first group of animals, the second group is tested for performance of the jumping response either one or sixty minutes after learning the response. Although both groups of rats receive equal training in jumping from the white to the black chamber, and even though

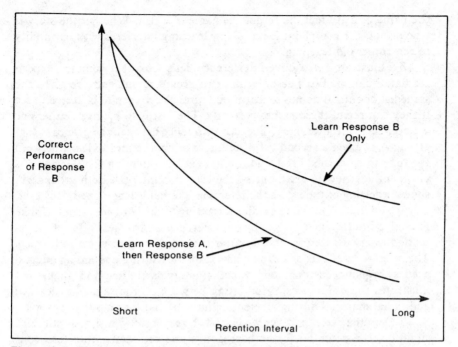

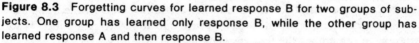

Figure 8.3 Forgetting curves for learned response B for two groups of subjects. One group has learned only response B, while the other group has learned response A and then response B.

both groups are tested after the same retention intervals, the two groups will not forget at the same rate. The animals trained only on the jumping response will exhibit some forgetting over the sixty-minute retention interval. However, the group that is trained to remain passive before being trained to jump will forget the jumping response much more rapidly than the group taught the jumping response alone. Notice that it is the *rate* of forgetting that is affected by prior learning. In other words, both groups will remember the jumping response reasonably well when tested shortly after learning, but the group with prior learning will then forget the response more rapidly. Figure 8.3 illustrates this difference in forgetting when one group has had prior learning and the other has not.

Not only is forgetting influenced by prior learning, but it is also affected by learning new responses during a retention interval. *An organism that learns two responses in a similar context and then is tested for performance of the first response will perform that response more poorly than if no second response had been learned.* This is called *retroactive interference.* We all are familiar with the effects of retroactive interference. There is, for example, the story of the marine biologist who was complaining about his job at a university. His complaint was that every time he had to learn the name of a student, he forgot the name of a fish. Whether the story is true or not, the complaint is real. New learning interferes with our ability to remember old learning.

To illustrate retroactive interference, let's look at a common experimental situation. We'll assume that two groups of subjects are given the same list of animal names to learn. Both groups are then to be tested to see if they can recite these names correctly. The test is to be given either one or seven days after learning. The only difference between the groups is that Group A is given a second list of different animal names to learn between the time they learned list 1 and the time of the retention test. Group B is given nothing new to learn during the retention interval. Both groups will show forgetting of the list as the retention interval is lengthened. However, Group A will exhibit much greater forgetting of the list 1 responses. Unlike proactive interference, retroactive interference is strongest after short retention intervals; that is, shortly after the interfering response is learned. The interfering effects of learning new responses during a retention interval are less pronounced when long retention intervals are involved. Figure 8.4 illustrates the differences in forgetting between a group that has learned additional material during a retention interval and a group that has not.

To summarize, whenever we learn two responses in a similar stimulus situation, the potential for both proactive and retroactive interference is present. If we attempt to remember the second response learned, the previously learned response will interfere with our ability to remember. If we attempt to remember the first response learned, the more recently learned response will cause forgetting. Such interference effects have a great deal of practical significance, especially for the student. Either through lack of foresight or because of circumstances beyond control, most of us have had to resort to "cramming" for an exam. Often, the result is that, on the exam, the material all seems to run together and we become confused. This confusion is usually due to interference effects because we learned all the material (several responses) in the same stimulus situation. Had we spread out our study of the material over time, different responses would have been learned in different stimulus situations and interference would have been minimized. Similarly, students who get a good night's sleep between studying and taking a test often perform better than students who stay up all night studying. Part of this difference is because a well-rested person can perform better than someone who is tired. Additionally, however, if the interval between studying and testing is filled with sleep rather than added study, retroactive interference and, hence, forgetting will be minimized. In effect, your ability to study and remember material almost always can be improved simply by taking care to minimize proactive and retroactive interference.

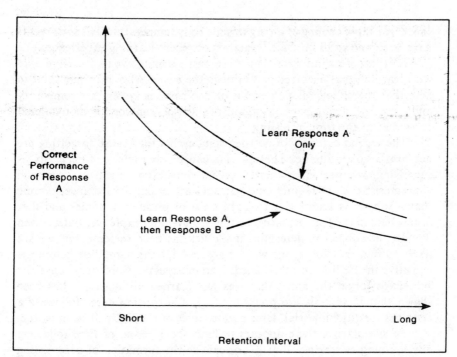

Figure 8.4 Forgetting curves for learned response A for two groups of subjects. One group has learned only response A, while the other group has learned response A and then response B.

Important Post-Learning Events

We all know that it is difficult to learn anything if there are constant distractions while we are trying to learn. During a learning experience, it is necessary for us to be relatively free to attend to the stimulus situation and to make appropriate responses. Apparently, to form an association that will be remembered later, it is equally necessary that the interval shortly *after* a learning experience be free from intrusion. If this interval is interrupted by certain distracting or intruding events, subsequent forgetting of the recently learned response is often dramatic. These dramatic cases of forgetting are usually termed *amnesias*.

Several events are known to produce amnesias if the events occur shortly (within seconds or minutes) after a learning experience. Most of these events fall into two general categories. The first includes a number of events that temporarily interfere with the normal operation of the nervous system and particularly with the activity of the brain. Bumps on the head, alcoholic blackouts, or epileptic seizures are natural examples of such events. In the laboratory, the normal activity of the brain can be altered artificially through certain drugs, electrical current (electroconvulsive shock), or rapid cooling of an organism's body temperature. All such events have been known to produce forgetting of recent learning experiences.

It is important to note that these post-learning events interfere *only* with learning that occurred just prior to the event. Also, it is important to note that the effects of such events on the nervous system are temporary and, thus, do not impair an organism's sensory, motor, or motivational capacities at the time of testing.

The second category of post-learning events that cause forgetting are not nearly so traumatic. These events can be characterized generally as surprising, unexpected, or unusual events. Such events all share a common characteristic: They require an organism's attention. For instance, assume that a subject is attempting to learn a list of presidents' names and that somewhere in the list we place a common four-letter expletive. Later, when we test the subject to determine if the list has been remembered, we are likely to find that forgetting will be greatest for the name just before the expletive in the list. In other words, the unexpected word may cause the subject to forget the name that was just learned. Similarly, it has been shown that if animals are presented with a surprising event following a classical conditioning trial, later performance of the CR will be impaired.

To summarize, there appears to be a short period of time following any learning experience that is critical for the formation of a persisting association. If during that interval an organism is sufficiently distracted, or if the normal operations of the nervous system are disrupted, the association formed often will be forgotten.

The Context of the Retention Test
Previously, in our discussion of stimulus context, we stated that if an organism learns to perform a response in one context, subsequent performance of the response will depend on whether or not that context has changed since learning. As a general rule, *the more similar the learning and testing contexts are, the better the performance of the learned response will be on the test.* Substantial differences between learning and retention test contexts usually result in greater amounts of forgetting than one normally would expect after a given retention interval. In this instance, we attribute the additional forgetting to a *stimulus generalization decrement*. In other words, a response acquired in one stimulus situation fails to generalize to a dissimilar stimulus situation. We will discuss the principles of stimulus generalization in more detail in the next chapter.

Although we shared in an earlier chapter several examples of how context change affects learned performance, at least one point should be reiterated. Stimulus context includes those stimuli inside an organism as well as stimuli in the external environment. Thus, if the internal state of an organism differs dramatically between the time of learning and retention testing, this change may cause as much forgetting as if the organism's external stimulus context were changed. An organism that learns a response, for example, while certain hormone levels are high will most likely perform that response best when those same hormones reach a high level again.

Retrieval Failure and the Permanence of Associations

On the one hand, we have characterized a learned association as being permanent. Yet in the present chapter we have discussed some of the factors that influence the forgetting of an association. These points may seem inconsistent on first examination. Doesn't the occurrence of forgetting indicate that associations are *not* permanent?

The best way to answer this question is with a familiar example. Suppose you have been invited to a party given in a neighborhood you have visited only once before. On your previous visit, you learned carefully the route between your house and your friend's neighborhood; but now, on the night of the party, you cannot remember how to get there. While driving around trying to decide whether to call your friend or to skip the party altogether, you see a sign that looks familiar. Suddenly you remember that if you turn right at the sign and then left at the next block, you will be at your friend's house. All of us have experienced situations like this one. We learn something, we forget it, and then the slightest hint allows us to remember it again. A facial feature may be all we need to remember a forgotten name, or the first few bars of a melody may allow us to reconstruct all the lyrics of a song we thought we had forgotten long ago.

The point of these examples should be clear. When we forget, it does not necessarily mean that previous learning has been lost so that we have to relearn the association to perform correctly. On the contrary, many cases of forgetting can be overcome if we are given even the slightest prompts or hints. This suggests that in many cases the correct associations are still present, but until we are given some kind of cue or reminder we are not able to use them.

The distinction between forgetting and the loss of an association is made clear in information-processing theories of memory. According to these theories, to remember anything we must go through at least two steps. First, we must *store* the information from a learning experience. By storing information, we mean that a learned association must become represented by some lasting change in the brain. In the terms we have used thus far, information storage is analogous to the act of learning itself or to the process of forming an association. Secondly, we must be able to *retrieve* information when we need it. By retrieving information, we mean that one must be able to search through the associations stored in the brain and select the appropriate one to determine performance in a given stimulus situation. In essence, information retrieval involves responding appropriately to stimuli that previously have been associated with some response.

According to research done within this information-processing framework, many cases of forgetting result from a problem with the second step, retrieval, rather than the first. Much of our forgetting seems to be due to failures in retrieving associations that clearly are stored permanently in the brain.

Evidence for this interpretation of forgetting is becoming increasingly strong. Animals that have forgotten how to run through a maze suddenly remember the response if they are placed briefly in the maze just before testing. Numerous instances of amnesia have been eliminated by presenting the subjects with cues concerning the information they cannot remember. Even the effects of proactive and retroactive interference have been decreased by giving subjects cues pertaining to the responses they are required to perform.

In sum, many instances of forgetting can be shown to result from a failure to retrieve associations rather than a failure to maintain associations in storage. Thus, it is clear that forgetting can occur, even though learned associations are permanent.

Extinction

Thus far, we have considered the conditions that affect persistence of learning over time. It is equally important for us to understand the factors that influence the persistence of learning when we are actively attempting to eliminate a learned response. For this reason, we will discuss two ways to eliminate learned responses—through extinction and through punishment—and will note the conditions under which these procedures are effective.

We have already introduced the concept of experimental extinction in the context of classical conditioning. In essence, *extinction results when an organism is exposed to nonreinforcement of a learned response.* By nonreinforcement of a learned response, we mean that the event that originally ensured the occurrence of the learned response is eliminated. In classical conditioning, this involves presenting the CS but eliminating the US. In the instrumental or operant situation, extinction consists of exposing an organism to the stimulus situation in which the response was learned but eliminating the reward for the correct response. As the discussion of extinction in classical conditioning indicated, we assume that although extinction decreases learned responding, it leaves the underlying associations intact. The theory is that extinction results in inhibition, which opposes the original learned association.

The technical dependent variable studied when one assesses the persistence of responding through extinction is called *resistance to extinction.* This is simply a measure of the number of times a response will occur after all reinforcement for the response is removed. We will now consider the factors that affect resistance to extinction.

Factors that Increase Resistance to Extinction

We can subsume a large amount of experimental research under a single principle: *Resistance to extinction is greater if the variability was greater during original learning.* Variability may involve the stimulus, the response, or the reinforcement; we will consider each of these factors briefly.

Stimulus Variability   The greater the variety of stimuli encountered during the learning of a response, the more persistent the response will be. Suppose we train some rats to run in a single straight alley for food, while another group of rats has the same number of rewarded learning trials but in several different alleys that vary in width, brightness, floor texture, and the like. If the reward is then removed for both groups and their running speed is measured over a series of extinction trials, the group running in a single alley will stop running significantly sooner than the group running in several alleys.

One way to understand this phenomenon concerns the number of habits involved. An organism trained to a single stimulus does have some generalized tendency to respond to similar stimuli, but this tendency will not be as strong as when the organism has actually learned to respond in a variety of situations. Hence, stimulus variation during training produces more habits in the sense of associating the response with several different stimuli . . . and each of these habits has to be extinguished before the response is eliminated. One of the reasons undesirable responses are especially persistent is that they are often learned in a number of different contexts. For example, the adult who does not like to go to parties has probably had unpleasant experiences in several such contexts.

Response Variability   The larger the number of response variations learned, the more persistent the response will be. One clear experimental demonstration of this fact involves training pigeons to peck at a particular location on a key. The experimenter first requires that the pigeons periodically vary the location they strike on the key to receive reward. After reward is removed, these pigeons will display considerably greater resistance to extinction of the pecking response than pigeons permitted to peck at a single location on the key.

Response variability may also be understood by considering the number of habits involved. In this case, each variant of the response entails a different habit, and the more habits learned, the more habits there are to persist during extinction. As each variant is partially extinguished, another is available to be tried; by the time the second has been extinguished, the first one has undergone spontaneous recovery and will recur again later.

Reinforcement Variability Perhaps no other phenomenon has received as much attention by experimental psychologists as the effect of reinforcement variability on resistance to extinction. Variability may be obtained in an operant situation by varying the schedules of reinforcement. In an instrumental situation, variability may be obtained by varying the amount or delay of reward or simply by giving partial reinforcement. So well-established is this principle that it is labeled the *partial reinforcement effect;* responses that are only occasionally rewarded during acquisition persist longer during extinction.

Reinforcement variability may be simply a special case of stimulus and response variability. On the one hand, reward is a stimulus which is part of the context in which learning occurs, and hence, variability in reward leads to more varied stimulus conditions. Furthermore, reinforcement variability often leads to greater response variability since the organism is less likely to become focused on a single way of responding. This is presumably because occasional nonreinforcement weakens each variant of the response enough that other responses are tried and receive occasional reinforcement. However, the generality of the partial reinforcement effect has led to a variety of special theories to account for it.

One of these involves the concept of *frustration.* Consider first extinction following continuous reinforcement. The organism has never encountered nonreinforcement in the situation prior to extinction, and when nonreinforcement does occur, two things are likely to happen. First, the organism is likely to react emotionally to frustration by making responses that are incompatible with the trained response itself; these responses tend to become anticipatory and interfere with smooth performance. Furthermore, the organism begins to anticipate frustration, and the natural response is then to stop responding and avoid the situation. In short, the continuously reinforced organism stops responding because it is highly frustrated by nonreinforcement and has not learned how to deal effectively with it.

In contrast, the organism trained with partial reinforcement *has* encountered nonreinforcement during original learning. Although this also is frustrating, the organism eventually tries again and is rewarded for doing so. In effect, the organism learns to accept nonreinforcement as part of the situation and to continue to respond in spite of occasional frustration. In the vernacular, we could call this result the development of frustration tolerance. In learning not to expect reward every time, the organism learns to "take no for an answer"; by contrast, in learning to expect reward only part of the time, the organism learns to "try, try again." Being accustomed to occasional nonreinforcement has, in effect, prepared the organism for the continuous nonreinforcement experienced during extinction.

Of special significance is the fact that the partial reinforcement effect can generalize from one situation to another. This means that extinction of one response that has received continuous reinforcement will be slower if a similar response has received partial reinforcement. Learning to tolerate frustration in one situation helps the organism to do so in other situations.

Punishment A final factor that produces increased resistance to extinction is, somewhat surprisingly, punishment. The role of punishment in eliminating responses will be discussed later in this chapter. But if punishment fails to eliminate a response, it will lead to greater persistence of that response than if punishment had never been involved. This concept is sometimes referred to as *fixation.*

To demonstrate fixation in the laboratory, we can, for instance, first train rats to turn to the right in a T–maze to obtain food. Enroute to the goal, electric shock punishment is given for turning in that direction, but the shock is not of sufficient intensity to prevent the rat from proceeding. After such training, the reward is placed in the left goal box. Rats that received shocks for making the right turn now take substantially longer to learn the new rewarded response than rats trained without the use of punishment.

Presumably the reason for fixation is that learning to respond even though one anticipates punishment is very similar to learning to respond even though one anticipates frustration; learning one therefore generalizes to the other. Consistent with this interpretation, partial reinforcement also makes organisms more resistant to the interfering effects of punishment.

Summary To summarize the factors that increase resistance to extinction, let's consider a father who deliberately wants to teach his son to persist in displaying an outburst of temper whenever the boy is denied his desires. (Perhaps no father would want to do this, but assume that this one does.) First, the father would ensure that denial occurred in a variety of situations and that various forms of temper displays were performed. He would not reinforce such displays regularly but would only occasionally give in to them. To further fixate the response, he would sometimes punish the boy, but not often enough or severely enough to eliminate the response. Several years of such diligent training could produce a person who would never be able to control his temper! The reason for giving this example may seem obvious: How many parents actually behave in this way, unaware that they are inadvertently training a persistent, undesirable response?

Factors that Decrease Resistance to Extinction

In one sense, we have already identified some of the factors that decrease response persistence. Constancy of learning conditions with respect to stimuli, responses, and reinforcements, coupled with the lack of aversive consequences, reduces resistance to extinction. There are, however, several other factors that reduce persistence even further.

Amount of Reward We have stated that large rewards lead to better performance than do small rewards when measured in terms of response vigor during acquisition. The opposite, however, occurs during extinction; extinction is faster following large rewards.

Perhaps the reason for this is again related to frustration. The person accustomed to consistently large rewards experiences greater frustration when reward is removed than the person who only expected a small reward in the first place. Accordingly, occasional large rewards may produce a high response level, but if persistence of that response is of concern, consistently large rewards will actually reduce resistance to extinction.

Extended Training A certain amount of training, during which rewards are administered frequently, may be necessary to bring the desired response to a high level of proficiency. Training may be continued beyond that point, however, with frequent reward provided even after there is no further evidence of improvement. While this is certainly effective in maintaining the response during that time, resistance to extinction is reduced by such extended training.

The reason why extended training reduces persistence is not yet well understood. One important factor, however, relates back to response variability. During continued training with reward, the response is likely to become increasingly stereotyped so that it is performed in a single, invariant way. Accordingly, the response will extinguish rapidly.

Summary To summarize, let's consider a mother who wishes to train her daughter to be a "quitter" when she faces the occasional failures that adults invariably experience. First, the mother would attempt to see that the girl always succeeded as she was growing up and would give her consistently large rewards for success. Not only might the mother "spoil" her daughter in this way, but she would also continue to protect the girl from failure well into adolescence and, insofar as possible, into young adulthood. Later, as an adult, that person's response to failure would be to quit trying. Again, one can reflect on the number of parents who so indulge their children, quite unaware of the behavior they are training.

Factors during Extinction that Affect Persistence

The preceding sections of this chapter have identified some of the conditions of the learning situation that affect resistance to response extinction. Not only does persistence depend on the way the response was learned, but factors within the extinction experience itself also affect resistance to extinction.

First, the rate of extinction depends on the distribution of the extinction trials over time. Learning (habit) occurs more rapidly if the experiences are widely distributed over time; extinction (inhibition) occurs more rapidly if the nonreinforced experiences are massed so they occur in rapid succession. Spontaneous recovery will, of course, still occur; but extinction is better accomplished by a series of highly massed episodes than if individual trials are spread out over time.

A second fact affecting persistence is that extinction is more rapid to a somewhat different stimulus than to the original stimulus itself. Not only is the response weaker to a different stimulus, but what strength it has is lost more readily than to the stimulus actually used in training. One practical application of this fact is evident in attempting to extinguish strong fears. It is often advisable to begin with a situation that produces only mild generalized fear and extinguish that fear before advancing closer to the situation in which the fear was learned. The shaping procedure that we described with respect to response training can be applied equally well to response elimination. In doing so, however, it is important to recall that inhibition does not generalize very broadly, so that smaller steps have to be taken in shaping extinction than in shaping acquisition.

Punishment

Whether we like it or not, punishment remains the most widespread method of attempting to eliminate responses. We are punished by parents, teachers, peers, society, and even ourselves in an effort to control the tendency to make responses deemed undesirable. The principle of punishment is similar to the principle of reinforcement: *Whenever a response is closely followed in time by an aversive event, the tendency for that response to occur in the future is decreased.* However, this principle must be understood in relation to the principle of the anticipatory response.

As with reinforcement, there are two types of punishment. *Negative punishment* occurs when a response is followed by the termination of a rewarding situation. For example, taking food from a rat, a toy from a child, or money from an adult constitutes negative punishment. *Positive punishment* occurs when a response is followed by the onset of an aversive event. Shocking a rat, spanking a child, or insulting an adult are positive punishments.

Also, note that the concepts of the conditions and schedules of reinforcement can be applied equally well to punishment. While the conditions of reinforcement include amount, the conditions of punishment include intensity. Punishment, like reinforcement, might be scheduled on a fixed-interval schedule. (A fixed-interval schedule of punishment would simply mean that the next response after a certain, constant period of time would be followed by an aversive event. Receiving bills at the end of each month is something like a fixed-interval schedule of punishment for the responses of consuming various commodities.)

The experimental analysis of punishment has not proceeded as vigorously as the analysis of reinforcement has, and the effects of the various possible conditions and schedules of punishment are not yet well understood. In part, this is a result of some early research leading to the belief that punishment suppressed behavior but did not actually modify it in terms of learning. In addition, the lack of research on punishment is due to the fact that punishment is inevitably more complicated because it must always be studied in the context of reinforcement; only after a response is made because it is rewarded will the topic of punishment be raised. Finally, the undesirable by-products mentioned earlier resulting from aversive control have led many psychologists to place more emphasis on positive methods of controlling behavior. Nevertheless, punishment is highly prevalent in modern society and an important topic of scientific inquiry.

The basic paradigm for analyzing the effects of punishment is shown in figure 8.5. It may be helpful to work through that paradigm before attempting to describe the ways in which punishment works. First, assume that the response in question is rewarded (em+S), and the tendency to make that response is indicated by the dashed arrow connecting the first stimulus (S) and the instrumental response (iR). This response also leads to punishment in the form of an aversive event (em−S), which reflexively elicits some unconditioned responses (uR)—including fear—and which may require some explicit escape response (eR). Let's consider the effect of the unconditioned response to the punishment (that is, the uR to em−S).

Note that the first stimulus (S) occurs in a regular temporal sequence with this unconditioned response. Hence, we have a classical-conditioning paradigm that invokes the principle of the anticipatory response; the unconditioned response to the punishment will tend to become anticipatory and to occur to the stimulus that elicits the punished instrumental response. This is shown by dashed arrow (1) in the figure. In effect, then, the first stimulus will come to elicit *both* the iR and the uR in the figure. The effect of this will then depend on the relationship between these two responses. If the unconditioned response to punishment is incompatible with the instrumental response producing the punishment, the anticipatory tendency of the unconditioned response may compete with the instrumental response. If, on the other hand, these responses are compatible, both may occur to the first stimulus without competition; in fact, if the responses are very similar, these tendencies combine to increase the response.

This analysis is much simpler than it sounds at first reading. Let's consider several examples, both from the laboratory and from everyday life, to help make the basic idea clear. First, assume that a rat has been trained to run down a short, straight alley to obtain food reward. Now punishment for running is introduced in the form of an electric shock. The principle of the anticipatory response helps to predict the effect of this punishment. Under normal circumstances, the electric shock will elicit as an unconditioned response a recoil or withdrawal from the goal end of the

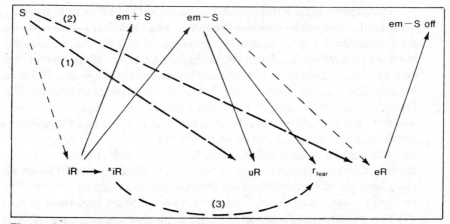

Figure 8.5 Schematic illustration of the punishment procedure. A stimulus (S) to which the organism has learned an instrumental response (iR) because it is followed by reward (em+S) is also followed by an aversive event (em−S). The latter event produces unconditioned responses (uR), fear, and at times, some escape response. The thick, dashed arrows indicate the effects of this procedure as described in the text.

alley; as the rat steps on the grid, it will stop and retreat. These responses, which become anticipatory, are incompatible with the learned instrumental response of running forward to the goal. On the next trial, then, the rat not only has the instrumental tendency to run forward, but the anticipatory tendency to withdraw. When the latter becomes stronger than the former, the rat refuses to run. Similarly, a parent may slap a child's hand as the child reaches for the forbidden candy bowl. This slap elicits withdrawal of the hand—a response that is incompatible with reaching and that, when it occurs as an anticipatory response, prevents the reaching response.

Through these examples we have simply shown how the principle of the anticipatory response fosters the respective conditioning and elimination of two competing responses. The importance of the principle of the anticipatory response in relation to punishment can be further emphasized by modifying one example. Returning to the rat running down the alley, suppose the rat is shocked in its hind paws as it approaches the goal. The unconditioned response to such a shock is not to retreat but instead to lurch forward—a response that is compatible with the punished running response. And, as implied by the principle of the anticipatory response, such a punishment does not eliminate the instrumental response but actually facilitates it. The rat runs faster if it is shocked in its hind paws; the animal is effectively making an anticipatory response by jumping forward when running into the shock area.

This leads to an important rule: The most effective punishment "suits the crime." This is accomplished when the response produced by the punishment is incompatible with the punished response so that, when the former becomes anticipatory, it will compete with the punished response. As a familiar example, consider the father who feels that if his young son cries when he is hurt, the boy is not being "manly." To eliminate that behavior, the father decides to spank the boy when he catches him crying. However, this punishment does not suit the crime; spanking actually elicits crying, which is the response the father wants to punish and eliminate. The father is thus sure to find that, at least initially, the boy's tendency to cry will increase, not only because the child has been hurt but as an anticipatory response to the spanking he will receive for crying.

It is not always easy to find a punishment that perfectly suits the crime. If, for example, a child has stolen a toy from a neighbor, there is no simple stimulus that will reflexively elicit the response of returning the toy. This fact makes the escape response (eR in figure 8.5) an important part of effective punishment. Even when the uR to punishment is compatible with the punished response, the agent controlling punishment can cause the organism to perform an escape response that is incompatible. This response, too, will tend to become anticipatory and to compete with the other responses, as shown by dashed arrow (2) in figure 8.5. In our example, the parent might withhold attention from the child until the toy is returned, thus ensuring that an incompatible response is made.

Another (and in the long run, more important) way in which punishment affects behavior involves the third response elicited by an aversive event—fear. To understand this effect, recall first that all responses produce feedback stimuli telling the organism what it is doing; these feedback stimuli, resulting from the instrumental response, are indicated in figure 8.5 by S_{iR}. Note that these stimuli regularly precede the fear response (r_{fear}) and should thus become conditioned to it. This is shown by dashed arrow (3) in figure 8.5. In short, an organism soon experiences fear when beginning to make a response that has been punished in the past.

Once fear has been conditioned, the organism is in a potential learning situation: The response of ceasing to respond reduces fear. When the organism ceases responding, the feedback stimuli that were eliciting the fear are eliminated. And, in turn, fear reduction is secondary negative reinforcement and thus will strengthen the response of ceasing to respond. This procedure may work even with a punishment that does not suit the crime, although, in such a case, the principle of the anticipatory response is working against the principle of punishment and reduces its effectiveness. The organism then has to learn how to behave to avoid punishment.

This discussion of the way in which punishment works, together with the principles we discussed earlier, enables us to state some basic rules to guide anyone administering punishment. The fact that we are providing such guidelines does not mean we advocate the use of punishment; but since punishment is probably an inescapable technique in the control of behavior, we feel it is essential to understand how to use it effectively.

1. *Avoid inadequate punishments.* If a response is not eliminated by punishment, it will become fixated and persist even after it is no longer rewarded. For example, states that impose too small a fine as a punishment for speeding may be teaching their drivers speeding habits that the drivers perform even when there is no reason to do so.

2. *If possible, punishment should suit the crime.* This means that the punishment should reflexively elicit a response incompatible with the punished response. Time in a penitentiary cell may elicit better planning of future crimes rather than socially acceptable behavior.

3. *Require an incompatible escape response.* This means that the punished person must engage in incompatible behavior to terminate the aversive state. A fixed number of days in jail is not proper punishment for vandalism; the person responsible should have to repair the damage, and punishment should last until the work is done.

4. *If possible, punish immediately.* Note that in regard to both the anticipatory response and fear response learning, we are dealing with classical conditioning. Such conditioning is maximally effective if the response is elicited very shortly after the conditioned stimulus occurs. Waiting until a "more appropriate" time to correct behavior provides little or no correction at all.

5. *If immediate punishment is impossible, reinstate the stimuli and the response.* Perhaps this can be done verbally by reminding the person of the behavior that is to be punished; an even better approach is to actually reinstate the cues. When relying on competing responses, re-play the scene. For example, a child who drops a coat on the floor upon entering the house should not simply be required to pick the coat up; rather, the child should put the coat back on, go outside, and reenter the house to hang up the coat. When relying on fear conditioning, feedback stimuli from the response must be present when the punishment is applied. The child who has hit a younger sibling earlier in the day might be required to act out the hitting response and then be punished.

6. *Avoid rewards after punishments.* We have noted that stimuli that precede rewarding events acquire secondary reinforcing value; even if the stimulus is initially aversive, it can become emotionally positive if it leads to pleasant consequences. Parents who employ punishment should therefore avoid letting guilt feelings lead them to lavish love and affection upon the child immediately after punishment. Otherwise, fear of punishment is reduced because punishment is a means to love and affection; in extreme form, this results in masochism, or a feeling of pleasure produced by pain.

7. *Finally, always provide acceptable alternatives to the punished response.* Punishment, even if it eliminates a response, leads to conflict. We have previously described conflict between habit and inhibition;

this potential problem is only intensified by punishment. If the motivation for making a response is left unresolved, the person cannot completely escape temptation; if performing that response is punished, the person cannot fully engage in the activity. This produces a state of continual conflict, leading to the misery that often culminates in neurotic behavior, inadequate solutions, and general maladjustment. Only if the person is provided with a way of reducing the drive that motivates an undesired response can he or she leave the situation and engage in normal behavior.

That this outcome is more than a remote possibility is amply illustrated in the clinical literature. In Western society, most neuroses involve sex because of the strong prohibitions surrounding some of the manifestations of this basic drive. The young person denied any form of sexual expression is inevitably left in conflict because of this persisting drive. Other cultures exist where, for example, guilt, shame, and secrecy surround hunger rather than sex; the neuroses in such cultures involve hunger because of the strong prohibitions surrounding what are considered the private activities involved in eating! In sum, a person should never be punished for desiring attention, love, affection, comfort, success, or the physical manifestations of sex. If the way the person desires to fulfill these drives is socially unacceptable, a socially acceptable alternative should be provided.

Response Persistence: Forgetting, Extinction, and Punishment

Multiple Choice Test Questions

1. When we forget one response more rapidly than usual because we have previously learned a similar response, what phenomenon has occurred?
   a. proactive interference
   b. retroactive interference
   c. post-learning interference
   d. amnesia
2. In most cases, the *rate* of forgetting for a response
   a. decreases as the retention interval is lengthened
   b. increases as the retention interval is lengthened
   c. stays the same no matter what the retention interval
   d. is greatest one to six hours after the response is learned
3. Among the factors during learning that increase subsequent resistance to extinction is
   a. deliverance of large rewards
   b. extended training
   c. response specificity
   d. mild punishment after a response

4. Among the factors that decrease response persistence is
   a. deliverance of small rewards
   b. extended training
   c. response variability
   d. punishment
5. Among the differences between the principles concerning acquisition and extinction is the fact that
   a. acquisition is faster with massed trials and extinction is faster with spaced trials
   b. acquisition is faster to a somewhat different stimulus and extinction is slower to such a stimulus
   c. acquisition should be shaped in relatively large steps and extinction should be shaped in small steps
   d. acquisition should be accomplished with large rewards and extinction should be accomplished with small rewards
6. One of the important principles concerning the use of punishment is to
   a. keep it mild
   b. wait until the appropriate time
   c. give rewards to counter the negative emotions produced
   d. provide an alternative response

Multiple Choice Answers

1. (a) Proactive interference is when more rapid forgetting occurs because of prior learning.
2. (a) The *rate* of forgetting is greatest shortly after learning and decreases as the retention interval is lengthened.
3. (d) The first three factors tend to decrease resistance to extinction. However, ineffective punishment may lead to greater resistance to extinction.
4. (b) Extended training involving reinforcement of the same stereotyped response reduces resistance to extinction. (Of course, many responses, such as the sum of two and two, are never subjected to nonreinforcement and, hence, are strengthened by extended training.) The other alternatives tend to increase response persistence.
5. (c) Because of differences in the degree of generalization, shaping needs to be more gradual when extinguishing a response than when acquiring it. The remaining alternatives are in error with respect to the principles of extinction.
6. (d) Whether or not punishment is an appropriate means of behavioral control, it is important to provide an acceptable outlet for various drives. The other alternatives are contrary to the stated guidelines for punishment.

True/False Thought Questions

1. Forgetting is any decrease in the performance of a response between the time of learning and a retention test.
2. The decrease in a learned fear over time is due to what is called the incubation of fear.
3. Often we can minimize forgetting by sleeping during a retention interval.
4. In a learning context, "resistance to extinction" is a technical term for the drive for self-preservation.
5. The worse the conditions for learning, the greater the persistence of a learned response.
6. The "partial reinforcement effect" is the emotional consequence of not receiving reward every time.
7. A person can be trained to behave according to the adage, "If at first you don't succeed, try, try again."
8. A response may become fixated by punishment.
9. Negative punishment tends to weaken a response; positive punishment tends to strengthen a response.
10. The principle of punishment is a special case of the principle of the anticipatory response.
11. Punishment makes the organism afraid to make the response.
12. The most effective punishment is given when you "count to ten" and calm down before punishing a response.

True/False Answers

1. (False) Forgetting is a decrease in performance since the time of learning that is not due to sensory, motor, or motivational changes in an organism.
2. (False) The incubation of fear is the apparent *increase* in a learned fear over time.
3. (True) Apparently, when we sleep, we decrease new learning during a retention interval and thus decrease retroactive interference effects.
4. (False) It would probably be better in a learning context to use the term "resistance to experimental extinction," since extinction relates to the number of times the response will occur during nonreinforcement.
5. (True) Learning is fastest if the organism can make the same response to the same stimulus and receive regular reinforcement for doing so. Persistence, however, is fostered by variability in the stimulus, the response, and the reinforcement. In addition, lots of training with large rewards promotes learning but not persistence.
6. (False) Partial reinforcement is, indeed, the condition in which some trials are not reinforced. The effect of this is to increase resistance to extinction. (The emotional consequences of nonreinforcement have been used to help account for the partial reinforcement effect.)

7. (True) If an organism encounters partial reinforcement in a variety of situations, persistence in the face of failure can generalize to new situations in later life.
8. (True) If an organism persists in responding in spite of punishment, the response may persist even when reward is removed and punishment is continued. This is called fixation.
9. (False) Both types of punishment lead to weakening. "Negative" punishment refers to the removal of something pleasant and "positive" punishment to the application of something aversive.
10. (False) Both principles influence the effect of punishment, but not in the same way. Punishment tends to weaken a response, but the responses produced by punishment also tend to become anticipatory. It is the net effect of these two tendencies that determines the final outcome of the punishment.
11. (True) Punishment associates fear with the feedback stimuli produced when a response is made. Thus, the organism may not respond in order to avoid this fear or may stop the response, once it begins, in order to escape this fear.
12. (False) Punishment is most effective if given immediately after an undesirable response. When that is not practicable, it is advisable to replay the scene, at least verbally, so that the appropriate cues are present at the time punishment is administered.

Essay/Discussion Questions

1. Frustration, as the term is used in everyday language, is produced by a wide variety of situations. Identify some situations that you find frustrating and relate them, insofar as possible, to the term frustration as it is used in this chapter (namely, as the result of nonreinforcement).
2. Our principal techniques for crime control rely on punishment. Critically evaluate these techniques in view of the principles described in this chapter (include controversial issues such as capital punishment in your discussion).

References

Forgetting

*Spear, N. E. Retrieval of memory: A psychobiological approach. In W. K. Estes (Ed.), *Handbook of learning and cognitive processes: Memory processes* (Vol. 4). Hillsdale, New Jersey: Lawrence Erlbaum Associates, 1976.
Wagner, A. R., Rudy, J. W., and Whitlow, J. W., Jr. Rehearsal in animal conditioning. *Journal of Experimental Psychology Monograph*, 1973, *97*, 407–426.

*Suitable for additional reading by the beginning student. The others are written at a more technical level.

Extinction

*Amsel, A. Partial reinforcement effects on vigor and persistence. In G. H. Bower and J. T. Spence (Eds.), *Psychology of learning and motivation.* New York: Academic Press, 1967.

Brown, J. S., and Bass, B. The acquisition and extinction of an instrumental response under constant and variable stimulus conditions. *Journal of Comparative and Physiological Psychology*, 1958, *51*, 499–504.

Brown, R. T., and Logan, F. A. Generalized partial reinforcement effect. *Journal of Comparative and Physiological Psychology*, 1965, *60*, 64–69.

Capaldi, E. J. Hypothesis of sequential effects. *Psychological Review*, 1966, *73*, 459.

Farber, I. E. Response fixation under anxiety and non-anxiety conditions. *Journal of Experimental Psychology*, 1948, *38*, 111–131.

Ferraro, D. P., and Branch, K. M. Variability of response location during regular and partial reinforcement. *Psychological Reports*, 1968, *23*, 1023–1031.

Guttman, N., and Kalish, H. E. Discriminability and stimulus generalization. *Journal of Experimental Psychology*, 1956, *51*, 79–88.

Reynolds, B. Extinction of trace-conditioned response as a function of the spacing of trials during the acquisition and extinction series. *Journal of Experimental Psychology*, 1945, *35*, 81–95.

Wagner, A. R. Effects of amount and percentage of reinforcement and number of acquisition trials on conditioning and extinction. *Journal of Experimental Psychology*, 1961, *62*, 234–242.

Punishment

Campbell, B. A., and Church, R. M. *Punishment and aversive behavior.* New York: Appleton-Century-Crofts, 1969.

Generalization, Discrimination, and Differentiation

We have previously indicated that learning is somewhat specific to the particular stimuli and responses involved during practice. Learning is partly restricted to the environment in which practice occurs, such as the room in which the student studies, and is partly restricted to the behaviors involved, such as the specific examples given in a text. But learning is not completely restricted to the original stimuli and responses. If, for example, you find a particular piece of fish distasteful, you are likely to generalize your reaction to other fish of the same species and even to other fish that look somewhat similar. People who "eat with their eyes" are those who generalize expectations about the taste of certain foods to the appearance of the foods, usually in relation to past experiences. Thus, stimuli other than the original can elicit a learned response. In acquiring table manners, we learn to use a knife and fork in a particular way, but we are not incapable of using different techniques if necessary. The American who normally scoops potatoes and vegetables onto his or her fork may feel embarrassed in a British home where they press food upon the back of the fork with the knife. Nevertheless, the American can use his or her utensils the British way if required to do so (although not so adeptly as if those responses had been practiced). Thus, we can make responses other than those we have practiced.

Accordingly, one of the basic principles of learned behavior is the principle of generalization: *Whenever a response has been learned in one stimulus situation, similar stimulus situations will also tend to elicit that response in proportion to their similarity, and that stimulus situation will also tend to elicit similar responses in proportion to their similarity.* There are two aspects to this principle. One is that of *stimulus generalization:* the greater the similarity of any situation to that in which practice occurred, the greater the likelihood that the learned response will occur. The other aspect entails *response generalization;* when the learned response is, for some reason, blocked, the organism will tend to make responses that are similar to the learned response. Both aspects of this principle apply to all learned habits, whether they are acquired through the process of classical, operant, or instrumental conditioning.

9

It should be recognized that this is an exceedingly adaptive principle. As a rule, similar situations require similar responses. Indeed, one could argue that since no stimulus situation is exactly identical to another, generalization is necessary in order to learn. In general, the response most likely to be appropriate in a new situation is the response most similar to one that was successful in a similar situation. Consider, for example, the behavior of dancing. Having learned to dance with one partner, it is probably best to make the same responses when confronted with a new partner. And having learned one particular type of dance, it is likely that many of those learned responses will be appropriate in learning a new type of dance. These generalizations are, of course, not always perfect; this is why we will also consider in this chapter the related processes of discrimination and differentiation.

The principle of generalization is also of considerable practical importance in understanding behavior. Racial prejudice, for example, whether positive or negative, is a familiar illustration of stimulus generalization. Emotional experiences with one person will involve responses that generalize to other people who have similar appearances. One obvious source of similarity is racial features, including skin color, nose shape, the slant of the eyes, or whatever.

Thus, the most fundamental principles involved in understanding interpersonal relations are classical conditioning and generalization; emotional responses become conditioned to people as stimuli and generalize to similar people.

The Concept of Similarity

As with other basic principles, there are complexities implicit in the principle of generalization that are not brought out in the simple definition. The most important complexity concerns the concept of *similarity:* How does one measure or estimate the extent to which two stimuli or two responses are similar to each other? There are three aspects to the answer to this question.

Continuous Dimensions
Many events vary in regard to natural, physical dimensions for which there are measures available. For example, in terms of stimuli, tones vary in pitch and loudness; lights vary in color and brightness; objects vary in height, length, and volume, as well as in shape. On the other hand, in terms of responses, behaviors vary in force, speed, and direction. For each of these examples a physical measure exists, and similarity can be measured along that continuous dimension. Thus, the closer two tones are in pitch, the more similar they are and the greater the generalization we expect between them. Particularly when dealing with simple stimuli, the most useful index of similarity involves a measure of physical attributes.

Common Elements

When events are complex and contain a number of elements, similarity is measured by counting the number of elements the events have in common. For example, the game of tennis is quite complex, containing elements such as a racquet, a ball, a court with a net, the responses of hitting the ball over the net into designated areas, and keeping score in a particular way. Many of the elements of this game are similar to those in Ping-Pong, although the size of the racquet, the ball, the court, and the net are different. Tennis is also similar to squash in that both games involve taking turns at hitting a ball with a racquet. Tennis is less similar to baseball and still less similar to football as the number of players, the nature of the ball, and the object of the game change. One way of measuring the similarity of complex events is to count the number of common elements or features that they share.

Learned Similarity

Not only may events be similar because of their inherent appearance, nature, or structure, but events may acquire similarity. This fact can be seen most clearly in the effects of language. All words have associated meanings, and insofar as the meanings of different words are similar, they tend to elicit similar responses. The words "couch" and "sofa," for example, have no sounds in common, but because they mean very much the same thing, they have acquired similarity. Similarly, the words "rocket" and "missile" may have acquired similarity for those who have not learned the distinction between them. Evidence for this assertion comes from the study of *semantic generalization;* if a human is conditioned to respond to a word as a stimulus, greater generalization will occur to words with similar meanings than to words with similar sounds.

This process is not restricted to language, although language is perhaps the most obvious source of evidence. More generally, *stimuli and responses may acquire similarity insofar as they become associated with similar responses.* If, for example, a rat is first trained to make one response to two different stimuli and then a second response is trained to one of them, that response will show generalization to the other stimulus as a result of the original training. Returning to the example of language, we respond similarly to all cats because we have learned to apply the same label to them.

Summary

We can summarize these approaches to estimating similarity by again considering people as stimuli. In the first place, we differ from each other along a number of continuous dimensions, including physical size; skin, hair, and eye color; voice pitch; and so on. Similarity can be measured for each of these dimensions in terms of physical units. In addition, people present a complex of elements; our similarity depends in part upon how many of these we share with another person. Two people whose eyes look very much the same, for example, may readily be distinguished if they have different hair color. And finally, we attach labels—such as Russian, dean, and doctor—to people, and these labels tend to increase the similarity among people who share them. The generalization of our learned responses is based on all of these sources of similarity.

Factors that Increase Generalization

As we have indicated, the amount of generalization is based primarily upon similarity. The concept of the *gradient of generalization* reflects the fact that the amount of generaiization can be placed on a continuum that relates to stimulus similarity, rather than being an all-or-none affair. Figure 4.7 shows such a gradient, demonstrating that as similarity decreases, generalization decreases. There are, however, two factors involved in the acquisition of an association that affect the amount of generalization between similar stimuli.

Reinforcement Variability

It is perhaps obvious that variability in the stimulus and response during practice will increase the amount of generalization. The larger the number of stimuli the response has become associated to, the wider the range of stimuli that will lead to that response; and the larger the number of responses practiced, the wider the range of behaviors that are learned. It is perhaps less obvious that the amount of generalization also depends on reinforcement variability. However, *responses acquired under conditions of variable reward generalize more extensively than responses acquired under conditions of constant reward.*

Punishment

It is also somewhat surprising that ineffective punishment (that is, punishment that does not successfully eliminate the behavior) leads to greater generalization than if the response is not punished. In fact, punishment may lead to a *greater tendency* to respond to different stimuli than to the original stimulus itself. This is the familiar phenomenon of *displacement*. A child first builds up a tendency to respond aggressively to a parent through reinforcement. On some occasions, however, such aggressive behavior against the parent is punished. The resultant behavior often takes the form of aggressive responses toward an object resembling the parent— for example, a brother or sister.

Factors that Decrease Generalization

Some aspects of the training conditions may also lead to less generalization than might otherwise be expected. Two of these, in particular, are worth noting.

Amount of Reward

The larger the amount of reward given during the acquisition of a response, the *less* the amount of generalization that learning will exhibit if the stimulus is changed or a different response is required. Although large rewards lead to vigorous performance, they also lead to more specific learning.

Extended Training

Rewarding training beyond the point at which no further improvement in performance takes place also leads to less generalization. Extended training progressively increases the specificity of the learning to the particular stimuli and responses practiced. This is shown most clearly in the context of compound stimuli. If a response is conditioned to a compound conditioned stimulus (composed, for instance, of a light and a tone), after a moderate amount of training either element alone will elicit the conditioned response. After extensive training, however, only the compound itself will elicit the response; the separate elements, although a part of and, hence, similar to the compound are no longer effective. The person who has "overtrained" may do worse in a test situation because the test may involve somewhat different stimuli or require somewhat different responses from those practiced, making the appropriate performance less likely.

Summary of Generalization

Although learning is somewhat specific to the particular stimuli and responses involved during practice, it also generalizes to fairly similar stimuli and responses in proportion to their similarity with the original situation. The degree of similarity may be measured along continuous dimensions for which there are physical measures; it may be estimated from the number of elements that complex events have in common; and it may be affected by learning similar responses to somewhat different stimuli. The amount of generalization not only depends on similarity but also on certain features of the training situation; generalization increases as a result of reinforcement variability and through the use of ineffective punishment and decreases as a result of large rewards or training extended beyond the point of improvement in performance. Note that these latter factors are the same ones that affect the persistence of learning. That is to say, the training conditions that increase persistence also increase generalization, and the conditions that decrease persistence also decrease generalization.

Discrimination and Differentiation

We have already anticipated the fact that generalization is not always adaptive. Two people may appear to be quite similar, even though they are markedly different individuals who should be responded to differently. Even identical twins are individuals; and although the rattlesnake and the western bull snake look very much alike, one is a menace to society and the other is beneficial. Similarly, although activities such as tennis and squash have many elements in common, they require somewhat different skills. In short, although generalization is often an adaptive and perhaps necessary principle for survival, organisms also need to be able to overcome the effects of generalization when generalization is inappropriate.

To do so, we distinguish between two types of processes. The process of *discrimination* arises when somewhat similar stimuli encounter differential reinforcement so that responding to them identically is not adaptive. The process of *differentiation* arises when somewhat similar responses encounter differential reinforcement so that the performance of one is more adaptive than the performance of the other. In effect, these are the processes by which an organism learns to offset the basic tendency to generalize, to respond only to those stimuli that are appropriate, and to make only those responses that are appropriate.

In the following discussion, we will confine ourselves to the process of discrimination. The primary reason for this is because considerably more experimental evidence is available on discrimination; one can more readily present and control the stimuli an organism is exposed to than one can control the responses the organism makes. However, insofar as comparable research has been done, the evidence suggests that the processes of discrimination and differentiation are fundamentally the same and that the principles of discrimination are matched by comparable principles of differentiation. In most instances, then, one could substitute the word "response" for the word "stimulus" in the following discussion and still arrive at an appropriate conclusion.

There is probably good reason for this set of shared principles. We have previously noted that all responses produce feedback stimuli, indicating to the organism what it is doing. *Differentiating* between responses may thus be thought of as *discriminating* between the feedback stimuli produced by somewhat similar responses. That is to say, responses are different because they feel different, and selecting which response to make is fundamentally the same as selecting which stimuli to respond to. The difference is only on the basis of whether the stimuli are external or response produced, and while at a molecular level there are theoretical reasons for distinguishing between the processes, for most purposes they may be treated as comparable.

Types of Discrimination Situations

Discrimination learning is the process resulting from the differential reinforcement of somewhat similar stimuli. By *differential reinforcement,* we mean simply that the consequences associated with these stimuli are not the same, so making the same response to them is not appropriate. In effect, the organism must learn to distinguish between the stimuli and respond differently depending on which stimulus is present. There are four basic contexts in which this process can be studied.

Differential Classical Conditioning   We have already described this process in our discussion of classical conditioning theory, but for completeness, this type of conditioning should be reviewed here. *Differential classical conditioning* occurs when there are two conditioned stimuli that occur in an irregular and unpredictable order, and when one of these is followed by the unconditioned stimulus and the other is not. For example, in the Pavlovian context, a 1000-cycle tone might be followed by food, while a 2000-cycle tone is not. Differential conditioning is demonstrated when the organism comes to salivate only to the former tone.

Differential classical conditioning is very important in everyday life. Again, in interpersonal relationships, we learn to like one person but may dislike another person who is somewhat similar to the first. The antidote for racial prejudice is, in fact, to arrange for differential conditioning so that the person learns that emotional responses generalized from one member of a race to another are not appropriate.

Differential Operant Conditioning   We briefly introduced the idea of differential operant conditioning as one of the more complex schedules of reinforcement. *Differential operant conditioning* occurs when on some occasions one stimulus is present and one schedule is in force, while on other occasions, a similar stimulus is present but a different schedule is in force. For example, a pigeon might encounter a fixed-interval schedule when the key to be pecked is red and a fixed-ratio schedule when a green key is to be pecked. Differential operant conditioning is demonstrated when the organism responds differentially to the two stimuli, responding appropriately to the schedule indicated by the stimulus.

To take an example involving interpersonal relations, consider the response of using slang expressions. This is, of course, a freely available response that may occur as a part of verbal behavior at any time. A high frequency of this response is not only permitted, but actually is expected and approved of in the context of many peer group activities. However, the use of slang expressions may be disdained when you are interviewing for a job or giving a professional presentation. All persons, then, are confronted with the necessity to discriminate between these contexts, coloring their language with slang when spending a relaxed evening with peers, but avoiding the use of slang expressions in professional encounters. To the extent that we are able to make this discrimination, we are displaying differential operant conditioning.

Differential Instrumental Conditioning   Recall that the principal variable of interest in instrumental conditioning is the condition of reinforcement. When the performance of a response is enabled for discrete trials, the speed or vigor of that response depends upon such variables as the amount and delay of reinforcement. *Differential instrumental conditioning* refers to the situation in which the consequences of making the response in one situation are different from those in another situation. For example, a rat might sometimes be placed in a black alley and rewarded with food for running to the goal box, while on other occasions, the rat is placed in a white alley where the goal box is empty. Differential instrumental conditioning is demonstrated when performance in the two situations is different and, in each case, appropriate to the reward or nonreward experienced there.

We have all experienced differential instrumental conditioning. Consider your response of accepting a dinner invitation. This is an instrumental situation since you cannot accept an invitation unless it is offered, but once the invitation is offered, you can accept or decline. Although dinner invitations to two homes may appear to be similar, you may have found in the past that you enjoy visiting one home and not the other. You display differential instrumental conditioning when you learn to accept one invitation and decline the other.

Simultaneous Discrimination   In each of the three types of differential conditioning just discussed, the stimuli to be discriminated between are presented one at a time. When only one stimulus is reinforced, the problem may be thought of as a "go/no-go" decision. By contrast, in *simultaneous discrimination learning,* the two stimuli are presented at the same time, but the consequences of responding to one are different from the consequences of responding to the other. This procedure, which may be thought of as *stimulus selection,* is illustrated when a rat confronts two doors, one black and the other white, with a food reward behind only one. Learning to choose the correct door by color, regardless of its position, illustrates simultaneous discrimination learning.

This is the type of problem voters confront during an election. Not infrequently, the candidates are in many ways similar. Each may appear to make pretty much the same promises, yet the voter must choose between them. The voter is thus confronted with a simultaneous discrimination problem.

Summary of Discrimination Situations

All four types of discrimination situations have one process in common: Two stimuli that are similar enough that generalization occurs between them are treated differently so that the organism must learn to distinguish between them and respond differently to each one. At this point, several more general features should be noted. In the first place, discrimination situations may involve more than two stimuli. Any number of somewhat similar stimuli might be embedded within any type of discrimination situation in a variety of complex combinations. We have restricted our examples to two stimuli because this provides the simplest illustration of the basic processes involved in discrimination learning. A second fact should also be noted: Discrimination situations are not always so simple that one stimulus is reinforced while the second stimulus is not. In the classical case, for example, one CS might be followed by a certain US, while a second CS is followed by another US. However, it is again easier to study first a simplified, restricted case of differential reinforcement.

In sum, then, experimental analysis has shown that organisms can learn to respond differentially even to highly similar stimuli when the consequences make such discrimination appropriate. There are certain limitations to this conclusion; some of them are indicated in the next section.

Factors that Affect Discrimination Learning

In discussing different types of discrimination situations, we have actually described the operations that may be performed by an experimenter. That is to say, differential reinforcement is associated with similar stimuli, but it is an empirical question as to whether and how rapidly an organism may learn to respond differentially. There are a number of factors that affect how readily performance adjusts to stimuli that are differentially reinforced.

Similarity The most obvious, but also most important, factors affecting the ease of discrimination learning concern the similarity of the stimuli and the reinforcement conditions. The more similar the stimuli are, the greater the amount of generalization that will occur between them, and, hence, the more difficult it will be for the organism to respond differentially. The more similar the reinforcement conditions associated with each stimulus, the less basis there is for differential responding and the less likely differential learning is to occur. In fact, if the stimulus or reward conditions are actually the same, or if they appear to be the same to the organism, then there is no basis for learning differential responses. On the other hand, as these differences increase, the ease of discrimination also increases. But if the differences are so extreme that there is no generalization in the first place, there is, again, no occasion for discrimination learning. The learning process takes place only when the stimuli are discriminably different to the organism, yet similar enough that generalization would normally occur.

Nondifferential Reinforcement Discrimination learning may be preceded by a stage during which the two stimuli are presented, but are not differentially reinforced. In the classical case, for example, both CSs might first be followed by a US, after which the US is omitted for one of them and continued for the other. The evidence shows that such *prior nondifferential reinforcement retards subsequent discrimination learning*. Having first learned to make the same response to two similar stimuli, the organism has difficulty overcoming the generalization between them.

Indeed, if nondifferential reinforcement is coupled with punishment during early trials, a subsequent discrimination may not be learned at all. For example, consider a rat that is first forced to choose between two stimuli, one black and the other white. Half of the time the reward is behind one stimulus, and half of the time it is behind the other; if the rat happens to choose the wrong stimulus, it experiences an aversive consequence. During this stage, the rat is likely to adopt a stereotyped solution, such as always going in the same direction, since there is no better alternative available. More importantly, however, if the conditions are subsequently changed so that reward is, for example, always behind the black door, the rat may never learn the discrimination! The rat's earlier solution, although no longer adaptive, persists not only because it initially received partial reinforcement but also because the response was fixated by partial punishment. Here is another situation in which organisms may learn *not* to learn.

Transposition Once a discrimination has been formed between one pair of stimuli, we may inquire as to how the organism will respond if a new, but similar, pair of stimuli is presented. We might, for example, first train a monkey to select the larger of two relatively small stimuli, then present two relatively large stimuli that also differ in size from each other. The term *transposition* refers to the fact that, in many situations, organisms tend to choose from between the two new stimuli on the basis of the relationship that was appropriate during the original discrimination. In this example, the monkey is likely to select the larger of the two new stimuli. This observation is true even when the smaller of the two new stimuli is actually the same size as the larger of the original pair; the monkey thus selects not the stimulus it was trained to choose, but rather, a totally new stimulus.

One cannot say in advance whether transposition will be beneficial or harmful to later discrimination learning; it depends on which response is correct in the new context. If the same relative choice is correct, then the organism will perform correctly in both trials. If the same relative choice is incorrect, however, the tendency to transpose on the basis of the relationship between the stimuli will be detrimental.

The term *transposition* was borrowed from music theory; in music, it means that the same piece can be played in different keys and still sound very much the same. Transposition is one of the bases for our earlier assertion that the relationships among stimuli qualify as stimuli themselves. It is also interesting to note that adult humans display a greater tendency to transpose a learned discrimination than infants or lower animals do. Apparently, learning words for relationships requires attending to these relationships and facilitates subsequent learning based upon them.

Transfer When the organism is confronted with a very difficult discrimination because the stimuli involved are highly similar, learning may be facilitated by first learning an easier discrimination involving the same dimension. For example, if we want to train a rat to choose between two very similar gray stimuli, the rat can learn the discrimination most readily if it is first trained to select between a black and a white stimulus and if these stimuli are then gradually made more similar. This transfer effect may be beneficial in terms of the number of training trials necessary; an organism learns a difficult discrimination faster by first starting on an easy problem and progressing to harder trials than by receiving the same amount of training only on the difficult problem. Indeed, in some cases a difficult discrimination can be learned only if preceded by pretraining on easier tasks along the same dimension.

The optimal procedures for facilitating learning through the transfer of discrimination have not yet been worked out experimentally. However, the student can profit from reviewing our discussion of shaping a response and noting that the transfer procedure is essentially the shaping of a discrimination. Because of the similarity between differentiating responses and discriminating stimuli, it will not be surprising if very similar rules apply. Specifically, for example, it is probably not advisable to spend too much time on the easier problems; once the discrimination process begins, it is best to move on rapidly toward the more difficult problems.

Imitation If a sighted organism is first given an opportunity to observe another organism performing a reinforced response, the observing organism's learning will be facilitated. People can be taught to imitate the behavior of a model, but there also appears to be an unlearned tendency to learn vicariously through observation. For example, a pigeon that has watched another pigeon peck a lighted key for food will later acquire the same response quickly. Indeed, if the observing pigeon has access to a key, it may begin to peck at the key even if not rewarded for doing so.

You can undoubtedly relate the relevance of the natural tendency to imitate to such current issues as violence on television and pornography in the streets. The tendency to imitate should also underscore the role of parents and teachers as models. For example, a child who has been raised primarily with aversive control will often be excessively punitive with dolls.

Learning to Learn The rate at which discrimination learning proceeds depends to a significant extent upon the amount of experience the organism has had with discrimination problems, even when these problems involved stimulus dimensions different from those the present problem involves. A monkey, for example, might first be required to learn to select the larger of two blocks of wood; forty or fifty trials might be necessary to train the animal to do so consistently. The monkey might then be required to learn to select a green ball instead of a red one; fewer trials will probably be required for the monkey to learn this discrimination. As the process is continued with new stimuli, each discrimination problem becomes progressively easier until, in the limiting case, the monkey will make at most one error. This process is called *learning to learn* or a *discrimination learning set*. Having solved a number of simple discrimination problems, the monkey is now readily able to solve comparable problems. Its first choice must be made by chance, but even if its choice is incorrect on that first trial, the monkey thereafter knows which stimulus is correct and will select it consistently.

The concept of learning to learn helps account for some of the quantitative differences between the adult human learning and the learning processes of other animals. During childhood, a person is taught a great many discriminations. In effect, we have learned to learn a wide variety of types of material through exposure to a graduated series of problems concerning different materials. Your ability to read and understand this book is heavily dependent on years of prior training, both in reading and in assimilating information of this type presented in this manner. Probably, as more is discovered about the learning process, better programs will be devised to take advantage of not only our capacity to learn, but also our capacity to learn how to learn.

Summary of Factors that Affect Discrimination Learning
It is intuitively obvious and experimentally demonstrable that organisms can tell the differences between stimuli even when the stimuli are similar enough that generalization between them occurs. How fine a discrimination an organism can learn and how rapidly it is learned, however, depends only partly upon factors in the situation itself, such as the similarity of the stimuli and reward conditions. Factors like speed and proficiency of learning also depend to a great degree upon the past experiences of the organism. Let's review these principles in a familiar context.

A child may learn to fear or dislike a teacher if the child has been embarrassed or frustrated by the teacher in the classroom. This negative feeling may generalize to other teachers or even to other adults who try to instruct or correct the child. This generalization is normal, natural, and inevitable, since most teachers share at least some characteristics and all share the same professional role. At the same time, the generalization is inappropriate, since a person's profession is not a perfect predictor of behavioral traits and since each person should be evaluated individually. We noted earlier that prior nondifferential reinforcement retards subsequent discrimination learning. In this context, then, a child who is exposed early in life to various teachers whose behavioral traits appear to be quite similar will later have more difficulty learning to discriminate between teachers on the basis of behavioral traits. We have also noted that learned discriminations transpose to new situations on the basis of the relative relationship between the early stimuli. Thus, if a child has learned that one teacher who moves around the classroom is more disquieting than another teacher who sits at a desk, the child will transpose this relationship so that the more physically active a teacher is, the more the child will fear the teacher's presence. Another observation we have made is that difficult discriminations are most readily formed by first learning easier discriminations involving the same dimensions. Hence, learning to discriminate among teachers whose profession inevitably makes them similar should be facilitated by early exposure to teachers with highly dissimilar behavioral traits. And, finally, we have seen that organisms can learn discriminations more easily if they have had the opportunity to solve similar problems of that type at an earlier time. Accordingly, explicit training in discriminating between people on some basis other than profession should facilitate a child's ability to discriminate between teachers on the basis of behavioral traits.

Errorless Discrimination Learning

Discrimination learning is demonstrated when an organism responds differently to stimuli that are sufficiently similar that generalization occurs between them. In each of the procedures we have discussed, the organism first learns to respond to one stimulus because doing so is reinforced. This tendency to respond then generalizes to the second stimulus. However, that response is not reinforced and, in time, the discrimination is learned. The reader might do well to review the theoretical description of differential classical conditioning, in which this process was described in detail.

Of considerable interest and usefulness would be a procedure in which appropriate differential responding could be achieved without the necessity for the organism to encounter the frustration resulting from responding and not being rewarded. An organism can build up enough inhibition as a result of nonreinforcement that the erroneous responses are eventually eliminated, but the aversive aspects of frustration and inhibition would lead one to favor a procedure in which errors never occur in the first place.

There is evidence that such procedures may, in fact, be possible. Working within the context of operant conditioning, we can, for instance, first train a pigeon to peck a key that is green in order to obtain food. Then, carefully watching the bird, we can present very dim and brief exposures of a red stimulus at times when the bird is otherwise engaged and unlikely to peck the key, returning immediately to the green. We can then gradually increase the brightness and duration of the red stimulus, all the while taking care that the pigeon is not likely to peck the red key. Through such a procedure, the bird's behavior may reach a stage very much like that of another bird trained in differential operant conditioning by standard procedures: Both pigeons peck when the key is green and don't peck when the key is red, with both stimuli now exposed equally often and at equal brightness.

It would be premature to generalize too extensively from this notion until a firmer experimental base has been laid. But the evidence does suggest that tasks such as toilet training can be accomplished without the use of obvious rewards for acceptable behavior or obvious punishment for unacceptable behavior; if the parent simply makes sure that the child uses the toilet by diligently observing the child's biological schedule for a while, the response and stimulus will become associated without further ado. For such a child, there is nothing particularly good about using the toilet nor particularly bad about not doing so—it is simply the way things are done. Similarly, the person who is addicted to nailbiting may eliminate this behavior without the trauma of shame and aversive control. If, probably with the help of others, the person consciously attempts to avoid that response for a while, the habit of not doing so will supplant the original habit, which will disappear simply because the person doesn't do it anymore. The possibility of controlling behavior without the use of emotionally negative consequences is one of the exciting possibilities that is only beginning to be revealed.

Generalization, Discrimination, and Differentiation

Multiple Choice Test Questions

1. As it is used in the psychology of learning, *stimulus generalization* refers to the
   a. tendency to make similar responses to similar stimuli
   b. formulation of very general principles
   c. elaboration of details in a complex stimulus
   d. presentation of redundant stimuli to an audience
2. Similarity among stimuli depends in part on
   a. the sensory modality involved
   b. the response system involved
   c. the number of dimensions involved
   d. prior experience

3. The degree of generalization to similar stimuli is increased by
   a. constant rewards
   b. large rewards
   c. punishment
   d. extensive training
4. Differential conditioning necessarily involves
   a. reinforcement
   b. nonreinforcement
   c. punishment
   d. stimulus intensity
5. Which of the following procedures is most likely to retard subsequent discrimination learning?
   a. nondifferential reinforcement
   b. transposition
   c. transfer
   d. learning to learn
6. Errorless discrimination learning is achieved by shaping the
   a. correct stimulus
   b. incorrect stimulus
   c. correct response
   d. incorrect response

Multiple Choice Answers

1. (a) The term *generalization* is indeed used for the process of formulating general principles from specific observations, but in the psychology of learning, the term refers to associations between stimuli and responses. The other two alternatives are not relevant.
2. (d) The concept of similarity does not differ for the sensory modalities or the response system involved; all of our sensory modalities may display generalization in regard to any learnable response. Furthermore, it is not the number of dimensions, but the number of common elements that determines similarity. Experience, on the other hand, may lead to learned similarity.
3. (c) Just as punishment increases the persistence of a response, it increases generalization. The other alternatives have the opposite effect—they decrease generalization.
4. (a) Differential conditioning may or may not be based on stimulus intensity, and punishment may or may not be included. Although nonreinforcement is often involved, differential conditioning can also be obtained by using different conditions or schedules of reinforcement.
5. (a) Learning to learn facilitates later discrimination learning. Transposition and transfer may retard later training but may also facilitate it, depending on the correct solution to the new problem. On the other hand, nondifferential reinforcement is detrimental to subsequent discrimination learning.

6. (b) There is only one response in discrimination learning. The task is to learn when and where to make the response, and when and where not to make the response. Learning when not to make the response can be achieved through nonreinforcing or punishing errors, but it can also be achieved wihout errors if the incorrect stimulus is gradually shaped.

True/False Thought Questions

1. A single situation cannot reflect stimulus generalization and response generalization at the same time.
2. Stimuli cannot be similar on the basis of continuous dimensions, common elements, and learned similarity at the same time.
3. Learning different responses to somewhat similar stimuli may increase their distinctiveness.
4. Because of displacement, a woman is likely to choose as a husband a man who is somewhat similar to her father, and a man is likely to choose as a wife a woman similar to his mother.
5. Responses that generalize very broadly do not persist very long.
6. Discrimination is responding the same way to similar stimuli while differentiation is responding differently to them.
7. What the organism learns about the difference between stimuli depends upon the type of discrimination situation employed.
8. In teaching children the distinction between "good" and "bad," it is best to treat their behavior indiscriminately until they are old enough to understand the difference.
9. In teaching a child the distinction between "good" and "bad," it is best to begin with examples that are extreme.
10. The rate of learning typically increases during childhood but then eventually decreases with age, largely as a result of prior learning.
11. A child's expectations from a Christmas package may well depend upon its size, largely as a result of transposition.
12. Stimulus control over behavior requires that errors occur so that they can be nonreinforced or perhaps punished.

True/False Answers

1. (False) If a new situation is encountered, the tendency will be to make the response learned in a similar situation; if, however, that response is impossible, the tendency will be to make a somewhat similar response.
2. (False) Two pizza pies may differ in the continuous dimension of the amount of a particular ingredient they contain, in the number of common ingredients they contain, and in the name associated with each pizza. Especially among complex stimuli, all bases for measuring similarity may be involved.

3. (True) Although we have emphasized the fact that learning similar responses to different stimuli increases their similarity, the reverse process also occurs. Stimuli become more different as an organism learns to respond differently to them.

4. (True) If a woman, for example, loves her father, similar men will be attractive to her because of generalization. However, the incest taboo leads her to avoid her father and, also by generalization, men very similar to him. Her strongest attraction will thus be a man who is similar to, yet distinctively different from, her father. This is an illustration of displacement.

5. (False) The truth is quite the reverse; factors that increase generalization also increase response persistence. This is fortunate, since we typically want to learn responses that will persist and generalize to new situations. It may also have unfortunate results, however, since we are likely to learn some undesirable responses under conditions that promote both persistence and generalization.

6. (False) In everyday language, we may say that racial discrimination means treating all members of a race alike. However, as used here, discrimination means distinguishing between somewhat similar stimuli, and differentiation means distinguishing between the feedback from somewhat similar responses.

7. (False) The different situations require somewhat different behaviors for an organism to indicate that it is discriminating between the stimuli. But what the organism is learning is very much the same, as is indicated by the fact that the experimenter can change the type of situation and still see some evidence of stimulus control.

8. (False) This approach would constitute prior nondifferential reinforcement and would thus make the discrimination more difficult to learn.

9. (True) Fine distinctions can be learned more readily if preceded by easier, but similar, distinctions. The converse may also be true: Starting with a difficult problem may make an easier one more difficult. In any event, the process of shaping applies equally to discrimination and differentiation learning.

10. (True) There may be important constitutional changes that occur during childhood and old age that affect the rate of learning. One important fact is that learning to learn during childhood enables us to solve new problems quickly. However, as we age, our accumulated habits may begin to interfere with learning new, incompatible responses. Hence, our prior learning history greatly affects how rapidly we can learn a new task.

11. (True) If, in the child's past, larger packages have contained better presents, this relationship will be learned, and the child's future expectations will reflect transposition on the basis of this relationship.

12. (False) Undesirable or inappropriate responses can be eliminated by nonreinforcement or punishment. However, it may also be possible to arrange conditions so that errors never occur in the first place and, hence, are never learned.

Essay/Discussion Questions

1. Elaborate on the distinction between stimulus generalization and response generalization. Illustrate the distinction in an original example in which both processes are involved.
2. Elaborate on the distinction between discrimination and differentiation. Illustrate the distinction in an original example in which both processes are involved.

References

The Concept of Similarity

Mostofsky, D. I. (Ed.). *Stimulus generalization.* Stanford: Stanford University Press, 1965.

Generalization

Logan, F. A., & Ferraro, D. P. *Systematic analyses of learning and motivation.* New York: Wiley, 1978. (pp. 315–339)

Maier, N. R. F. *Frustration, the study of behavior without a goal.* New York: McGraw-Hill, 1949.

*Razran, G. A quantitative study of meaning by conditioned salivary technique (semantic conditioning). *Science*, 1939, *90*, 89–91.

Wickens, D. D. The transference of conditioned excitation and conditioned inhibition from one muscle group to the antagonistic muscle group. *Journal of Experimental Psychology*, 1938, *22*, 101–123.

Discrimination and Differentiation

Harlow, H. F. The formation of learning sets. *Psychological Review*, 1949, *56*, 51–65.

Kendler, H. H., & Kendler, T. S. Vertical and horizontal processes in problem solving. *Psychological Review*, 1962, *69*, 1–16.

Riley, D. A. *Discrimination learning.* Boston: Allyn and Bacon, 1968.

Spence, K. W. The differential response in animals to stimuli varying within a single dimension. *Psychological Review*, 1937, *44*, 430–444.

Terrace, H. S. Discrimination learning with and without errors. *Journal of Experimental Analysis of Behavior*, 1963, *6*, 1–27.

*Suitable for additional reading by the beginning student. The others are written at a more technical level.

An Overview of Learning

We have now completed a survey of the fundamental principles of learning. In doing so, we have by necessity submerged ourselves in a large number of technical terms and details that may have made it difficult to see the overall organization of these materials. Let's now try to regain a general perspective of the topic of learning.

We began by defining learning as a relatively permanent process resulting from experience with some task and reflected in a change in performance under appropriate circumstances. We acknowledged that no one yet knows what learning is in a physiological sense and that we therefore must treat it as a *hypothetical process* that is functionally *associative* in nature. Within this framework, we can say that all organisms learn one thing: that stimuli occur regularly in the environment. Learning means to come to anticipate or expect the occurrence of stimuli and to respond appropriately.

Learning is what is called in the study of logic an "if-then" relationship—if something happens, something else happens. Regularity may occur simply over time; the sun rises and then sets each day. More commonly, however, a stimulus is more or less regularly preceded by another stimulus that occurs irregularly over time. The adage, "where there's smoke, there's fire," captures one such regularity among stimuli. Similarly, thunder regularly "follows" lightning. Learning that results from pairing two stimuli in temporal order is called *classical conditioning*. The response occasioned by the second stimulus tends to become anticipatory and to antedate its initial time of occurrence.

A second type of regularity is present when a stimulus follows a response—if you do something, and then something happens. If you turn on a radio, you may hear music. You may also hear music when you go to a dance. We can distinguish between two types of situations in which this learning process is studied experimentally. These two types of situations are known as operant conditioning and instrumental conditioning. In *operant conditioning,* the response is freely available and can be made repeatedly, at least for some period of time. Listening to music on the radio is such a freely available behavior. In *instrumental conditioning,* there are discrete trials or opportunities to engage in the behavior. Going to a dance is such a behavior because the response can only be made when a dance has been scheduled.

Although we have distinguished between operant and instrumental conditioning, the same fundamental principles are involved in each situation; in each case, the organism learns that a stimulus follows a response. The distinction between the two types of conditioning situations is necessary because somewhat different methods and procedures apply to each. When a response is freely available, the *rate* of the behavior is measured over time. This behavior depends to a great extent on the schedule of reinforcement; for example, how frequently a friend invites you to dinner depends in part upon how frequently you have accepted the friend's past invitations. On the other hand, when a response is only periodically enabled by circumstances, the behavior is measured in terms of how rapidly or vigorously the response is made. How rapidly you accept a dinner invitation depends in part on how pleasurable previous occasions have been.

All of the same basic procedures can be used with emotionally negative stimuli, leading to what is called aversive control. Although similar principles apply in the sense that organisms learn to escape or avoid noxious events and are restrained by punishment, such side effects as aggression, maladjustment, and learning not to learn are encountered in aversive control.

At a more complex level, adjustment to the environment may require that the organism distinguish between (respond differently to) similar stimuli; we call this *discrimination learning*. Discrimination learning may be studied in each of the conditioning situations—classical, operant, or instrumental. A dark cloud may signify impending rain, while a lighter cloud may only obscure the sun for a moment. A visitor to a foreign country may find that drinking tap water is safe in some hotels but not in others. And the appropriate response to a cutting remark may depend on whether it was made in jest or whether it was intentionally malicious.

Discrimination learning can be viewed as a conditional if-then relationship. That is, if something happens, then something else happens— *provided the conditions are right*. When an organism has learned a conditional relationship, we say that behavior has been brought under stimulus control because the response depends on which stimulus is present.

Differentiation learning is a closely related process in which regularity depends on how a response is made. *Differentiation learning* occurs when the organism learns that responding in one way leads to one outcome and responding in another way leads to another outcome. Most of our skills reflect not only learning what to do but also how to do it to get the most reward.

Equal in importance to learning itself is the extent to which learning will *generalize* to somewhat different situations and persist not only over time *(forgetting)* but when reinforcement is removed *(extinction)*. Paradoxically, as a general rule, the poorer the conditions for learning, the more general and persistent that learning will be. Actually, we believe that *all* learned associations are extremely persistent and possibly even permanent, but the conditions of learning determine the number of associations formed and the ease with which they can be retrieved in different situations. Even persistent associations, however, can be superseded by new learning if circumstances change and new contingencies prevail.

We should note that, because our focus has been on the process of learning, we have paid little attention to unlearned behavioral tendencies and predispositions. All organisms, including humans, are born with various reflexive and instinctive tendencies to behave in particular ways in response to particular environmental events. These unlearned behaviors are very important to a complete understanding of learning because the ease with which associations are formed depends on whether they are consistent or inconsistent with our natural tendencies. What is more, there is good reason to believe that, given a normal environment, organisms are predisposed to certain types of behavior. For example, we may well have been "prewired" to learn to walk, to distinguish visual patterns, and to acquire the complex syntactical and grammatical rules involved in our everyday language.

Accordingly, our analysis of the fundamentals of learning has dealt with only a part of what is already known about the learning process, which, in turn, is only a very small part of what can be discovered by further experimental analysis. We may be quite confident that these basic principles will still be relevant as the science of learning progresses, but we can be equally confident that our understanding of them will be refined in the process. As a case in point, there is little doubt that emotional responses can be classically conditioned to a wide variety of stimuli, but we are still a long way from accounting for the complexity and diversity of our likes and dislikes, attitudes and opinions, and hopes and fears.

The goal of psychology is to understand behavior, which is evidenced by the ability to predict and control behavior. In a similar sense, learning enables us to predict and control our environments. We learn to predict our environment when stimuli follow stimuli, and we learn to control our environment when stimuli follow our responses. We may also learn fine stimulus discriminations and response differentiations to better predict and control the environment. It is for this reason that the topic of learning is of intimate, personal importance to everyone. And the better we understand the learning process itself, the better we learn, the better we help others learn, and the better off we will all be.

Introduction to Motivation

11

Our natural manner of speaking predisposes us to distinguish between learning and motivation. When you ask the question, *"How* did someone do something?"* you are typically asking a question about learning. How did the murderer commit the crime? How did the mountain climber scale the peak? How did the scientist discover some new phenomenon? In all such cases, you are impressed by the fact that someone has learned to do something that you do not know how to do.

When you ask the question, *"Why* did someone do something?"* you are asking a question about motivation. Why did the murderer commit the crime, the mountain climber scale the peak, or the scientist discover some new phenomenon? Even knowing how the feat was accomplished is often not enough . . . we want to know what motivated the person to do it. Why do some people spend so much time and effort jogging or engaging in other physical fitness activities? Why do collectors covet paintings, stamps, or phonograph records? Why do alcohol addicts drink so much, and gambling addicts gamble so much, and work addicts work so much? The answer in all cases is, of course, that they are "driven"—or motivated—to do so.

Accordingly, we already have a pretty good intuitive idea of what the term *motivation* means. *Motivational factors are relatively temporary and reversible states that tend to energize or activate the behavior of organisms.* The term *primary motivation* refers to those factors that have these properties without any special learning experiences. Primary motivational factors are characteristic of all normal members of the species.

It is appropriate to think of primary motivation as a set of unlearned motivational dispositions. That is to say, an organism is predisposed to become motivated in specific environmental circumstances. A baby gets hungry without any training and becomes frightened by the loss of physical support, but these motives are aroused only if the appropriate conditions occur. Furthermore, even a motivated organism does not persist indefinitely in displaying activity, but rather responds to stimuli in the environment only when appropriate. A food-deprived rat confined in a cage, for example, becomes aroused into activity only when signals appear that feeding time is approaching.

This basic conception of motivation bears further illustration. You are not now actively motivated by the fear of loss of physical support; but were an earthquake to begin, your predisposition toward being motivated by that fear would probably become apparent—most likely in vigorous responses to any stimuli that offered hope of self-preservation. In less violent circumstances involving the arousal of fears such as fear of inferiority, inadequacy, or helplessness, you may be especially sensitive to the remarks of others and especially eager to respond to any stimulus offering relief. Charlatans, quacks, and "con men" prey upon such unresolved motives. One of the dramatic ways to illustrate this two-stage image of motivation (the disposition to become motivated if something happens and then the disposition to respond vigorously to relevant stimuli) is to observe a group of people facing each other at a cocktail party when there is an occasional lapse in the conversation. Silence is a very powerful motivator in a social setting, and the increasing anxiety as silence continues becomes more and more apparent in the mannerisms and postures of the people involved as everyone tries desperately to think of something to say. This motivation is even more apparent when someone finally does start a new train of conversation; the others are eager to listen and may even blurt out interruptions once a new stimulus is provided.

Biological Needs and Psychological Drives

It is important to distinguish between the concepts of *psychological drive* and *biological need*. All organisms require certain conditions to survive, and these conditions may be thought of as *biological needs*. Humans, for example, must eat food, drink fluid, eliminate wastes, breathe air, and copulate if the species is to survive. Other biological needs are less obviously necessary, such as the requirement for an adequate supply of vitamins and minerals. Biological needs differ for different species, but each species has some requirements for survival.

Psychological drives impel the organism to respond. Most biological needs give rise to psychological drives; for example, the need for food produces the primary drive of hunger, which activates the organism to seek food. Of course, if this were not the case, the organism would not respond in the ways necessary to obtain the commodities essential to survival.

It is necessary to distinguish between biological needs and psychological drives because these concepts are not always perfectly related to each other. There are biological needs that do not give rise to psychological drives—for example, the need for oxygen (as distinguished from the need to breathe). It is a surprise to many people that they are not motivated by a lack of oxygen as long as breathing of nontoxic gas is not restrained. This fact became apparent when certain types of airplanes permitted pilots to reach altitudes where the oxygen supply was inadequate for human survival. The pilots did not become aware of the lack of oxygen until they began to black out. A psychological drive impels the organism to respond in some way to correct the deficiency. The lack of oxygen or of some specific vitamins, although these materials are vital for survival and thus are biological needs, simply does not motivate the organism.

Furthermore, there are some psychological drives that cannot be traced to any obvious biological need. Among the most important and familiar examples of such drives is the "curiosity" or "exploratory" tendency. A person whose biological needs are completely satisfied may explore the environment and undertake tasks simply out of curiosity. The evidence shows that not only humans but many other organisms as well, including rats, are motivated by curiosity.

The lack of correspondence between certain biological needs and psychological drives can be understood by considering the natural environment of our ancestors. According to evolutionary theory, it is likely that only those psychological drives that favored the survival of the species would persist. Suppose, then, that mutation occurred and an organism that *was* motivated by a lack of oxygen was born. Since the air supply near the surface of the earth contains a supply of oxygen sufficient for survival, such a mutant would not be at any particular advantage in the fight to survive. An organism that was not motivated to *breathe,* however, would, of course, not consume the air containing the oxygen and would not survive.

Curiosity may be considered in a similar light. When an early organism was born with a mutation that caused curiosity to motivate, it is reasonable to suppose that this organism discovered facts about the environment that were subsequently valuable in the struggle to survive. Although curiosity might also "kill the cat," as the saying goes, the tendency to explore the environment, tempered with a reasonable degree of caution, most likely enhanced the odds of survival.

Thus, it is useful to consider biological needs and their possible significance in terms of evolution, but it is important not to confuse these needs with psychological drives. Psychological drives are states that impel the organism into action, that activate behavior, and that provide the energy that converts potential behavior into actual performance. As such, motivation is a hypothetical construct, just as learning is—in other words, we cannot actually observe motivation directly.

An Experimental Distinction between Learning and Motivation

Let's suppose that we want to train two groups of rats to obtain food by pressing a bar in an operant-conditioning situation. During this training phase, both groups are treated identically; each is given a small amount of training each day until their response rates are high and equal.

Then suppose that one day we decided to treat the two groups differently. For one group, we will disconnect the feeder so that the bar pressing no longer produces food. This operation should result in experimental extinction—the response rate should decrease gradually until the rat stops pressing the bar altogether. For the other group, we'll continue to reward the same response. Now, if we leave the subjects in the second group in the apparatus for a while, we will observe that their rate of bar pressing also begins to decrease and eventually stops altogether. The reason for this is simple: These rats are becoming full of food.

The reason we believe the first group of rats was affected in terms of learning while the second group was affected in terms of motivation can be demonstrated by waiting a day and then returning both groups of rats to the apparatus. For the animals whose responses were extinguished, only a low rate of response will be observed (that resulting from spontaneous recovery). For the animals that were rewarded, the response rate will return to the high level that was obtained before satiation. The learning effects have persisted in the first group; the motivational effects have dissipated in the other group.

This illustration shows that we cannot determine simply from a change in behavior whether a change in learning or a change in motivation has occurred. Learning is inferred only when a relatively persisting change results from practice in the situation. Motivation, on the other hand, can be increased or decreased rapidly, and these changes do not necessarily require practice in the situation (we could have easily reduced the rats' rate of bar pressing by stuffing them with food in their home cages before putting them in the apparatus). Motives may change from moment to moment; learning changes are gradual, cumulative, and persistent.

How Do Learning and Motivation Combine?

The logic of the distinction between learning and motivation concerns their conceptual status. Learning is viewed as a potential for behavior—as habits (or knowledge) available for execution. Motivation is the force that activates or energizes these habits into actual performance. This conceptualization is captured mathematically by saying that learning and motivation combine multiplicatively to determine performance.

A multiplicative combination rule has one significant property: If either term is zero, the combination is zero. This property is presumed to apply to behavior. You won't perform if habit is missing (stated loosely: you don't *know* what to do) or if motivation is missing (stated loosely: you don't *want* to do it). Performance occurs only when some degree of both learning and motivation are present, and the more of each, the greater the performance.

The importance of this combination rule lies in the fact that the same level of performance may result from different combinations of the two factors, and the way to deal with or to understand behavior depends on the strength of each of these factors. Suppose, for example, that you are turning the pages of this textbook very infrequently. This poor performance could be caused by one of two problems. On the one hand, the problem may be due to learning; for example, you may have gone through an educational system in which slow reading was inadvertently taught. If this is the difficulty, then proper treatment must also involve learning—such as a remedial speed-reading course. On the other hand, the problem may be due to motivation; perhaps you're disinterested in the task and are dividing your attention between the reading assignment and more appealing daydreams. If this is the difficulty, perhaps a reminder that you will be tested on the reading material tomorrow will suffice to increase your page-turning rate noticeably. Note that a learning factor requires time and practice to correct, while a motivational factor can be changed rapidly. This is the essence of the distinction between learning and motivation and is the basic reason for trying to separate the two concepts.

How Does Motivation Affect Learning?

Although we have taken some pains to distinguish between learning and motivation, these two factors are not entirely independent of each other. One question that might be raised in regard to their relationship is the way in which motivation affects learning. A categorical answer to this question is simple: *Motivation has no direct effect on learning.* The word *direct* in this statement is critical since there are several ways in which motivation *indirectly* affects learning. Still, the initial proposition remains: Learning does not depend on motivation.

Some older psychologies, along with some popular beliefs about learning, ascribe to motivation a kind of "stamping in" role in the learning process. According to such views, information may be passing through the individual's system, but it is not stored permanently for retrieval unless the individual is intent upon learning, is motivated to learn, and is rewarded for learning. This belief is almost certainly in error—actually, a much simpler principle probably applies: *Organisms learn everything that they actually notice or practice.* In short, some learning occurs whenever a response is made or whenever a stimulus is noticed. Witness, for example, how many advertising jingles you know simply because you have heard them so many times.

The implications of this fact are widespread and of great practical importance. To give one familiar example, suppose you are so anguished over a personal problem one evening that you are unable to study or concentrate on anything else—so you go to bed. Being emotionally upset prevents sleeping, of course, so you lie in bed, fitfully worrying about your problem. Since it is unlikely that you will solve it that night, and since you may have caused other problems by not working or sleeping well, the next evening you are still overwrought and again, you eventually worry yourself to sleep. The basic principles of learning would hold that through such experiences, you will learn to worry about problems in bed! Once the response is well learned, you may find that although when you sit at your desk or in front of a television you're so sleepy you can't keep your eyes open, when you climb into bed, your eyes pop open and your mind becomes alert to worry about problems. In this situation, insomnia is largely self-taught.

Insofar as motivation affects the extent to which we attend to stimuli and practice responses, motivation will indeed affect how much we learn about any particular topic. If motivation leads us to spend more time reading a textbook, preparing and rehearsing a speech, or practicing the piano, we will certainly learn more. But it is the time we spend engaged in these activities that determines how much we learn and not our motivation, at least in a direct sense. You may not be highly motivated to attend a lecture and may do so only because you have nothing better to do, and yet you may learn just as much as another student who has foregone very attractive alternatives because of a burning desire to attend the lecture. As long as you listen equally well, you will learn equally well, even if you find the subject personally irrelevant.

Although motivation does not directly affect learning, *motivation does indirectly affect the responses learned.* Just as motivation can affect how much you learn by determining how much you expose yourself to the material, it can also affect what you learn. Recall that what is practiced is what is learned. If motivation is poor, and the response is thus practiced in a sloppy and inaccurate manner, the response learned is sloppy and inaccurate! Again, realize that the function of motivation is *not* to impress the experience into you so that it will be learned; whatever is experienced is learned. But motivation is partly responsible for what is experienced and practiced, and in this way, motivation indirectly affects what is learned.

A somewhat curious fact is that motivation can be too high for efficient learning. There appears to be an optimal level of motivation for the learning of any task; this optimum depends on the task's difficulty. In general, *the more difficult the task, the lower the level of motivation that will promote efficient learning.* The reason for this is not yet completely clear, but it is presumably related to the energizing effects of motivation. When motivation is low, performance is slower; the person is thus more likely to observe fine distinctions, relationships, and details that might be obscured by approaching the event pell-mell. Furthermore, if a high level of motivation leads to extended practice on the same stereotyped responses, the extent to which the learning will generalize to different situations is actually reduced.

A very practical advantage of understanding these facts is that you can assess your own state of motivation for any action and compensate accordingly. If you know that your motivation is low, then you should know that you are vulnerable to developing bad habits. Return to the earlier example of attending a lecture you find uninteresting. Naturally, you will have a tendency to slouch back in your seat and let your mind wander during the lecture. These same tendencies will then be likely to occur in other, more important lectures. To prevent this, you might deliberately practice attentive responses, even when your motivation is low. Conversely, when you know that your motivation is very high, you should know that you are vulnerable to overtraining on the most conspicuous aspects of the event or material. To prevent this, you can deliberately slow down and try to take different perspectives on the material. The important point is that motivation affects what you observe, the way you practice, and what you do—and these are what you learn.

Another important point to remember is that *motivation affects the stimuli that are learned.* Although the primary role of motivation is to energize habits into performance, *drives also have stimulus properties.* You know when you're hungry, thirsty, or afraid. This is because distinctive internal stimuli are produced whenever a motive is aroused. These internal events are called *drive stimuli.*

It is important to recognize the existence of drive stimuli because they are present at the time learning takes place, which means that they are part of the stimulus context in which learning occurs. Your behavior is not only energized but is also partly guided by motivating forces. You may respond to the same external stimulus differently depending upon what drive stimuli are present at the time. A creak in the house at night as it cools from the heat of the day is treated with indifference unless you are anxious because of a newspaper story reporting burglaries in your neighborhood.

Drive Motivation and Incentive Motivation

It is important to distinguish between two sources of motivation even though both are necessary for performance. *Drive motivation* refers to the internal source of psychological energy that drives the organism to do something. Organisms are impelled to reduce drives; as we have seen, many of these drives are based upon biological needs. *Incentive motivation* refers to the organism's expectation of reward for making a particular response. Incentive motivation may be thought of as the force that pulls one toward a goal, but it should be carefully distinguished from the goal itself. In everyday language, we often speak of a goal as "incentive." In the psychological context, we are not talking about the goal, but rather about the motivation to respond arising from past rewards for the response.

These two sources of motivation are relatively easy to separate in the animal laboratory. Consider, for example, a rat running down an alley.

The rat's drive motivation is based on the need for food resulting from being deprived of food for some period of time. Its incentive motivation is based on prior experiences of finding food at the end of the alley. Each motivational condition can be manipulated independently: The longer the rat has been deprived of food, the higher its hunger drive; the larger the reward the rat has previously received, the higher its incentive motivation. For the rat to run, both conditions must be present. If the rat is not hungry, no amount of food will induce it to run; if there is no food in the goal, no amount of hunger will induce the rat to run there. Drive motivation pushes the animal out of the start box, while incentive motivation pulls it toward the goal.

A simple physical analogy may help make this concept clear. Consider the way a flashlight bulb is illuminated by a battery. The battery has two poles, positive and negative; electric energy flows from the positive pole toward the negative pole. If these two poles are connected through the light bulb, energy flows and the lamp is lit. Learning is like the light bulb in this analogy. Drive motivation corresponds to the positive pole of the battery, and incentive motivation corresponds to the negative pole. Performance will occur (the light bulb will light) only if the circuit is complete to both sources of motivation. And we know that the stronger the battery or the bigger the light bulb, the brighter the light. So too, the better the learning and the stronger the sources of motivation, the greater the performance.

It is not always easy to make the distinction between drive and incentive motivation in everyday contexts, but it is nevertheless important to do so. For example, we not infrequently say that an individual knows perfectly well what to do but simply lacks motivation to do it. If that is true, it is necessary to determine which source of motivation is weak. Suppose, for example, that a student appears to be unmotivated to study. The typical interpretation of such a problem is that the student does not want to learn or is not interested in the subject. That interpretation is based on the assumption that the deficit is in drive motivation, and, indeed, it may well be. But it is at least equally likely that the student really wants very much to learn but is unable to learn through the teaching program being used. In such a case—and this problem is probably more common than realized, the deficit is in incentive motivation. The student simply does not expect to learn by paying attention to that particular teacher or studying that particular textbook. The appropriate treatment also depends on the source of the motivational deficit. If drive motivation is low, offering rewards or even making threats may improve the student's performance. But if incentive motivation is low, such approaches may only aggravate the situation; the student needs a better program! In everyday language, organisms must both *want* and *expect* something in order to be motivated to get it. These two sides of the coin reflect drive and incentive motivation, respectively.

Summary

Our most general view of behavior can be stated as follows: Performance requires both learning and motivation; motivation, in turn, involves drive and incentive. No one of these ingredients is sufficient alone; to understand behavior, we must understand all three fundamental processes. The preceding chapters of this book described the most basic types of learning situations, and the remaining chapters are devoted to some of the basic principles of motivation. Altogether, they comprise an oversimplified but invaluable way to conceptualize what "makes us tick."

Sometimes we want to understand why people are not doing things we think they should be doing. For example, voter apathy is a contemporary plague in our society, with frequently less than half of the eligible voters casting ballots. By referring to the problem as apathy, we imply that the problem is motivational; but before we can make that assumption, we must first ensure that everyone of voting age has, indeed, learned how to register and vote. If everyone eligible to vote has had such learning, the problem is motivational; one might focus on drive motivation by appealing to the voter's sense of civic responsibility. However, in general, *in trying to increase the tendency for desired behavior, it is best to concentrate on incentive motivation.* In other words, be sure something rewarding can be expected from the response. In the present context, the voter needs a candidate he or she can vote for with enthusiasm and the expectation that the election will bring beneficial results.

On other occasions, we want to understand why people are doing things we think they should not be doing. For example, vandalism is another serious problem in our society, with schools, homes, and scenic attractions frequently and wantonly damaged. Since this behavior is occurring, all three ingredients (learning, drive, and incentive) must be present. In general, *in trying to decrease the tendency for an undesired response, it is best to concentrate on drive motivation.* Since learning is persistent, it cannot be eradicated easily, and if some drive is being serviced by the behavior, then the drive must either be eliminated or satisfied in some more acceptable way. In the present context, society must find some way to curb the drive that motivates vandals (be it rebellion against authority, too much time on their hands, or whatever) or provide alternative outlets for that drive.

This same approach is an equally good way to analyze your own behavior. The analysis is not always easy, and you may not be particularly proud of the results. But if it is true that understanding the problem is at least half the battle, then insofar as you can identify the learning, drive, and incentive processes involved in any facet of your behavior, you are well on your way to ensuring the kind of behavior you consider appropriate.

Introduction to Motivation

1. As described in the text, motivation is
   a. a generic term for survival needs
   b. the source of physical energy that makes it possible to respond
   c. actually unrelated to evolution
   d. hypothetical
2. Learning and motivation are assumed to combine
   a. additively
   b. subtractively
   c. multiplicatively
   d. divisibly
3. Because we learn everything we practice, it follows that motivation
   a. directly affects what is learned
   b. indirectly affects what is learned
   c. does not affect what is learned
   d. may or may not affect what is learned
4. Drive motivation and incentive motivation differ in that they are, respectively,
   a. hypothetical and observable
   b. temporary and permanent
   c. based on deprivation and based on reward
   d. necessary and unnecessary for performance
5. For the purpose of understanding behavior
   a. drive is more important than incentive
   b. incentive is more important than drive
   c. drive and incentive are both indispensable
   d. the relative importance of drive and incentive depends on the situation
6. In dealing with motivational problems, the recommended procedure is to concentrate on
   a. drive
   b. incentive
   c. drive and incentive equally
   d. drive or incentive depending on the problem

Multiple Choice Answers

1. (d) Both survival needs and evolution are relevant to the concept of motivation presented in the text, but the concept itself remains hypothetical since it cannot be directly observed. Motivation in this sense is psychological and not physical.

2. (c) Although neither learning nor motivation, as hypothetical concepts, have been quantified, the assumption is that they combine in a multiplicative manner so that at least some strength must be present in each to produce a response.
3. (b) Motivation partly determines what we practice and, hence, indirectly affects what is learned. The effect is considered indirect because we do not need to be specifically motivated to learn.
4. (c) Both drive motivation and incentive motivation are hypothetical and necessary for performance; neither is permanent if conditions change. The basis for the distinction rests in the factors that produce each type of motivation—specifically, deprivation and reward. (Stimulation and punishment will be included in the complete picture.)
5. (c) It is true that in some situations, either drive or incentive may pose the larger problem. But in any situation, both components of motivation are important to an understanding of behavior.
6. (d) Some problems implicate drive, some incentive, and some both. But the important thing is to determine the nature of the problem and concentrate on that aspect that is causing the problem in adjustment.

True/False Thought Questions

1. Motivation is a hypothetical process that combines multiplicatively with the hypothetical process of learning.
2. The same level of performance can result from different combinations of learning and motivation.
3. Motivation has no direct effect upon learning.
4. Motivation can be both too high and too low for efficient learning.
5. The drive stimulus is the event that produces motivation.
6. A person who gets mad easily has a motivational disposition.
7. The biological need for food is equivalent to the psychological drive of hunger.
8. The principal operational distinction between learning and motivation concerns permanence.
9. Drive motivation is the internal push and incentive motivation is the external pull.
10. If you find yourself frequently trying to avoid reading assignments, you must not like the subjects the assignments cover.
11. Students would definitely work harder if they were paid for "A" grades.
12. The authors' practical advice is this: When trying to obtain a response, increase incentive motivation; when trying to eliminate a response, decrease drive motivation.

True/False Answers

1. (True) Neither learning nor motivation can be observed directly; they are thus hypothetical constructs inferred from observations of performance. The assumption that both are necessary to produce behavior leads to the assumption that they combine multiplicatively.

2. (True) Both learning and motivation vary in strength—the former on the basis of practice, the latter on the basis of deprivation and prior reward. Hence, the combined value may be obtained through different proportions of the strengths of the two underlying processes.

3. (True) We have taken the position that learning results simply from practice so that habits are formed whenever responses occur. Motivation is necessary for responses to occur and, hence, indirectly affects what is practiced and learned, but learning itself does not require motivation.

4. (True) Motivation tends to energize behavior. If motivation is low, the response may be practiced slowly and ineffectually, leading to poor learning. On the other hand, a high level of motivation may lead to fast and stereotyped practice that detracts from fine discriminations and differentiations. Hence, there is an optimal level of motivation that depends on the difficulty of the task.

5. (False) There is a drive stimulus associated with each drive, enabling the organism to discriminate between stimuli and respond adaptively to its needs. The drive stimuli, however, do not produce the motivation; they are simply associated with it. Motivation is produced by deprivation or painful stimulation.

6. (False) We have not used the term *disposition* in the sense of a person's personality traits. Rather, we have said that organisms are *disposed* (or *ready*) to become motivated when certain events occur.

7. (False) It is important to distinguish between needs and drives. Needs are the conditions necessary for survival and drives are the source of energy that motivates behavior. Drives are often based on needs, but the relationship is not perfect.

8. (True) Habits are acquired gradually during repeated practice, while motivation can be changed relatively rapidly; and habit must be acquired in the learning situation, while motivation may be changed outside the situation. Nevertheless, the principal basis for the distinction between learning and motivation concerns permanence. Habits are at least somewhat permanent, while motivation is more transitory.

9. (False) Both motivational processes are internal. Drive motivation is the internal force that drives the organism to act, and incentive motivation is the organism's *expectation* of reward—not the reward itself. Motivation is inside the organism, even though it represents an attraction toward a goal.

10. (False) Although it might be true that your avoidance of an assignment stems from a dislike for the subject, it is also possible that the assigned text is not suitable for your needs. You might eagerly read a better text on that subject.

Introduction to Motivation

11. (False) Whether or not students would work harder if offered money for "A" grades depends on whether the students believe that harder work will increase their chances of actually getting high grades. If there was no hope of getting an "A" in a particular class (or if the students know they can easily get such a grade without hard work), the offer of payment would not have any practical effect on diligence.

12. (True) Both drive and incentive are integral parts of motivation, and a change in either changes performance accordingly. However, as a matter of practicality, lack of performance is usually due to too little incentive motivation, and adding drive motivation is of little value and may even intensify the person's conflict. Hence, it is better to increase the expectation of a reward for responding. Conversely, undesirable responses are inevitably both drive and incentive motivated, and removing the reward leaves the organism's drive unresolved. Accordingly, it is better to provide an acceptable alternative for reducing that drive, or, if the drive itself is undesirable, to remove it.

References

Biological Needs and Psychological Drives
Berlyne, D. E. *Conflict, arousal and curiosity.* New York: McGraw-Hill, 1960.
Revusky, S., and Garcia, J. Learned associations over long delays. In G. H. Bower (Ed.), *The psychology of learning and motivation* (Vol. 4). New York: Academic Press, 1970.

How Do Learning and Motivation Combine?
*Prokasy, W. F. Do drive and habit multiply? *Psychological Bulletin,* 1967, *67,* 368.
Spence, K. W. Learning and performance in eyelid conditioning as a function of the intensity of the UCS. *Journal of Experimental Psychology,* 1953, *45,* 57–63.

How Does Motivation Affect Learning?
Hull, C. L. Differential habituation to internal stimuli in the albino rat. *Journal of Comparative Psychology,* 1933, *16,* 255–273.
Yerkes, R. M., and Dodson, J. D. The relation of strength of stimulus to rapidity of habit formation. *Journal of Comparative Neurological Psychology,* 1908, *18,* 459–482.

Drive Motivation and Incentive Motivation
*Logan, F. A. *Incentive.* New Haven: Yale University Press, 1960. (Chapter 1)

*Suitable for additional reading by the beginning student. The others are written at a more technical level.

Primary Motivation

We have said that primary motivation refers to unlearned motivational dispositions—conditions that tend to arouse the organism without any special training or experience. The most important of these dispositions to the student of learning are pain, hunger, thirst, and sex. There are certainly, other primary drives, such as those based on the need to breathe air and the need to eliminate wastes from the body. However, these are generally of less interest simply because the appropriate drive-reducing responses are normally freely available to the organism; thus, little learning is motivated by these drives.

This is not to say that *no* learning occurs with respect to such primary drives. Although breathing is automatic, some people, such as opera singers and deep-sea divers, must practice special techniques to control their breathing. And, of course, all socialized humans have learned where the response of elimination should normally occur and where it should not occur.

Our focus on the primary drives of pain, hunger, thirst, and sex is not meant to infer that other primary drives are not important in understanding behavior. Pain, hunger, thirst, and sex simply provide the principal occasions for learning and, hence, are the drives that have received the most attention from experimental psychologists interested in the learning process.

The Pain Drive

There is little to add to our previous discussions involving the pain drive. The descriptions of aversive control, especially in terms of escape and avoidance learning, suffice to demonstrate the motivating power of noxious stimuli. It may be useful, however, to review escape learning as a model of motivation.

A painful stimulus first arouses the organism into action; this obviously reveals the fact that pain is motivating and that the pain drive energizes or activates the organism's behavior. The drive stimulus provided by pain is explicit and clearly leads to a variety of unlearned reflexes or automatic responses. If none of these responses are effective in terminating the drive state, a new response, one that is effective, will be learned; this illustrates the fact that drive reduction is a rewarding event. Pain can be turned on and off rapidly, can energize behavior, can help guide behavior by way of the distinctiveness of the painful stimuli, and can provide an opportunity to reward responses that terminate the pain, thus fostering the learning of these escape responses. This encapsulates one view of motivation.

It is worth noting that pain itself is mediated by a separate system in the body. That is to say, although some degree of discomfort may be experienced by overstimulating other receptors (through touch, temperature, light, or sound), pain per se is experienced only when special receptors located rather deep under the surface of the skin are stimulated. That these receptors are not evenly distributed around the body may easily be seen by pinching the body in various places. The same pressure is noticeably more painful in some areas than in others; for example, the bottom of the elbow is essentially devoid of pain receptors. The eye is extremely sensitive to pain from even a minute particle, the genitalia are relatively insensitive, and many internal organs such as the kidney and liver do not respond with pain to injury. Thus, *the intensity of pain and the degree of drive motivation produced by an aversive stimulus depends on the nature of that stimulus and on where it is applied.*

The Concept of a Dual Control System

We have said that drives energize behavior. There are, in general, two ways in which the energy controlling any system may be arranged. One is in a single control system, in which there is a natural resting state of the system and one source of energy that tends to drive the system from that state. The kitchen oven is an example of a single control system: Its natural temperature is that of the kitchen, and there is a heating coil by which the temperature may be raised.

In contrast, a dual control system has two opposing sources of energy so that the state of the system depends on the relative action of each of these two sources. An oven could be made into a dual control system by adding refrigeration coils so that the temperature would depend on the extent to which the heating and cooling coils were energized at any given point in time. The advantage of a dual control system is perhaps obvious: It enables the system to be changed rapidly in either direction. An automobile, for example, is a dual control system containing both an accelerator and a brake for controlling speed. This system allows the driver to adjust the automobile's speed rapidly in an emergency.

By and large, humans are constructed on a dual control principle. For example, each joint has both flexor and extensor muscles, enabling, by a fascinating process of reciprocal inhibition, the movement of those joints.

So, too, most bodily glands are controlled by two opposing nervous systems. In this context, recall our theory of classical conditioning and recognize it as assuming a dual control process of learning: Habit tends to activate a response, and inhibition tends to reduce that activation.

Many motivational systems are also under dual control. Body temperature, for example, may be raised through exercise or simply through shivering, burning up sugar to produce heat in the process; on the other hand, the body may be cooled by the evaporation of sweat. It is now well known that sleep is also under neurological control and that anatomically distinct areas in the brain tend to lead to either sleep or wakefulness; whether we are asleep or awake depends on the relative activity in these areas. This is why, originally, sleeping pills were unsatisfactory; although they activated the sleep areas, they left the wakefulness areas aroused so that sleep was less relaxing. Modern sleeping potions instead inhibit the wakefulness areas, enabling the sleep areas to dominate more naturally.

The Hunger and Thirst Drives

The evidence that both hunger and thirst are under dual control is now well established. The intricate details are not yet fully understood, but it is appropriate to review the evidence available as a background for describing some of the behavioral effects of hunger and thirst.

Biological Bases

It is obvious that food deprivation produces the hunger drive and water deprivation produces the thirst drive. Let's look now at some of the known biological bases for these effects.

1. First, to remove one common misconception: Contractions of the stomach (hunger pangs) are not the principal basis of the hunger drive. These contractions normally accompany hunger, but eliminating them by distending the stomach with an inflated balloon does not reduce the hunger of a food-deprived person. Similarly, dryness of the mouth and throat are not the principal bases of the thirst drive. Hunger and thirst are mediated more centrally and these familiar stimuli are only indicators that the drives are present.
2. There are areas in the brain that, when stimulated electrically, produce hunger in a normally satiated organism. Stimulation of these hunger areas not only induces the organism to eat but will motivate it to learn and perform instrumental responses to obtain food. Other areas in the brain can induce drinking in a water-satiated organism.
3. Consistent with the notion that certain portions of the brain constitute hunger and thirst areas is the effect of their surgical removal or destruction. Removing the hunger areas produces an organism that never

displays normal hunger, does not eat, and that must be fed intravenously. Similarly, removal of the thirst areas removes evidence of normal thirst, and removal of both areas eliminates both eating and drinking.

4. That the normal control of these areas in the brain is biochemical can be demonstrated by injecting a small quantity of one hormone into certain brain structures. A fully satiated organism will display all the signs of a hungry organism when stimulated chemically in the brain. However, when another hormone is injected into the same area, this chemical now produces evidence of thirst! In short, the same area of the brain may produce different drives, depending on the way in which the area is chemically stimulated.

5. Electrical stimulation of anatomically different areas in the brain eliminates hunger. Stimulation of the "satiety" areas will cause a food-deprived organism to stop eating. Stimulation of comparable areas can eliminate drinking.

6. Consistent with the notion that these second types of areas might be classified as satiety areas is the effect of the surgical removal or destruction of such portions of the brain. An organism that has undergone such surgery is insatiable and stops eating only to the discomfort of an extremely full stomach. Given an unlimited food supply, such an organism will reach a weight several times larger than normal and, if sensory feedback from distention of the stomach is disrupted, the organism is literally likely to burst.

The pattern which thus emerges runs something like the following: Food or water deprivation causes a biochemical change in the blood through which the drives of hunger and thirst are mediated. (That this is true has been shown by transfusing blood from a food-deprived animal into a satiated one, and vice versa. The deprived animal now behaves as if satiated, and the satiated animal now behaves as if hungry.) Through the biochemical changes in the blood, hunger and thirst areas in the brain are aroused, giving rise to psychological drives. The mechanism of this activation is not yet known, although, for example, differences in the pressure around certain cells in the brain have been implicated in the case of thirst. But in any event, the drive is experienced as a result of the activation of distinct brain structures.

These drives then energize behavior until consummatory responses are made, and these responses lead to stimulation of the appropriate satiety areas, terminating the psychological drive. In view of the drive-reduction hypothesis concerning reinforcement, it is interesting that the satiety areas are indeed locations where electrical stimulation of the brain is rewarding. Activation of these areas can eliminate the drive long before the digestive processes that restore the biochemical balance of the blood are able to stimulate these areas to shut off the hunger and thirst drives.

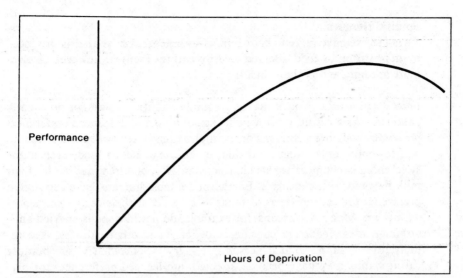

Figure 12.1 The effect of food or water deprivation on performance. In general, the longer an organism has been without food or water, the higher its level of performance to obtain them, except after such severe deprivation that physical weakness occurs.

Hunger and Thirst as Psychological Drives

Normally, hunger and thirst are induced simply by depriving an organism of food or water. Presumably, the greater the length of deprivation, the greater the drive. The effect of different degrees of deprivation on instrumental performance is shown graphically in figure 12.1. This figure compares the response strength of different groups of subjects trained under different degrees of deprivation. The greater the deprivation (and hence, presumably, the greater the drive), the stronger the observed performance up to the point where physical weakness begins to occur. Short of that point, however, *performance is an increasing function of drive*—a fact consistent with our statement that drives energize the performance of habits.

Changes in Drive Level

After training has been completed at one level of drive, what are the effects on performance of changing the drive level to either a higher or lower value? When only the energizing role of the drive is taken into consideration, one would expect an immediate change in behavior to a performance level in keeping with the new drive level. But we must also consider the drive stimuli, which are changed when the drive level is changed. Since the organism learned to respond in the presence of one set of drive stimuli, these changed stimuli will produce some generalization decrement. *Hence, when we change to a new drive level, subjects normally perform more poorly than they would if the new drive level had been in effect all along.*

Specific Hungers

Thus far, we have talked about hunger as a general drive that is produced by deprivation of food and reduced by eating. Hunger, however involves more specific factors than thus far implied.

Food Preferences   Foods that are equally nutritious may not be equally palatable. As a result, most organisms demonstrate unlearned preferences for some foods over others. For example, rats prefer sweetened food and will eat more of a sweet food than of an unsweetened food, even if the sweetening is nonnutritive saccharine; similarly, children may prefer their milk flavored with chocolate. Furthermore, most humans have acquired a preference for certain types of foods as a result of their early experiences with them. Many Americans, for example, do not like snails or fried ants, although these foods are considered delicacies in other cultures. Accordingly, to say simply that a person is hungry is somewhat vague because eating habits may have become directed into learned preferences for particular kinds of foods.

Specific Deprivation   It has also been demonstrated that specific hungers may be aroused by depriving an organism of specific substances. For example, a rat that is fed a salt-free food diet will drink salty water, even though rats normally prefer plain tap water. Similarly, pregnant women may occasionally express a craving for a particular type of food. However, it should be noted that the "wisdom of the body" with respect to such specific hungers is not perfect—some important substances do not give rise to drives motivating their consumption. But the fact that salty popcorn sometimes tastes especially good indicates that one may not simply be hungry, but rather may be hungry for particular foods.

The Sex Drive

Contrary to common belief, *the sex drive is among the weakest of the primary drives.* That is to say, hunger, thirst, and pain can achieve compelling proportions far exceeding those produced by even complete sexual abstinence. Nevertheless, the sex drive is a very important one in American life. A British characterization of the Yank soldier during World War II captured this idea; the Americans were viewed as being "overpaid, overfed, and oversexed." This description also confirms an important point: preoccupation with sex only occurs after the other primary drives are satisfied. Furthermore, the cultural prohibitions surrounding sexual expression prior to marriage virtually ensure that this drive will be emphasized among young people.

   The other primary drives, as noted earlier, may be based upon the biological survival needs of the individual organism. This is not true of the sex drive since an individual could presumably go through an entire lifetime without ever experiencing overt satisfaction of the sex drive. The principle of natural selection still applies, however: The sex drive is essential to the survival of a species. Were a species devoid of a compelling sex drive ever produced, the lack of offspring would obviously mean that the species would quickly become extinct. In a larger sense, then, the sex drive is indeed based on a survival need.

Biological Bases

The biochemical control of behavior is clearly illustrated in the case of sex. Hormones produced in the testes, the ovaries, and the pituitary gland have profound effects upon our masculinity or femininity. This has been demonstrated to the extreme by Frank Beach. He has injected pregnant dogs with male hormones, removing the ovaries from any female pups at birth and injecting the same pups with male hormones. Such dogs become truly bisexual and develop a rudimentary penis and prostate gland. Both male and female organisms produce both male and female hormones; it is the relative balance of these hormones that not only determines our physical sexual characteristics but also affects the extent to which our everyday behavior conforms to what are considered masculine or feminine characteristics. The removal of the testes or ovaries has less pronounced effects if the person is older at the time of surgery; sexually experienced adult males, for example, continue to behave in a "masculine" manner, sexually and otherwise, for years. If not treated with male hormones, however, such men gradually develop increasingly feminine features and traits. The story of hormones and behavior is a fascinating one that is only now beginning to unfold to experimental analysis.

To describe the neurological control of sexual behavior, it is necessary to review first some highlights of neuroanatomy. Mammals contain two distinct nervous systems: the somatic and the autonomic. The somatic nervous system is comprised of pathways that help control voluntary muscle movements. Anatomically separate is the autonomic nervous system, which controls the more internal processes and organs. This latter system, in turn, has two distinct branches: the sympathetic and the parasympathetic, which oppose each other in the control of these internal processes. When the parasympathetic is dominant, as in times of rest and relaxation, breathing is regular, the heart rate is slow and steady, and digestive processes such as conversion of starches into sugar by the liver take place. When the sympathetic is dominant, as in times of stress or arousal, breathing becomes more rapid, the heart rate increases the blood supply to the muscles, and digestive processes are reversed (for example, the liver releases sugar to provide extra energy for action). The autonomic nervous system is thus under dual control.

The term *sexual arousal* refers to male erection, female tumescence, and secretion of precoital fluids by both. These behaviors are mediated by the parasympathetic branch of the autonomic nervous system. At times, you have probably awakened early in the morning in a state of apparent sexual arousal without any accompanying sexual thoughts or desires. This is because the parasympathetic system acts diffusely over its entire course, and when it is in complete control of the body, as in some stages of sleep, sexual arousal is a normal and natural condition.

Sexual climax refers to male ejaculation and orgasm by both male and female. These events are mediated by the sympathetic branch of the autonomic nervous system. You may have had some degree of orgastic experience occurring in a nonsexual context when the sympathetic is aroused by anxiety. This is also a normal and natural reaction to the diffuse action of the sympathetic system.

The inner events accompanying sexual behavior thus run the following course: Erotic stimulation first activates the parasympathetic system, leading to sexual arousal. Continued stimulation increases the activation of this system but also begins to activate the sympathetic. In time, the parasympathetic reaches the limit of its activation and then the sympathetic becomes dominant, leading to orgasm as the parasympathetic is subdued. The antagonism within the autonomic nervous system is nowhere better revealed than in the sexual arena.

There is one important additional part of the story. The time required for these events to take place is not necessarily the same in male and female. One can only speculate about the evolutionary basis for this difference. Presumably, the original purpose was to enable the female to accommodate a number of different males during her maximal fertility, thus increasing the probability of conception and the perpetuation of the species. However, the rate at which these processes occur is not invariant; it depends in part on learning and concurrent emotions. This will be illustrated later in our discussion of drive incompatibility.

Sex and Early Experience

Freud startled the world by asserting that people do not wait until puberty to initiate a sex life. It is not necessary here to debate the correctness of his description of infantile sexuality and the persisting effects of early conflicts. It is, however, appropriate to note that the picture of childhood innocence is somewhat misleading. Babies derive pleasure from erotic stimulation. Children are certainly interested in and curious about their genitalia, and various kinds of sex-related contacts do occur during the years before puberty. The importance of these experiences should not be underestimated.

One source of evidence on this topic has come from the work of Harry Harlow. He first developed successful procedures for breeding monkeys in captivity, separating the infant from its mother at birth, and raising it on a surrogate mother. It was this line of research that led to the important discovery that contact comfort is a very powerful source of primary reward and promotes the development of emotional security. But more relevant to the present topic are the results of raising monkeys in an environment in which they are not permitted to play with other infant monkeys during the first six months of life. Total isolation during this period has profound effects upon the monkeys' adulthood; specifically, they are incapable of indulging in mature sexual behavior. Comparable isolation at a later age has no such deleterious effect. Six-month-old monkeys certainly do not engage in actual sexual activity, but they do enter into miniature forms of social interaction and rough-and-tumble play that are apparently essential to normal development.

A second source of evidence concerning the importance of early experience comes from rats. If a thirty-day-old male rat (who is still prepubescent) is exposed to a receptive female rat, he will engage in some investigatory behaviors even though he is incapable of copulation. During this exposure, a series of electric shocks can be applied after which the rat is returned to his home cage to reach maturity. When he is later exposed to a receptive female, the male rat will not even attempt to copulate. Aversive events occurring in association with sex-related stimuli, even though overt sexual behavior is not yet involved, are sufficient to modify the natural sexual responses of the adult!

Although it may appear to be rather cruel to perform such experiments on animals, it is probable that many parents are guilty of comparable actions in dealing with their own children. A human infant may be essentially isolated during the first few years of life as a protection from danger. And virtually all children play "doctor" or some such activity and discover that about half of all people look pretty much as they do and the other half look interestingly different. A parent, catching the child in such a scene, may unconsciously reveal his or her own anxieties about sex and describe the behavior as naughty or something nice children don't do. Little do such parents realize the lasting effects that such treatment may have.

Sex and Learning
Mating behavior provides the most convincing evidence of instinct, or the unlearned tendency to perform a complex behavior chain. However, it is also a general principle that experience plays an increasing role in behavior the higher the order of the species. Insects, fish, birds, and many mammals perform intricate series of activities culminating in reproduction. For example, the adult but sexually naive male rat will likely copulate successfully the first time he is exposed to a receptive female rat. Certainly unlearned tendencies exist, but the question remains, to what extent are such behaviors learnable? Even the rat demonstrates three ways in which the learnability of sexual behavior can be observed.

First, *sexual arousal* is learnable. If a male rat is repeatedly placed into an arena into which a receptive female is subsequently introduced, the arena will become associated with sexual activity. The male will learn to orient toward the location where the female will be introduced and then to initiate sexual approaches more rapidly. Second, *sexual behavior is itself learnable*. The experienced male rat is more adept at achieving intromission than is his naive counterpart. Finally, *the orgastic response itself is, to some extent, learnable*. If the male rat is allowed only a limited amount of time with the female, he will learn to reach sexual climax more quickly than normal.

This point is at least equally true for the female rat. As with the male, her actions are largely instinctive. But an experienced female rat can "seduce" a reluctant male rat just as clearly as an experienced male rat can "entice" a reluctant female rat to engage in sex. This fact is underscored by observations of female dogs. Apparently, the male dog is irresistably attracted to any female dog in heat, but the female dog is selective as to which males she will copulate with. Animals still higher in the phylogenetic scale, such as monkeys, learn to masturbate if isolated, to acquire homosexual tendencies if confined with same-species, same-sex animals, and to establish rudimentary familial relationships if given the opportunity.

We must be very cautious in attempting to extrapolate to humans our presumed knowledge of the sexual behavior of animals. In the first place, our observations are likely to be anthropomorphic (colored by our own human experiences). But more importantly, although we should accept our sexuality as a natural biological fact, there is every reason to believe that learning plays an even more important role in human sexuality. Arousal and orgasm are, indeed, reflexive responses to erotic stimulation. But arousal is also learnable and may become associated with particular places, times, or scenes. And the great variety of sexual practices observed cross-culturally clearly attests to the fact that humans are not committed to an instinctive mating pattern.

Drive Interactions

In discussing some of the more important primary drives, we have described each drive as if it occurs in isolation from all the others. Of course, this is not the case. Seldom are we *just* hungry or *just* thirsty. More often than not, when one drive is aroused, another will also be present. An important question, then, is how these drives interact with each other when they occur together. The answer is complex and requires that we consider two aspects of drive interaction: the combination of relevant and irrelevant drives and the incompatibility of certain drive states.

Irrelevant Drives
In the view of motivation we developed in the previous chapter, drives were seen as acting indiscriminately on habits. We characterized drives as general energizers; that is to say, *any source of drive is capable of potentiating any habit,* regardless of the drive conditions that were present when the habit was acquired.

The area of study concerning this view deals with irrelevant drives. An irrelevant drive is one that is not appropriate to the nature of the reward given for making a response. Note that we are not saying that the drive is irrelevant to the organism; presumably, all motives are important. We are saying only that an irrelevant drive is not reduced by the goal event. If you are working at a job for money and are at the same time anxious about an upcoming examination, anxiety is an irrelevant drive with respect to your performance on the job. Money does not help you pass the examination (we hope). Nevertheless, your anxiety may affect your work.

To summarize the results of the experimental analysis of irrelevant drives, let's consider the hungry rat trained to run down a short alley to obtain food. In this situation, hunger is a relevant drive because the goal object is food, which reduces hunger. But suppose, after training the rat under these conditions, we add some degree of thirst to its hunger. Now the rat is both hungry and thirsty, but thirst is an irrelevant drive because the dry food reward does not reduce the rat's thirst. The question is what effect the addition of thirst to the rat's motivational complex will have upon performance of a response learned only for food.

The answer to that question is shown graphically in figure 12.2. Adding moderate degrees of thirst to the rat's prevailing hunger increases performance of a response rewarded with food. However, if the degree of thirst is increased still further, performance begins to get weaker, eventually reaching a level below that which would be expected had there been no irrelevant thirst drive at all. Clearly, the performance of a response depends to some degree on the presence of drives unrelated to the reward for that response.

There are two principles necessary to understand this phenomenon. The first is that drives serve as general energizers; in other words, thirst must be able to help potentiate a response based on hunger for food, or the rat's performance would never show an increase as a result of adding thirst. How much effect the irrelevant drive will have depends on the strength of the original drive. Were drive motivation already maximal on the basis of hunger alone, adding thirst could not be expected to increase performance. But this type of study does show that a learned habit can be potentiated by an irrelevant drive.

To understand the eventual decrease when thirst is very strong requires an understanding of a second concept, that of the drive stimulus. Recall that drives not only potentiate behavior, they also produce internal stimuli that may help to direct behavior. We learn what to do in the presence of particular drive stimuli. The stronger the irrelevant thirst drive, the stronger the thirst drive stimulus and the more it changes the total stimulus situation from the conditions that were present during training. We know that a change in the stimulus situation leads to lower performance because of stimulus generalization decrement. In effect, then, adding an irrelevant drive does two things: It increases the total drive, which in itself would lead

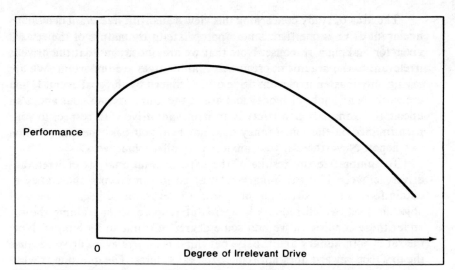

Figure 12.2 The effect on performance of adding an irrelevant drive. Above zero is the performance with only the relevant drive; for example, a hungry rat's running speed toward food. Moderate amounts of an irrelevant drive, e.g., thirst, will increase performance; more intense irrelevant drive will decrease performance.

to increased performance; and at the same time, it adds a new drive stimulus, which, by changing the situation, tends to lead to lower performance. The combination of these two actions produces the results observed in figure 12.2. As long as the increased drive can offset the decreased habit, performance is increased by adding an irrelevant drive. Beyond that point, however, further change in the situation leads to progressively lower performance. The irrelevant drive stimuli may begin to elicit responses appropriate to that drive that then interfere with the original behavior.

According to this analysis, if the original response was the same as the response produced by the added drive, we would not expect a decrease in performance even if the added drive became very strong. For example, a group of adolescent girls may have learned to giggle at the antics of a nearby group of boys for social reasons. They may also have learned to giggle to help conceal anxieties when their conversation takes on sexual overtones. If both conditions occur at the same time, their giggling will be doubly potentiated.

With this background, return now to the situation in which you are working at a job and are simultaneously anxious about a forthcoming exam. So long as that anxiety is reasonably moderate, you will actually work faster and harder than usual. If, however, your anxiety is very strong, you will work more slowly and less effectively because the anxiety makes you think and worry about the test, the material you must learn, and the test's outcome—and all of these responses interfere with attending to your job.

Fear or anxiety is probably the most common irrelevant drive in human behavior, and understanding its effects and how they operate is important in controlling behavior. How will anxiety affect a student's performance on an examination, an actor's performance on the stage, or behaviors such as driving, playing tennis, or thinking? In many cases, a small amount of anxiety is beneficial; when the relevant drive is not terribly strong, the added drive will help potentiate practiced habits. In other cases, anxiety interferes with performance—and the reason it does so is because it causes new responses associated with the anxiety that compete with the appropriate behavior. In many cases, however, anxiety's detrimental effects can be reduced or even reversed by learning adaptive responses to fear and anxiety.

This knowledge can be applied to drives other than fear. Suppose you are going to attend a lecture, a sermon, a show, or go on a date that you expect to be dull and boring, but you feel it is your duty to attend and to appear to be attentive. You can carry this off more effectively if you arrange to be mildly hungry at the time. Suppose you are going to a party at which you expect to be rather anxious and you're afraid you might drink and talk too much. You can reduce the probability that this will happen by ensuring that no irrelevant drives (such as hunger and thirst) further potentiate your drinking and talking behaviors. Indeed, you can discover for yourself in various situations that such a trivial matter as wearing moderately uncomfortable shoes may be beneficial or detrimental to the behavior you desire, depending on the strength of the other drives motivating your behavior.

Drive Incompatibility

We have seen the effects of arousing more than one drive at the same time. There are situations, however, in which the arousal of one drive is incompatible with the arousal of another drive. In other words, in some instances the presence of one drive tends to override or inhibit the arousal of another. In a sense, this incompatibility is highly adaptive since it forces the organism to attend toward one type of activity at a time. In this way, an organism is able to satisfy the dominant drive without being distracted by competing responses connected with another drive. There are many instances of drive incompatibility.

Hunger and Thirst   There is now clear evidence that high levels of hunger and thirst are biologically incompatible. An organism cannot be intensely hungry and intensely thirsty at the same time, even if deprived for some time of both food and water. That this incompatibility is a central process can be seen by returning to the procedure of inducing hunger or thirst by injecting chemicals into the brain. If a food-deprived organism is eating and is injected with a hormone to make it thirsty, it will stop eating. Similarly, if a thirsty organism is drinking and is injected with a hormone that makes it hungry, it will stop drinking. Note that these observations further rule out the notion that hunger depends on stomach contractions and thirst on dryness of the mouth. The water-deprived animal's mouth is still dry, but the animal will not drink if it is made hungry. In effect, arousing the hunger drive tends to inhibit the thirst drive and vice versa.

Hunger and Fear   There is also an incompatibility between the processes involved in the ingestion of food and those involved in fear or anxiety. Each may interfere with the other, depending on their relative strengths. A person who is mildly anxious, for example, may find it satisfying to nibble more or less constantly since this constant ingestion seems to inhibit anxieties to some extent. Alternatively, however, intense fear essentially eliminates hunger and may preclude proper digestion. If bad news arrives just before your regular mealtime, you probably won't have a desire to eat.

   This incompatibility can be demonstrated experimentally. Rats that are deprived of food for several hours will quickly learn to lick a metal tube to receive sugar-water solution. One indication of how strongly motivated the food-deprived animals are is that many animals will lick the tube in excess of seven times per second to receive the solution. Yet, even under these conditions, animals that have previously learned to fear some stimulus will suppress their licking entirely if the feared stimulus is presented. Fear apparently suppresses the behavior that is so strongly motivated by hunger. On the other hand, if a rat has learned to fear a particular spatial location, one of the best ways to suppress that fear is to make the animal hungry and allow it to eat *only* in the feared location. In this instance hunger suppresses the fear normally elicited by the spatial location.

Sex and Fear   Fear may also have far-reaching effects upon sexual behavior; this is especially true when the fears concern sex itself. This fact can be illustrated through the two most common fears people take to bed with them. One is the fear of failing to become sexually aroused. For males, this is called impotence and completely precludes sexual intercourse; for females, it is called frigidity and reduces the likelihood of sexual satisfaction. The second fear is of premature orgasm, which is more common in the male but is certainly of concern to both.

   These fears may produce feedback that eventuates in self-fulfilling prophecies. To understand this, it is only necessary to know that fear reflects activity in the sympathetic branch of the autonomic nervous system. Sexual arousal requires dominance by the parasympathetic and is thus more difficult to achieve if the sympathetic is aroused by fear. Sexual climax reflects eventual dominance of the sympathetic and is thus more readily achieved if erotic stimulation occurs in the context of fear arousal.

Consummatory Behaviors as Learnable Responses

We normally think of eating, drinking, and indulging in sexual behavior as consummatory responses motivated by hunger, thirst, and sex and hence performed in their service. While this is certainly true, it is important to note that these are also learnable responses in their own right. This conclusion has already been implied in our earlier discussion, but it is worth repeating.

A new situation that demonstrates this fact involves placing a hungry rat in an operant situation in which the rat is working for food. Periodically a signal appears, indicating that pressing a bar will now be rewarded. If a water bottle is also available, the rat may learn drinking as well as bar pressing. The reason for this is as follows: If the dry food eventually leads the rat to become thirsty, the animal may be drinking water as the food signal occurs. This reinforces the drinking response so that the rat is likely to repeat it during the next interval between signals. The response, in effect, becomes a superstition; the rat may consume three or four times its normal daily consumption of water during an hour or so in an operant conditioning situation where it is working for food.

The point is this: Although consummatory responses are intrinsically rewarded by drive reduction, *the frequency of consummatory behavior may also depend on extrinsic rewards.* That is to say, we may eat for reasons other than hunger, we may drink for reasons other than thirst, and we may engage in sex for reasons other than sexual deprivation. Chefs, wine tasters, and prostitutes perform these responses for money. But we all may learn to eat, to drink, and to engage in sex to help reduce our anxieties. We may even develop superstitions about the effects of these behaviors. And, like all habits, consummatory responses are learned permanently. Many middle-aged people gain weight simply because they have carried their adolescent eating habits into adulthood, when the need for food actually decreases—such people often eat to be eating and not to reduce hunger. In the same way, early preoccupations with sex may persist. In short, all the principles of learning apply to consummatory behaviors.

Primary Motivation

Multiple Choice Test Questions

1. One of the notable features of pain is that it
   a. only energizes instinctive responses
   b. is not a good guide to behavior
   c. has little bearing on reinforcement
   d. varies across regions of the body

2. One advantage of the type of dual control system described in the text is that it can
   a. accelerate twice as fast
   b. decelerate twice as fast
   c. control the speed of acceleration and deceleration
   d. shift to a backup control system .
3. The psychological drives of hunger and thirst
   a. are based on the stomach and mouth respectively
   b. are based on the blood and the brain
   c. are based on the eyes and the skin respectively
   d. actually have no known biological bases
4. An irrelevant drive is one that is not appropriate to the
   a. organism
   b. stimulus
   c. response
   d. reward
5. Two drives are considered incompatible when the
   a. strength of one affects the strength of the other
   b. consummatory responses cannot be made simultaneously
   c. conditions which give rise to the drives are different
   d. reduction of one also reduces the strength of the other
6. One of the important features of consummatory responses is that they are .
   a. inherently incompatible with instrumental responses
   b. inherently incompatible with operant responses
   c. determined by biological conditions
   d. subject to the principles of learning

Multiple Choice Answers

1. (d) The first three alternatives concern properties of all drives, including pain: They energize and guide behavior and set up occasions for reinforcement. However, one unique aspect of pain is that different regions of the body differ in sensitivity to it.
2. (c) A dual control system as described in the text has two opposing sources of energy whose combined effect controls the state of the system and the rate at which it changes in either direction. The rate is not necessarily twice that of a single control system. And dual control in the sense of a backup system is a completely different concept.
3. (b) It is known that hunger and thirst are related to the chemical state of the blood and its effects on the brain. The conditions of the stomach and mouth are normal concomitants of hunger and thirst. Tempting food and parched skin may contribute to our tendency to make consummatory responses, but are not the basic sources of the hunger and thirst drives.
4. (d) A drive is irrelevant if it is not appropriate to the reward one gets for a given response. An irrelevant drive may, however, be intensely appropriate to the organism.

5. (a) The last three alternatives may all be true in particular instances, but the defining feature of incompatible drives is that they cannot both be present in an intense form.
6. (d) A consummatory response may be compatible or incompatible with a requisite instrumental or operant response; for example, you may be chewing one bite of food while preparing the next. Biological conditions do affect consummatory responding, but the feature stressed in this chapter is that consummatory responses are modifiable by learning.

True/False Thought Questions

1. There are only four primary drives: hunger, thirst, sex, and pain.
2. Pain is produced by overstimulation of the basic senses of touch, sight, sound, taste, and smell.
3. Stomach contractions and dryness of the mouth are actually unrelated to hunger and thirst.
4. Hunger depends on the activity in a single, specific center in the brain.
5. One sure way to increase performance is to increase drive.
6. The concept of hunger is an aggregation of our desires for a variety of specific commodities.
7. Sex is the weakest primary drive and yet is very important in the understanding of behavior.
8. Adult sexual behavior is greatly affected by nonsexual activities that occur before puberty.
9. One reason for distinguishing between sexual arousal and sexual climax is that arousal is learnable and climax is not.
10. Sex is really not a psychological drive because indulgence in sex is not necessary for survival.
11. Hunger and thirst combine together because they are both consummatory responses made with the mouth.
12. Eating, drinking, and engaging in sex are instinctive responses to the hunger, thirst, and sex drives and, hence, are not learnable.

True/False Answers

1. (False) These are the four primary drives that are most often considered in relation to learning because the drive-reducing responses appropriate to these drives may not be freely available. However, there are other primary drives, and some learning may occur in relation to them.
2. (False) Overstimulation of these sensory systems produces discomfort, which is indeed aversive. Pain, however, is mediated by a separate sensory system.
3. (False) Under normal conditions, these experiences do arise as a result of food or water deprivation and hence are related to these drives. They are not, however, the principal basis for the hunger and thirst drives.

4. (False) There are hunger areas in the brain that partly determine hunger. However, there are also satiety areas in the brain and the hunger drive depends on the relative activity in each of these areas.
5. (False) Increasing drive does lead to increased activation of the organism. However, by changing the drive stimulus, it may also change the stimulus situation enough that the loss in habit offsets the increase in motivation.
6. (False) We do develop specific hungers for some specific commodities but hunger also exists as a general state.
7. (True) Sex is the weakest primary drive; organisms will tolerate more pain and do more work to eat or drink than to copulate. However, when the other primary drives are reasonably satisfied, sex may become the dominant drive motivating behavior. Preoccupation with sex may also result from anxiety. Hence, the topic is extremely important to an understanding of behavior.
8. (True) Infants engage in social interactions and exploratory activities involving their bodies that are important in maturing toward adult sexuality.
9. (False) Both arousal and climax are reflexive responses to adequate erotic stimulation; however, not only can arousal become associated with initially ineffective stimulus situations, but climax may also be affected by learning.
10. (False) Although sex is not a survival need of the individual organism, it does give rise to a psychological drive motivating behavior. Perhaps its relative weakness is understandable in that only individuals that were capable of reducing their other primary drives would experience the sex drive at sufficient intensity to motivate reproduction.
11. (False) Although eating and drinking are both done with the mouth, and may even overlap (as when eating moist foods), the psychological drives of hunger and thirst are biologically incompatible.
12. (False) These consummatory responses do provide intrinsic rewards for these drives. However, the responses are also learnable in the sense of being associated with other drives or desires, and may occur habitually in the absence of the relevant drive.

Essay/Discussion Questions

1. Discuss the possibility of primary drives other than those mentioned in the text (pain, hunger, thirst, sex, breathing, and elimination). Consider, for example, love, lust, hate, and other strong emotions.
2. Discuss some ways in which the consummatory responses associated with the sex drive are learnable. Take care to distinguish between intrinsic and extrinsic rewards for these responses.

References

The Pain Drive

*Hilgard, E. R. Pain perception in man. In R. Held, H. W. Leibowitz, and H. L. Teuber (Eds.), *Handbook of sensory physiology. Vol. 8: Perception.* Berlin: Springer Verlag, 1978.

*Trapold, M. A., and Fowler, H. Instrumental escape performance as a function of the intensity of noxious stimulation. *Journal of Experimental Psychology,* 1960, *60,* 323–326.

The Hunger and Thirst Drives

Grossman, S. P. Role of the hypothalamus in the regulation of food and water intake. *Psychological Review,* 1975, *82,* 200–224.

Kimble, G. A. Behavior strength as a function of the intensity of the hunger drive. *Journal of Experimental Psychology,* 1951, *41,* 341–348.

Rozin, P., and Kalat, J. W. Specific hungers and poison avoidance as adaptive specializations of learning. *Psychological Review,* 1971, *78,* 459–486.

Stellar, E. The physiology of motivation. *Psychological Review,* 1954, *61,* 5–22.

Yamazuchi, H. G. Gradients of drive stimulus intensity generalization. *Journal of Experimental Psychology,* 1952, *43,* 298–304.

The Sex Drive

*Alexander, B. K., and Harlow, H. F. Social behavior of juvenile rhesus monkeys subjected to different rearing conditions during the first six months of life. *Zoologische Jahrbucher-Physiology,* 1965, *71,* 489–508.

Beach, F. A. Instinctive behavior: Reproductive activities. In S. S. Stevens (Ed.), *Handbook of experimental psychology.* New York: Wiley, 1951.

*Beach, F. A. Sexual attractivity in females. *Hormones and Behavior.* 1976, *7,* 105.

Drive Interactions

Grossman, S. P. Effects of adrenergic and cholinergic blocking agents on hypothalamic mechanisms. *American Journal of Physiology,* 1962, *202,* 1230–1236.

Kendler, H. H. Drive interaction: II. Experimental analysis of the role of drive in learning theory. *Journal of Experimental Psychology,* 1948, *35,* 188–198.

*Suitable for additional reading by the beginning student. The others are written at a more technical level.

Secondary Motivation

13

One way to characterize primary drives is to say that they arise naturally or automatically when certain events that produce biological needs occur. The automatic responses to an aversive event are pain and fear. Hunger and thirst result naturally when we are deprived of food and water. There are, however, certain occasions when drives do not arise naturally from events in our environment. In other words, in some situations stimuli that *do not* naturally produce any biological need *do* produce drives. We call such drives *learned* or *secondary drives* because the stimuli that produce them do so because of prior learning.

The term *secondary drive,* like the term *secondary reinforcement,* is often misunderstood by the inexperienced psychology student. It is thus worth repeating that such drives are labeled *secondary* not because they are of less importance than primary drives, but because their arousal depends on prior learning. As a matter of fact, in most advanced societies, secondary drives may have even greater importance than primary drives in influencing our behaviors. In a society in which food and water are freely available, few of our behaviors are directly energized by the hunger or thirst drives. Likewise, in a society that places some restrictions on when and where sexual activity can occur, the sex drive directly influences very few of one's daily activities. On the other hand, secondary drives such as frustration or the need to avoid failure play a pervasive role in how we behave and interact with one another on a daily basis. We are much more likely to attend a social function because of a fear of loneliness (a secondary drive) than we are to attend because we are hungry and the hosts have promised that food will be served. Secondary drives are not secondary when we consider their impact on human behavior.

We have said that secondary drives are learned responses to stimuli, but we have not yet discussed how such drives are learned. How might a stimulus that is originally neutral, that does not naturally produce a drive, come to arouse a secondary drive? Such stimuli acquire their motivating properties through classical conditioning, by regularly preceding events that do naturally produce drives. Thus, we can view these originally neutral stimuli as CSs, the events that naturally produce drives as USs, and the secondary drives themselves as CRs. It is important to note, however, that not all events that naturally produce drives can serve as effective USs. For reasons that are not yet well understood, it is only *aversive* drive-producing events that function well as USs and facilitate the learning of secondary drives. Therefore, we can state the following generalization: *Any stimulus that, more or less regularly, precedes in time the occurrence of an aversive event will itself come to function as a motivating event.* The presumed mechanism for this learning is the fear response, which is part of the response initially made to any primarily aversive event and which becomes associated with the neutral stimulus.

A familiar illustration of a secondary drive is the motivating power of a parental threat. Assuming the parents at least occasionally follow through with punishment if their child continues to misbehave, the words "or else," which precede the punishment, acquire strong motivating value. Depending on the relative strength of the adversary, such threats come to be as effective as the subsequent punishment would be.

There are three basic laboratory demonstrations of the fact that stimuli that precede aversive events acquire motivating properties themselves.

Drives Energize

In our discussion of drive motivation, we presented the argument that drives serve as general energizers; that is, they activate or potentiate any habits associated with the existing stimuli. We have also noted that adding irrelevant drives may reduce performance because of the incompatible responses produced by their drive stimuli. However, when the responses to the irrelevant drive are compatible with the habit being studied, the energizing value of an irrelevant drive can be readily observed.

To illustrate this in the context of secondary motivation, consider the following study. Rats are placed individually in a small enclosure, often called a "jiggle cage" because it is suspended on a spring so that the motions of the rat jiggle the cage. This type of apparatus permits the experimenter to measure the vigor of any gross responses that occur. The observed behavior is the startle response to a sharp noise—specifically, the "pop" of a cap pistol. Rats show a distinct startle to an occasional noise.

The second stage of the study consists of pairing a tone with an electric shock according to the basic classical conditioning paradigm. A tone is sounded, followed shortly by an unavoidable electric shock, and this sequence is repeated a number of times. The tone should thereby acquire motivating value. This is demonstrated by the energizing properties of drives during the third stage of the study. The tone is sounded, but instead of the shock, the cap pistol is fired. The vigor of the startle response to the cap pistol is significantly greater than it was prior to the pairing of the tone and the shock. The tone, in effect, energizes a more vigorous response, as would be expected if it were a motivating force.

Illustrations of comparable experiences in everyday life are easy to find. For example, all houses occasionally creak or make other noises, all of which typically pass unnoticed by the occupants. If, however, you are reading a murder mystery, your response to these noises may be noticeably greater. The story produces some degree of anxiety, which then potentiates your reactivity to the noises. In a similar vein, if you are tense or otherwise frustrated, you will react more violently to criticism than when these learned drives are not present. In general, stimuli paired with aversive events will increase responsiveness in situations where the responses are compatible.

Drive Reduction Is Reinforcing

Although we have stated that not all reinforcing events entail drive reduction, the reciprocal proposition is certainly true: Reduction of a drive is reinforcing. Accordingly, if a stimulus can acquire motivating properties, its termination should reinforce a learned response. We encountered this notion earlier in the context of secondary negative reinforcement, but we can now consider a more direct demonstration

For the purpose of illustrating this feature of secondary motivation, let's examine a study by Neal Miller. He first observed rats exploring a two-compartment apparatus and noted that there was no particular preference for either compartment. The rats were then locked in one compartment and given an occasional electric shock. Miller then observed that the rats, if given a chance, would not only quickly scamper out of that compartment into the other one but would, if necessary, learn a new response (such as pressing a bar) to get out of the compartment in which they were shocked. Since this new learning took place even when no shock was given, the rats must have been reinforced simply by getting out of the compartment that had earlier contained shock. This observation is consistent with the argument that the stimulus situation of that compartment had acquired motivating properties through the conditioning procedure. Termination of the stimuli would thus serve as a secondary negative reinforcement.

Again, there are countless everyday illustrations of comparable phenomena. The small boy who has been bitten by a dog may run away in the future at the very sight of the dog. The student who has had unpleasant experiences in a class with a particular professor may learn a variety of methods to avoid that teacher. In general, stimuli that have been classically paired with aversive events not only motivate behavior in general but lead to learning of responses to terminate them.

Some Drives Are Biologically Incompatible

The pain-fear drive is inherently incompatible with the vegetative drives such as hunger, thirst, and sex. This can be demonstrated in the laboratory. We first observe the quantity of water that rats drink during a timed exposure period each day. Subsequently, we pair a tone with an electric shock a number of times while the rats are not permitted to drink and then observe the effect of presenting the tone while the rats are drinking. As expected from the incompatibility of fear with thirst, the rats quit drinking during the tone presentation.

Summary of Procedure and Experimental Results

The procedure whereby a stimulus acquires motivational properties is classical conditioning: Any stimulus, even a previously positive one, that is regularly followed by an aversive event will become a secondary motivator. This can be demonstrated in (1) the ability of such a stimulus to potentiate compatible responses such as startle; (2) the ability of such a stimulus to become a negative reinforcer for escape learning; and (3) the suppression such a stimulus exerts over incompatible drives such as hunger, thirst, and sex. All of these situations occur in everyday life and reflect the learned motivation property of stimuli.

Frustration

There is a second type of aversive event other than pain that appears to give rise to a learnable drive. This is the frustration induced when an organism fails to receive an expected reward. Everyone is familiar with frustration as a personal experience, and there are various references to frustration in the experimental literature. Rats that sit placidly on the experimenter's shoulder while being carried back from the goal to the start of a maze may begin to bite once extinction begins.

A more formal way to demonstrate the effects of frustration is to run rats in a "double runway," so called because it consists of two runways in sequence. That is to say, the rat leaves the start box and runs to a first goal box, where it is detained briefly and then is released to run on to a second goal box. In one demonstration procedure, food reward is initially placed in both goal boxes. After a number of such experiences, food is omitted from the first goal box and interest centers on the speed at which the rats run from there toward the second goal box. The finding is that they now run significantly faster; the frustration produced by failing to find the customary food in the first goal box persists as a drive and further potentiates running in the second portion of the maze.

With this demonstration that frustration has the energizing function of a drive, we can return to a phenomenon that we introduced earlier.

Recall that partial reinforcement (reward given on only some of the trials) leads to more vigorous performance, at least during the early portions of a behavior chain. It is this finding that most clearly suggests that the frustration drive is learnable. Since the frustration produced by occasional nonreinforcement becomes anticipatory, it begins to occur earlier in a behavior chain and helps potentiate the response. We also noted that occasional nonreinforcement during training makes the behavior more persistent. This is, in part, because occasional nonreinforcement provides experience with continuing to respond in spite of frustration.

Our understanding of frustration is essentially identical to our understanding of fear; indeed, they are quite similar responses. Both are produced by aversive events, fear by pain and frustration by nonreinforcement. Both are drives that potentiate behavior. Both provide drive stimuli that help guide behavior, depending on what the organism has learned to do in the presence of these drives. And both drives are learnable in the sense that they can become associated with originally neutral events. In fact, because of their similarity, fear and frustration transfer to each other. Training to tolerate frustration facilitates fear toleration, and training to perform in the face of fear facilitates performance in the face of frustration.

Other Sources of Secondary Motivation?

There are some who argue that this account of secondary motivation, while true, is incomplete—at least for humans. The contention is that we humans are not so base that our learned motives are based entirely on fear and frustration. Rather, there are positive learned drives, such as honesty and courage, which evolve in socialized humans and motivate much of their behavior.

People with this position are arguing for a source of learned motivation based on secondary reinforcement. The assumption is that, once events acquire secondary reinforcing value, they become intrinsically valuable so that the person desires them in their own right. Specifically, for example, we first learn that social approval is secondarily reinforcing because it is paired with pleasant events. Thereafter, we are presumed to develop a desire for social approval in its own right and work for it even when subsequent rewards are not given.

The first argument against this position is one of parsimony, or the preference for economy and simplicity. We all agree that fear is a source of secondary motivation and, hence, that fear of social disapproval will be learned because such disapproval is often followed by undesirable consequences. Our apparent desire for social approval can thus be understood simply as a desire to *reduce* our fear of social disapproval. This analysis can be made without appealing to any new principle.

Secondly, what little evidence there is runs counter to a positive source of secondary motivation. Recall the study in which chimps worked for poker chips, which had acquired secondary reinforcing value because of their association with grapes. The poker chips were perfectly good reinforcers when the chimps were hungry, but the chips had no intrinsic value— the chimps would not work for them when satiated.

Finally, in most (if not all) cases, the fear analysis provides a better understanding of the behavior. Are people motivated by a drive for honesty, or are they honest as a rule because of a fear of dishonesty and its consequences? Are people courageous in the face of danger, or are they instead afraid of being thought a coward? Are people moral because morality is good, or are they moral because immorality is bad? Do people achieve because they need to achieve, or do they achieve because they need to prove that they are not inferior? Perhaps there is no single answer to all of these questions, but the extent to which these behaviors are motivated by fear must first be recognized before proposing additional sources of secondary motivation.

In doing so, it is important to add that the rules and customs of society may become internalized, and the members of the society may punish themselves for the failure to comply with these rules. For example, students may know perfectly well that they can get away with cheating on an examination but do not do so because they would feel guilty about the deception and the untrue grade.

How to Deal with Fear

One of the most common questions asked by many people is how they can deal with their fears. The typical approach is "How can I get over my fear of . . . ?" and the feared scene may be anything—examinations, dates, other people, or animals, to name a few. The golfer may make a hundred two-foot putts in a row on the practice green and then feel her stomach tighten when faced with such a putt in a match. The student may know the material forward and backward but become so anxious during an examination that his mind goes blank. While we cannot yet give a completely adequate solution to such problems, there are several potentially useful procedures we can discuss.

Fear Is Not Always Bad

Let's begin by recognizing that fear is not inherently bad from a behavioral point of view. Fears provide motivation and, as such, can both energize and guide behavior. Fears are useful when they inhibit socially undesirable behavior; dishonest behavior is largely prevented by the fear of being caught and punished. Fears are also useful when they facilitate performance of socially desirable behavior; fear of being thought a coward may motivate us to perform tasks that risk well-being. Fears provide an important mechanism through which society controls the behavior of its members.

Even in many situations in which fear may appear to be detrimental, the difficulty is not with the fear itself, but with the way we have learned to respond to fear. Since fear is a drive, it can help motivate behavior and arouse us to our best possible performance. But it can do so only if the response we have learned to the drive stimulus of fear feeds into the required response. For example, if you know that you are going to be anxious in a test situation, then one adaptive approach is not to try to overcome these fears, but rather to practice the required responses under conditions of anxiety. In this way, you learn to respond with fear present and available to help motivate performance. Stage performers generally do not overcome their stage fright; instead they teach themselves to respond in spite of fear and, in fact, may not be able to perform as well unless they are somewhat anxious. The same would apply to training soldiers to respond in combat or to teaching students to respond during examinations. Even if it were possible to eliminate completely the fear of those situations, it is often more advantageous to respond with some fear present.

When Is Fear Detrimental?

There are occasions, however, when fear is clearly detrimental to personal well-being. If you are afraid of certain aspects of yourself as a person, there is no way to avoid or escape them. Fear then becomes chronic and leads to continual misery. Fearing dishonesty is adaptive: You can avoid this fear by behaving honestly. But fearing inferiority is maladaptive because you cannot get away from yourself. So too, fears concerning your physical appearance or inescapable motives for pleasure lead to persisting anxiety, shame, and guilt, which almost inevitably interfere with good adjustment.

In like fashion, fearing unavoidable and actually harmless events in the environment is undesirable. Being afraid of the dark, of small enclosures (such as elevators), or of heights (such as tall buildings) can preclude normal behavior. Although you can successfully avoid some of these fears, such as flying in an airplane, other situations are an inevitable part of modern life and fear of them is maladaptive.

Perhaps the worst effect of fear is when it becomes involved in a vicious positive feedback circle. Many people, for example, are afraid of being sick; for them, sickness is a sign of personal weakness or threatens them with death. Such people may respond to minor stomach pain with the fear that they have an ulcer, and yet they are afraid to find out the truth. Their silent worry interferes with digestion and leads to secretions of acids that do produce ulcers. The effect of this fear is thus to increase the abdominal pain, which further increases the fear that there is an ulcer. In time, such people may indeed develop ulcers and be forced to see a doctor when an early examination could have prevented the entire affair.

President Franklin D. Roosevelt stated in his inaugural address: "The only thing we have to fear is fear itself." By now, the reader should be better able to understand the full meaning of such an expression. We are indeed in trouble if we are afraid that we will behave badly when fearful. A little anxiety, coupled with the least thing that goes wrong, leads to an increased fear that we are, indeed, becoming afraid, which may progressively feed upon itself to the point of panic. The major reason for learning to deal with fear is so that one will not be afraid that fear will ruin performance.

How to Control Fear

There are several things a person can do about fear. The first—and this should not be dismissed too lightly—is simply to avoid the situation you are afraid of. Although many feared situations, such as examinations and social contacts, must be faced, a surprising number of people continue to expose themselves to avoidable situations they are anxious about. Persons concerned about their appearance can consult an expert for advice on hairstyling and selecting a wardrobe that will almost certainly eliminate their imagined problem. Students who are having difficulty in one school because they are constantly fighting the long-remembered superior exploits of their parents there can simply change schools. Before embarking on the job of eliminating a fear, first explore the possibility of realistically avoiding the stimuli that elicit the fear.

It is, however, maladaptive to avoid all of the situations people are afraid of. Marriage, social gatherings, and public appearances are important to social life. In dealing with these, the first thing to recall is that fears are learned by the principles of classical conditioning, and they can be extinguished by the same principles. This is not easy because of repeated spontaneous recovery and the possibility of disinhibition. Nevertheless, exposure to a feared stimulus without aversive experiences eventually will lead to the extinction of fear. In following this procedure, gradual exposure may be much more effective than "sink or swim" techniques.

Punishment, however, does not produce responses incompatible with fear and hence does not eliminate fear. Indeed, we can demonstrate that punishment may make matters worse. We first train rats to run from a start box down a short alley to a goal box by shocking them in the alley if they fail to get to the goal in time. They readily learn to run rapidly. We can then attempt to extinguish this fear-motivated avoidance response. For some of the animals, the shock is simply disconnected; over repeated trials, they will gradually slow down and stop running. For other animals, shock punishment is given in the last foot of the alley if they get there, but they can now avoid the shock by simply staying in the start box. These animals, who are punished for responding to their learned fear, require considerably more trials before they stop running. Since they do not know at first that they will receive no shock if they stay put, they run. This puts them into the alley, where they are now shocked, which induces them to run on to the goal box. Things are pretty much as they had been, only worse. Punishing fears produces more fear and confirms the expectation of aversive experiences in the situation.

Despite the common belief to the contrary, fears can be brought under at least some degree of voluntary control. The reason that this is not easily taught is that we are dealing with private experiences that cannot be readily exposed to others for training. But relaxation is a learnable response, although few people even know how to relax physically. If you repeatedly clench your fist tightly and then relax it, you will learn what it feels like to relax your muscles. And if you say to yourself, "relax" as you do so, you can teach yourself to relax to verbal command. A similar process can be used with fear. First, think of a situation fearful enough to arouse your anxieties; then think of a pleasant situation, and, at the same time, attend to what it feels like to relax from fear while telling yourself to "settle down." Deliberate practice of this kind can enable you to gain control over responses you might think are completely involuntary.

Finally, alcohol appears to work selectively to suppress the sympathetic system and hence reduce fear. This is not to recommend the use of alcohol for this purpose; indeed, using alcohol in this way poses many dangers. But it is important to understand alcohol's effects. Alcohol is often thought of as a behavioral stimulant, but it stimulates not by arousing the nervous system but instead by inhibiting inhibitory systems. That alcohol is a general depressant is also clear; it increases reaction time, blurs vision, and, in sufficient quantity, causes the person to pass out. By depressing the sympathetic system, alcohol leads directly to a reduction in fear. The difficulty is that drinking is a learnable response. The person who begins to drink as a way of dealing with personal fears may thus be beginning a vicious positive feedback circle leading to alcoholism. For example, the student who is afraid of a forthcoming examination might visit a nearby bar. This indeed reduces fear and reinforces drinking behavior. But it also interferes with effective performance and may do so even the next day since it requires about two hours for the liver to process a single ounce of alcohol. Accordingly, fears of failure are increased, leading to a need for more alcohol to reduce them. In short, drinking alcohol may be learned as a simple expression of the principle of reinforcement.

Secondary Motivation

Multiple Choice Test Questions

1. A drive is called "secondary" when it is
   a. weaker than the other drives present
   b. inappropriate to the reward
   c. not necessary for survival
   d. based on learning
2. For a stimulus to acquire secondary motivating properties, it must be
   a. paired with an emotionally positive stimulus
   b. paired with an emotionally negative stimulus
   c. contingent on a positively rewarded response
   d. contingent on a negatively rewarded response
3. According to the analysis developed in the text, fear and frustration differ primarily in the
   a. aversive conditions on which they are based
   b. types of feedback stimuli they produce
   c. types of responses they produce
   d. situations in which they may be aroused
4. According to the position adopted in the text, which of the following would best illustrate a source of secondary motivation?
   a. morality
   b. honesty
   c. responsibility
   d. failure
5. With respect to adaptive behavior, fear is
   a. beneficial
   b. detrimental
   c. beneficial or detrimental, depending on the source of the fear
   d. beneficial or detrimental, depending on the responses made to the fear
6. With respect to maladaptive behavior, fear is
   a. controllable
   b. uncontrollable
   c. desirable
   d. undesirable

Multiple Choice Answers

1. (d) A secondary drive such as fear may be the strongest drive present, and it may be quite appropriate and necessary for survival. Such a drive is called *secondary* only because it is learned.
2. (b) Response contingencies may be involved, but simple pairing of stimuli is sufficient. Emotionally positive stimuli lead to secondary reinforcement. Emotionally negative stimuli lead to secondary motivation.

3. (a) Both fear and frustration may be aroused in the same situation, may produce similar feedback stimuli, and may produce similar responses. Some teachers produce fear in their students and also frustration due to lack of reinforcement; these may combine to produce self-defense responses such as maligning the teacher. The distinction between fear and frustration, then, is based on the different conditions of pain and nonreinforcement.

4. (d) The text focused on immorality, dishonesty, and responsibility because of their aversive consequences. Failure may also have aversive consequences that a person learns to fear, thereby motivating efforts to achieve.

5. (d) Fear may be either beneficial or detrimental, depending on whether it enhances adaptive or maladaptive responses, regardless of its source.

6. (a) Fear may or may not be desirable depending on the situation; it is appropriate to fear an unwanted pregnancy, but not appropriate to fear sex because of this fear. Fear is, albeit with difficulty, controllable. People can learn to overcome fear of the dark, fear of a barking dog, fear of flying in an airplane, and so on.

True/False Thought Questions

1. Originally neutral stimuli acquire motivating power through classical conditioning.
2. That stimuli can acquire motivating power is attested to by two facts: that such stimuli energize behavior and that their termination reinforces behavior.
3. Secondary motivation cannot be based on the primary drives of hunger, thirst, or sex.
4. Frustration is similar to fear.
5. The authors contend that all learned drives are based on aversive events.
6. One way to improve society would be to eliminate all fears.
7. Fears inevitably give rise to a vicious positive feedback situation.
8. The authors advise to never try to control fear by avoiding feared situations.
9. Extinction more effectively eliminates undesirable fear than punishment does.
10. One of the difficulties in dealing with fears is that fears are completely involuntary.
11. One danger of alcohol is that it stimulates the nervous system.
12. One danger of alcohol is that drinking is self-reinforcing.

True/False Answers

1. (True) The process of classical conditioning involves pairing two stimuli in temporal order. Secondary motivation is established by following an initially neutral stimulus with an aversive one.

2. (True) These are two basic properties of all drives that must be demonstrated to prove that an originally neutral stimulus has acquired motivational properties.
3. (True) This is apparently true with respect to thirst and hunger, since experimental data are available. It is possible that sexual arousal leads to an increase in motivation, and arousal is learnable. However, there are no experimental data establishing this source of learned motivation.
4. (True) Frustration is based on nonreinforcement, and fear is based on painful events. Both sets of conditions are aversive and involve similar processes; this is demonstrated by the transfer of training with one to the performance of the other.
5. (True) That aversive events can be used to establish secondary motivation is experimentally established. Other learned drives have been proposed, but their proponents have failed to demonstrate that a fear/frustration analysis is inadequate. Unless this is done, there is no reason to favor the new theories.
6. (False) Fears are not always harmful. They may facilitate desirable responses or help deter undesirable responses. Hence, it would not be appropriate to try to design a society in which there is no fear.
7. (False) When fear produces responses that lead to a further increase in fear, a positive feedback circle is established. This is a not an uncommon result; but fear can also produce adaptive responses that lead to a reduction in fear.
8. (False) There are many situations people can be afraid of that would be maladaptive to attempt to avoid—even though people sometimes do try to avoid them. Hence, avoidance is not a general solution. The authors, in fact, advised *not* to neglect the possibility of avoidance when it is appropriate.
9. (True) Fears are learned by classical conditioning, and the principles of classical conditioning apply to the elimination of fears. Extinction effectively eliminates fears, but punishment is ineffective because it can never "suit the crime" of becoming fearful and only intensifies the fear.
10. (False) Although the principle of the anticipatory response inevitably applies to fear, some degree of voluntary control can be exerted over conditioned responses, including the internal ones associated with fear.
11. (False) Alcohol is a neural depressant. It may appear to be a behavioral stimulant because it depresses the sympathetic branch of the autonomic nervous system, where inhibitions and fears reside.
12. (True) Assuming that any degree of fear or anxiety is present, alcohol inhibits the sympathetic neural system and directly reduces those drives. Hence, the response is directly reinforced by its neurological effect.

Essay/Discussion Questions

1. This chapter has concentrated on the learned drives of fear and frustration. Try to think of other possible sources of secondary motivation, such as the desire for knowledge, money, or social approval. Discuss the adequacy of the alternative understanding based on fear of ignorance, poverty, or social disapproval.

2. The text's description of dealing with fear focused on the fear motivation as a learned drive. Discuss the possible relevance of these principles for dealing with unlearned fears such as the fears of loss of physical support, restriction of breathing, and threat of violence.

References

Hunger and Secondary Motivation
Myers, A. K., and Miller, N. E. Failure to find a learned drive based on hunger; evidence for learning motivated by exploration. *Journal of Comparative and Physiological Psychology,* 1954, *47*, 428–436.

Fear
Brown, J. S., Kalish, H. I., and Farber, I. E. Conditioned fear as revealed by magnitude of startle response to an auditory stimulus. *Journal of Experimental Psychology,* 1951, *41*, 317–328.
*Miller, N. E. Studies of fear as an acquirable drive: I. Fear as motivation and fear reduction as reinforcement in the learning of new responses. *Journal of Experimental Psychology,* 1948, *38*, 89–101.
*Miller, N. E. Some recent studies of conflict behavior and drugs. *American Psychologist*, 1961, *16*, 12–24.

Frustration
Amsel, A., and Roussel, J. Motivational properties of frustration: I. Effect on a running response of the addition of frustration to the motivational complex. *Journal of Experimental Psychology,* 1952, *43*, 363–368.
Wagner, A. R. Conditioned frustration as a learned drive. *Journal of Experimental Psychology,* 1963, *66*, 142–148.

How to Deal with Fear
*Brown, J. S., Martin, R. C., and Morrow, M. W. Self-punitive behavior in the rat: Facilitative effects of punishment on resistance to extinction. *Journal of Comparative and Physiological Psychology,* 1964, *57*, 127–133.

*Suitable for additional reading by the beginning student. The others are written at a more technical level.

Incentive Motivation

In previous chapters, we have maintained that motivation is not necessary for learning, that learning results simply from experience. We have also made repeated reference to the principle of reinforcement: that the tendency for responses to occur depends to a great degree upon the schedule and condition of reward. Resolution of this apparent ambiguity comes from understanding that *the principle of reinforcement is a performance principle, not a learning principle.* The principle correctly asserts that the vigor, speed, rate, or simple likelihood of a response depends upon reward. But reward does not effect learning itself; rather, organisms come to expect or anticipate rewards that follow responses, and this expectation is the source of motivation to make those responses.

In like fashion, *the principle of punishment is a performance principle.* The occurrence of an aversive event following a response does not weaken the learning process but, instead, leads to an expectation of punishment that tends to inhibit making the response. The means whereby both reinforcement and punishment affect performance is best understood in terms of a *cybernetic*, or feedback, analysis. When you start to make a response, or even think about doing so, the response-produced feedback stimuli are associated with the consequences that you have previously experienced. If those consequences were pleasant, your motivation is to continue with that train of thought or that course of action. If, however, those consequences were unpleasant, your motivation is to stop. Accordingly, the expectation of reward increases and the expectation of punishment decreases the tendency to perform.

Evidence that Reward Affects Motivation

In reviewing the evidence that leads to this conception of the role of reward, it is important to keep in mind the fundamental distinction between learning and motivation. For a variable to affect learning, it must be experienced repeatedly and must lead to a relatively permanent change in behavior. Motivation, in contrast, is more transitory and can be increased or decreased rapidly. We will see that the effects of reward on performance conform to a motivational interpretation of the role of reward.

Latent Learning

Suppose hungry rats are allowed to wander through a maze that does not contain food. When they ultimately get to the goal box, they are removed, and the experience is repeated a number of times. During such trials, there is very little improvement in the rats' performance; they persist in entering as many blind alleys as correct paths and, hence, do not appear to be learning the maze. Recall that learning can only be inferred from a change in performance. We can show that the rats have indeed learned something about the route to the goal, even though their performance does not indicate it—this phenomenon is thus called *latent learning.*

To demonstrate the rats' latent learning in this particular context, reward, in the form of food, is introduced the next time the rats run to the goal box. Performance then shows a very rapid improvement, much more rapid than would be expected were they learning the maze from scratch. Within a very few trials, the rats perform as well as other rats that have been receiving reward in the goal box from the very beginning. We thus can conclude that reward is not necessary for learning, and that the nonre-warded rats were learning the maze equally as well as their rewarded counterparts. However, their learning was not evident in performance until incentive motivation was added by the introduction of reward.

Changes in Reward

Latent learning involves a special case of changing the reward; the case of going from no reward to some reward. But one can also observe the effects of other changes, such as increasing or decreasing the amount of reward. We have already noted in our discussion of instrumental conditioning that the speed of a response depends upon the amount of reward that is received, and that changes in the reward lead to changes in performance appropriate to the direction of the change in reward. Here we need only note how these findings indicate that reward functions as a motivational variable.

Although larger rewards lead to better performance, they do not lead to better learning. This is clear from the fact that decreasing the amount of reward leads to a decrease in performance; since learning is persistent, it would not be lost from a decrease in the reward. Furthermore, the changes in performance following a change in the reward are very rapid, much more rapid than could reasonably result from learning. Instead, it appears that the amount of reward affects performance in a motivational manner since the change can occur so rapidly in either direction.

Direct Placement

Finally, there is some evidence that the effects of reward on performance can occur without the actual response occurring. Clearly, if one can change performance without practice, the manipulation cannot involve learning. There are two variants of this procedure. In one, rats are first permitted to explore a maze without reward; they are then placed directly in the goal box and given food there. Following this, they are released from the start box and show an immediate improvement in running speed and in the number of correct turns they make. Again we have an instance of latent learning, in this case made manifest by simply exposing the rat to food in what was previously an empty goal box.

The other variant is just the reverse and is called *latent extinction*. Rats are first trained to run through a maze with reward. After they are making few, if any, errors and are running rapidly to the goal box, they are placed directly in the goal box—but now without food. Following these direct placements, the rats are replaced in the start box of the maze. They now run more slowly and make more errors. Hence, simply being placed in the empty goal box results in some extinction, which manifests itself as a decrease in the incentive motivation to run.

The direct placement studies are analogous to telling a person that the reward conditions have been changed—that where you used to be rewarded, you will no longer be, or where you used to get nothing, you will now be rewarded. The latter case is like saying, "Now, let's play for keeps." As with the rats, your performance would probably change accordingly. For example, if the evening news reports that the fish are not biting at your favorite spot, you will be less inclined to go there the next day.

Summary

The conclusion is that reward affects performance not as a learning variable, but as a motivational variable; the expectation of reward provides incentive motivation for making a response. This conclusion is supported by the observations that organisms can learn from exposure to a situation without reward, that their performance can be changed rapidly, for better or worse, by a change in reward, and that some such changes can be produced without the response itself occurring. In short, rewards motivate behavior.

Comparable studies involving punishment have not yet been run, but what evidence there is points in the same direction. For example, a single traumatic experience in the goal box of a maze can disrupt a rat's performance even more dramatically than direct placement without reward. Similarly, reading that the police have been ordered to clamp down on enforcing the speed limit may promptly suppress your tendency to speed.

Review of Positive Reinforcement

This understanding of the role of reward applies to all of the situations discussed in previous chapters. We cannot review all of these situations here, but let's return to the operant situation in which a hungry rat is working for food by pressing a bar. We know that the rat's rate of responding depends a great deal on the schedule of reinforcement. We are now in a better position to see why this is true. The rat presses the bar at a rate depending on its expectation of reward; that is, depending on the momentary level of incentive motivation.

If, for example, the reinforcement schedule is a variable-interval one, so that responding may be rewarded at any time, there is no basis for incentive motivation to vary over time. Responding is not always rewarded, but it is as likely to be rewarded now as later. This steady level of incentive leads to a steady response rate; the more frequent the reward, the higher the incentive and the higher the rate. This situation involves the maximal amount of uncertainty about when to respond.

If, alternatively, the situation involves a fixed-interval schedule, then the rat is never rewarded for responding immediately after receiving reinforcement. Hence, the rat learns not to expect another reward right away; its incentive motivation is low and its response rate is low. But as time passes and the next scheduled reward becomes imminent, incentive to respond should increase and should lead to an increasing response rate. Thus, the scallop generated by a fixed-interval schedule reflects the rat's changing expectation of reward over time, corresponding to the regular, periodic availability of reinforcement. If an external stimulus, such as a light, is added to the situation to signal when responding will be rewarded, incentive motivation will come to be high in the presence of the stimulus and low in the absence of the stimulus. As a result, the discriminative behavior characteristic of differential operant conditioning occurs.

Thus, incentive motivation determines *when* a freely available operant response will occur. Incentive motivation also helps determine *how* a response is made. To understand this, return to the instrumental conditioning situation in which a hungry rat is running down an alley for food. We know that the rat's running speed depends to a large extent on the condition of reinforcement, and will generally be faster the larger, more immediate, and better-quality the reward. These conditions lead to a high level of incentive motivation and hence a high level of performance.

This interpretation can be made most clearly when the condition involves correlated reinforcement. Typically, reward is simply at the end of the alley and the sooner the rat gets there, the sooner it gets the reward. In *correlated reinforcement*, some quantitative dimension of the reward, such as its amount, depends upon some quantitative dimension of the response, such as its speed. Specifically, for example, the rat might be given a larger reward if it runs slowly than if it runs fast. Under such a condition, the rat learns to run slowly, more slowly than the amount of reward received would produce under typical conditions. In effect, if the incentive motivation for a slow response is greater than that for a fast response, the former will be the one performed. Response differentiation is therefore attributable to incentive motivation, which is, in turn, associated with the optimal way of making the response.

Conditions of correlated reinforcement are very prevalent in everyday life and account for all skilled performance. Not only the speed but the vigor and rate of responding can be precisely controlled if reward is correlated with them. Thus, the skilled lecturer has learned not only how fast to talk but also how loudly to talk and how often to repeat points, depending on the size and background of the audience. This same principle has equally important implications for the design of optimal training programs. For example, when fast responses are desirable, they can be encouraged by explicitly giving greater rewards for faster responses. This is most obviously true in situations such as athletic races, but also applies to more mundane activities such as reading and writing. More generally, in controlling the behavior of ourselves and others, excellence is most likely to result from correlating reward with the degree of excellence observed. Within reason, the greater the differential reinforcement accorded outstanding performance, the greater the incentive motivation to perform in an outstanding manner.

Hopefully, it is clear that our interpretation that rewards affect behavior by determining the level of incentive motivation is *not* incompatible with the principle of positive reinforcement. That principle and the more specific facts describing its applications are empirically sound. The concept of incentive motivation is a way of conceptualizing how rewards work to produce observed results. Incentive motivation guides the organism toward those behaviors that have historically been associated with the most reward. As with learning and drive motivation, incentive motivation is hypothetical; none of the three can be observed directly. But they are, presumably, the underlying processes determining behavior.

Other Effects of Incentive Motivation

With the role of reinforcement established as being motivational in nature, we can more readily explore various other types of situations involving reward and punishment. In the simpler situations such as those just described, positive incentive motivation depends on the condition and schedule of reinforcement, while negative incentive motivation depends on the condition and schedule of punishment. Specifically, the larger the reward, the greater the positive incentive; and the more intense the punishment, the greater the negative incentive. But this description is an oversimplification of the richness of the concept of incentive motivation; several other effects should give a more complete perspective.

Incentive Contrast

In our discussion of the principle of positive reinforcement, we noted that the performance of an operant or instrumental response is an increasing function of the amount of reward. Specifically, a rat presses a bar more frequently or runs down an alley more rapidly the larger the reward contingent on such behavior. Although that proposition is true in general, it is even more true for organisms that have been exposed to several different amounts of reward in past experiences. Functionally, a small reward is less effective for an organism who has previously received large rewards, and a large reward is more effective for an organism who has previously received small rewards. This symmetrical effect is called *incentive contrast.*

For example, if a rat is sometimes run in a black alley, receiving a small reward, and is also sometimes run in a white alley, receiving a large reward, the rat runs slower in the black alley and faster in the white alley than do rats who have only received either the small or the large reward. In comparable fashion, if a rat is on a variable-interval schedule of small rewards when a low-pitched tone is sounding, and is on the same variable-interval schedule of large rewards when a high-pitched tone is sounding, the rate of responding is lower with the low-pitched tone and higher with the high-pitched tone than would be true if the rat were only accustomed to one amount of reward.

This phenomenon is called incentive contrast because it is similar to perceptual contrast and, indeed, may be a special case of that effect. If you are asked to judge how big a medium-sized rock is, you will perceive it as being large if it is surrounded by pebbles and small if it is surrounded by boulders. An average person looks tall in the company of horse jockeys and short in the company of basketball players. So too, a reasonably large reward may simply look larger to an organism who has been exposed to small rewards, and vice versa. An important point to note is that it is the *apparent* or *perceived* size of the reward that matters. Rats perform more vigorously for the same total amount of food cut up in several pieces, or if they encounter a very large pile of food, even though they cannot eat it all.

Accordingly, the incentive value of a reward is as great as the organism perceives it to be. In the not-so-good old days, unscrupulous employers paid very low wages; but the workers were apparently content because they had never known higher wages. Even today, people are loathe to return to a lower standard of living when they thought it was quite comfortable at an earlier period of their lives. In sum, *incentive value is relative*; what seems large or small depends on your experiences.

Probability Matching

In chapter 9, we discussed two types of *selective learning*—discrimination and differentiation. In discrimination learning, the organism selects between stimuli based on differential reinforcement associated with the stimuli, and in differentiation learning, the organism selects between responses based on differential reinforcement associated with the responses. In either case, the usual procedure is for reward to be associated with only one of the alternatives, the other being nonreinforced.

Let's now consider situations in which the reward is not consistently associated with either of the two alternatives. In a black-white discrimination, for example, reward is sometimes associated with the black stimulus and sometimes associated with the white stimulus, or in a right-left differentiation, reward is sometimes to the right and sometimes to the left. In either case, reward is available on every trial. Assume that 75 percent of the time the reward is associated with alternative A, and 25 percent of the time with alternative B, but that there is no meaningful pattern to the reward association. For example, we might toss two coins before each trial, rewarding alternative B if both coins turn up heads and alternative A if any of the other three equally likely combinations turn up. In that way, the probability of reward is greater (75 percent) for alternative A, and it is strictly up to chance as to when alternative B will be rewarded.

Under such circumstances, it is impossible to *learn* which alternative is correct; rather, one must choose on the basis of relative incentive value. The optimum strategy for choosing between the alternatives is, of course, to *always* choose the more frequently rewarded alternative—A. In this way, you are assured of being right 75 percent of the time. Any other strategy (short of supernatural clairvoyance) will, in the long run, result in a lower percentage of reinforcement. This is simply because you will be wrong 75 percent of the time when you choose alternative B. Nevertheless, few organisms, whether rats or humans, adopt this optimum strategy. Instead, the preponderant tendency is to match the probability of choice with the probability of reinforcement. That is to say, the typical organism in this situation will choose alternative A about 75 percent of the time and alternative B about 25 percent of the time, even though this results in a lower (actually about 62.5 percent) incidence of reinforcement. This tendency has been labeled the *matching law*; organisms tend to distribute their choices according to the probability with which rewards are distributed. When incentive motivation is associated with several alternatives, organisms tend not to stick with the best alternative—they try to beat the odds.

A comparable tendency can be seen in an operant conditioning situation. If the schedules of reinforcement provide a rat with twice the rate of reinforcement for pressing on one bar as for pressing on another bar, the rat will press about twice as much on that bar as on the other. Organisms can be induced to violate the matching law by making drive motivation very high or by imposing penalties for selecting the poorer alternative part of the time, but the fundamental matching tendency is very pervasive.

Perhaps the most familiar place to observe this tendency is in your behavior when taking a multiple choice examination. If there are four alternatives for each item, you have a tendency to presume that about one-fourth of the correct answers will appear in each of the four positions and most likely will distribute your answers accordingly. Similarly, your past experiences have probably set you to expect that about half of the items on a true-false test will be true, and you might even complain if a teacher deviates very much from that expectation in constructing the test. In these and many other situations, such as rolling dice, our expectations tend to match the probabilities of the events as we have experienced them in the past, and we tend to behave in accord with those expectations, even at the expense of being wrong more often.

Information Value

In the context of learning, *information means the occurrence of stimuli that are* differentially *associated with the occurrence or nonoccurrence of emotionally significant events.* In a black-white discrimination, for example, the brightness of the cue has information value because it tells the organism where the reward is. In avoidance conditioning, the conditioned stimulus has information value because it forewarns the organism that an aversive event is impending unless the avoidance response is made. In a very general sense, learning in all its facets can be conceptualized as behaving adaptively on the basis of information conveyed by stimuli in the environment.

What is more, organisms appear to value information. Let's review several examples to make this point clear. First, consider a pigeon given a choice between pecking on two keys, one of which is reinforced on a fixed-interval, thirty-second schedule and the other of which is reinforced on a variable-interval, thirty-second schedule of reinforcement. Now in the long run, these schedules are equivalent in the sense that the pigeon will receive, on the average, one reward per every thirty seconds. But there is some information available in the fixed-interval schedule about when the reward can be obtained—namely, precisely every thirty seconds. That the pigeon values information is revealed by the fact that the bird prefers the fixed-interval schedule.

Indeed, organisms even make responses just to obtain information. Attending to the relevant cue in a discrimination problem is an example of such an information-seeking response, but attention is a covert process that we can only infer from the fact that the organism behaves adaptively with respect to the relevant cue and nondifferentially with respect to any irrelevant cues in the situation. It is possible to make such responses overt by requiring the organism to make an *observing response* to obtain the information.

For example, suppose that a pigeon is pecking on a white key and the schedule of reinforcement changes occasionally between a fixed-interval and a variable-interval schedule. Under such circumstances, the pigeon has no way of knowing which schedule is in force at any particular time. But suppose we also provide a small treadle on the floor of the apparatus and arrange things so that, if the pigeon steps on the treadle, the key will change briefly to either red or green, with red conveying the information that the current schedule is fixed-interval while green signals the variable-interval schedule. Notice that stepping on the treadle is not, in itself, rewarded. Nevertheless, the pigeon frequently makes this observing response to gain information about which schedule is in force on the reinforced key.

Presumably, the incentive value of information is based on the fact that the information permits the organism to adjust optimally to the environment. In the preceding situation, the pigeon can peck the red or green key appropriately, rather than pecking the white key haphazardly. In a totally different situation, it has been shown that if rats are placed in an apparatus in which they are scheduled to receive occasional electric shocks, their preference is to have a signal shortly precede each shock, presumably so that they can brace themselves for it. The negative incentive value of the shock is, in effect, reduced if there is a warning signal.

All of these sorts of evidence suggest that *useful information has positive incentive value.* This is probably not surprising to you. Most students prefer to know, in advance, what kind of a test will be given; a great deal of time and money is spent in trying to forecast the weather; and it is usually important to know what kind of dress is appropriate for a party. Humans also seem inclined sometimes to garner apparently useless information, although such information may prove to be useful some time in the future. Be that as it may, organisms of all types clearly seek information that improves their adjustment to the environment.

Decision Making

The concept of incentive motivation can be further enriched by a discussion of decision making. In a sense, our earlier descriptions of discrimination and differentiation could have been described as decisions. A rat at a choice point, where food lies in one direction and not in the other, certainly has to decide which way to go. So does one confronting two stimuli, behind only one of which is a reward. But these are not thought of as decision problems because the outcome is obvious in advance. The hungry rat that knows where the food is will certainly go there; not much decision making is involved. A *decision-making situation* is in effect when the outcomes are arranged so that one choice produces one reward or aversive event and the other choice produces another reward or aversive event.

Decision making is typically studied with humans, but animals have been shown to be consistent decision makers. For example, if a rat receives a larger reward in one alley than in another but has to wait longer for the reward in that alley, the rat's choice depends on the difference between the amounts relative to the difference between the delays. In similar fashion, if a rat must choose between a small, certain reward and a larger, but more uncertain reward, its choice depends on the difference in amount relative to the difference in probability. As a final illustration, if a rat has a choice between two alternatives, one of which contains a larger reward, but also entails a mild shock punishment, its choice depends on the difference in reward relative to the strength of the shock. In effect, the rat weighs the two alternatives and behaves accordingly.

We can use this knowledge to determine equal-incentive differences. This is done by using a *titration schedule* and observing the point of indifference. Specifically, assume that pressing on one bar provides a rat with one pellet one second later, and pressing on another bar provides two pellets, delayed for some length of time. We titrate the length of delay as follows: Each time that the rat chooses the two-pellet bar, we increase the delay by a second for the next trial; each time the rat chooses the one-pellet bar, we decrease the delay on the two-pellet bar by one second for the next trial. The idea is that, if the delay of the two pellets is too short, so that the rat prefers it, we make the delay longer; if the delay is too long, we make it shorter. Using this schedule, we ultimately find a point where the rat is pressing each bar about equally often, with the delay on the two-pellet bar hovering around some value (say, five seconds). This is the point of indifference and we then know that, to that rat under those conditions of deprivation, the *difference* in incentive value between one and two pellets is equal to the *difference* in incentive value between one and five seconds delay. In effect, one additional pellet is worth waiting four more seconds.

The important implication of such research is the concept of *net incentive motivation*. If a response is followed by several events, these events combine into a single value upon which decisions are made. Suppose, for example, that you are given a choice between a sure one dollar or a one-in-five chance at five dollars. Clearly these alternatives would be equivalent over the long run, but given a single choice, you might prefer one over the other. What you do is judge the difference in subjective incentive value between one and five dollars against your subjective estimate of the chances that a five-to-one shot will pay off. Interestingly enough, humans' subjective estimates of probability do not always perfectly equal the objective probability; people tend to overestimate low-probability events and to underestimate high-probability events. (This is why novice gamblers usually lose to experts—the latter don't bet the "long shots" when the odds are actually longer than the wager would indicate.) Your choice will depend on the net incentive value of the two choices.

Most theories assume that decisions will display the property of *transitivity*. Specifically, if you indicate a preference for *A* over *B*, and also a preference for *B* over *C*, then you should indicate a preference for *A* over *C*. This property has held true in all situations studied with animals and most of those studied with humans. However, a lack of transitivity has sometimes been found when humans are choosing among complex alternatives, such as when a smoker is stating preferences for different brands of cigarettes. It thus appears that attempts to measure the incentive values of different outcomes by studying them in a decision-making situation may reveal important interactions within the concept of net incentive motivation.

Reprise

The only people with no drive motivation are dead. Under some conditions of deprivation, we are motivated to eat, to drink, or to engage in sexual activity. We may be curious and even have a primary drive to learn about ourselves and our environment. In the absence of these drives, there are a host of socially acquired drives to fall back upon. We have learned the value of money, of social approval, of knowledge. And when we rest, it is not because we have done everything we would like to do, but because fatigue gives rise to a drive for sleep.

Thus motivated for self-preservation and self-actualization, we respond; and as we respond, we learn. The biblical saying, "As ye sow, so shall ye reap," applies to our own behavior. We learn habits of overt action, from walking and talking through a countless number of everyday behaviors to the virtuoso performance of our special skills. We learn more covert habits of thinking, of developing attitudes, beliefs, and dreams. If there is a limit to how much the human can learn, it is doubtful that anyone has ever tested that limit.

These habits are called into play by their consequences. If emotionally significant events follow a response in any particular situation, incentive motivation is generated and affects the future likelihood that we will make that response in that situation. These events feed the drives the process began with, leading on to new situations. Behavior is a continual progression of choice points, confronting us with stimuli we have learned to discriminate between, requiring responses we have learned to differentiate between, through which we act because of drive motivation, guided by incentive motivation.

Sometimes we are consciously aware of these processes. We know what we want, we canvas the alternatives one by one, and then we deliberately select the one offering the greatest hope of success. But the same processes are taking place even when we are unaware of them and, indeed, even when we can't figure out why we do what we do. Understanding the fundamentals of learning and motivation is important precisely because behavior is inescapably controlled by these processes.

Incentive Motivation

Multiple Choice Test Questions

1. Which of the following is *not* evidence that reward affects motivation?
   a. Performance improves gradually over rewarded trials.
   b. Learning occurs during nonrewarded practice.
   c. Changes in reward lead to changes in performance.
   d. Organisms can learn about the presence or absence of reward without making the response.

2. The scallop characteristic of performance on a fixed-interval schedule reflects the changing incentive motivation associated with the
   a. external stimulus
   b. overt response
   c. reward
   d. passage of time
3. Grades in school are intended to provide
   a. correlated reinforcement
   b. correlated punishment
   c. increased learning
   d. increased drive
4. The concept of net incentive motivation is most evident in the context of
   a. operant conditioning
   b. instrumental conditioning
   c. differential conditioning
   d. decision making
5. Organisms tend to value
   a. information about positive events
   b. information about neutral events
   c. information about negative events
   d. useful information regardless of whether the events are positive, neutral, or negative
6. Which of the following best describes the function of incentive motivation?
   a. initiating behavior
   b. maintaining behavior
   c. guiding behavior
   d. terminating behavior

Multiple Choice Answers

1. (a) The last three alternatives suggest that rewards do not directly affect learning, but instead act in the transitory and reversible manner of motivational factors. That performance improves gradually over rewarded trials could be attributed to learning.
2. (d) The stimulus, the response, and the reward are all involved in the situation, but the passage of time since the previous reward leads to a progressive increase in the expectation of reward for responding again.
3. (a) Although some students think of grades as punitive, the intent is to provide reinforcement that is correlated with the effort expended in mastering the material. Grades do not directly affect learning, and any effects on drive are the result of unintended emphases placed on them.
4. (d) Rewards and punishments always have several features such as amount, delay, quality, and probability. These features would presumably

combine into a net incentive value in any situation. But the concept is most evident when a choice must be made between events that differ in several ways.

5. (d) Information is useful if it enables you to prepare for upcoming events. It has incentive value even if the impending event is aversive.

6. (c) Incentive motivation is involved in all of the listed functions. However, its unique function is to guide behavior in the direction that will optimize reward and minimize punishment.

True/False Thought Questions

1. The better the reward, the better the learning.
2. Learning may occur yet not be reflected in performance.
3. The tendency to make a response can be changed without ever having actually made the response itself.
4. Incentive motivation controls behavior only in special situations such as decision making.
5. The incentive motivation to make a response may change from moment to moment.
6. Practice makes perfect.
7. Racing is an instance of correlated reinforcement.
8. Humankind is the only species capable of making real decisions.
9. The fact that people take gambles that must lose in the long run contradicts the notion of net incentive motivation.
10. Transitivity is a necessary quality of decision making.
11. The optimal strategy when the probability of reward varies between two alternatives is to match your response probabilities to the reward probabilities.
12. Incentive motivation affects our decisions even when we are not consciously aware that we are evaluating the alternatives.

True/False Answers

1. (False) Reward affects performance as a motivational factor. As with drive motivation, incentive motivation may be too high for efficient learning of difficult material, although this fact has not been clearly established. In any event, better rewards do not ensure better learning unless they lead to practicing better responses.

2. (True) We can correctly infer that learning has occurred only from a change in performance. However, the learning resulting from practice may be latent and not demonstrated unless the organism is motivated to demonstrate it.

3. (True) While there must be some habits upon which to base performance, behavior can be radically altered by independent changes in incentive motivation. For example, a youth may never have stolen a woman's purse before, but could be induced to do so if offered sufficient reward.

4. (False) The situations described in this chapter are those that have led to the view that rewards affect motivation rather than learning. If this view is to be adopted, it must apply to all situations involving reward or punishment.
5. (True) If the likelihood that a response will be rewarded changes from moment to moment, and if you are aware of these changes, then your incentive motivation will mirror the changes so that you respond only when appropriate.
6. (False) Whether practice makes perfect depends upon what is practiced. No amount of practice in responding slowly will lead to an ability to respond fast. Indeed, extensive practice at a slow pace may interfere with learning to respond fast later.
7. (True) In a race, whether you win, place, or show depends on how fast you run. Reward is therefore correlated with excellence, and practice under such conditions tends to lead to learning excellence.
8. (False) Decisions are required when several differences among alternatives are pitted against each other. Other animals are capable of making consistent decisions, at least in simple situations.
9. (False) People will sometimes take bets even if they have proven mathematically that they are on the losing end of the odds. Nevertheless, we assume that there is sufficient net incentive to motivate these people, perhaps contained in what is sometimes called the "utility of gambling."
10. (False) It would appear that rational decision makers would always display transitivity in their choices; each alternative has a value that determines the choice. However, lack of transitivity does sometimes occur in complex decisions.
11. (False) Organisms frequently do match response probabilities to reward probabilities, but this strategy results in less reward than if the organism always chose the most frequently rewarded alternative.
12. (True) Doing something may make us "feel better" even though we don't know why. It is the exception rather than the rule when we contemplate the alternatives; instead, we typically react automatically on the basis of past experiences of success and failure.

Essay/Discussion Questions

1. Explain the difference between a learning principle and a performance principle. Think of original examples of performance principles. (Hint: Return to the initial definition of learning.)
2. Review your behavior for the past hour or so. Identify the sources of incentive motivation that guided your decisions as to which activities to engage in at each step along the way.

References

Evidence that Reward Affects Motivation

Blodgett, H. C. The effect of the introduction of reward upon the maze performance of rats. *University of California Publications in Psychology*, 1929, *4*, 113–134.

Moltz, H. Latent extinction and the fractional anticipatory response mechanism. *Psychological Review*, 1957, *64*, 229–241.

Review of Positive Reinforcement

Logan, F. A. *Incentive*. New Haven: Yale University Press, 1960.

Other Effects of Incentive Motivation

Herrnstein, R. J. Frequency of reinforcement on relative and absolute response rate. *Journal of Experimental Analysis of Behavior*, 1961, *4*, 267.

*Padilla, A. M. Incentive and behavioral contrast. *Journal of Comparative and Physiological Psychology*, 1971, *75*, 464.

*Wyckoff, L. B. Observing response in discrimination learning. *Psychological Review*, 1952, *59*, 531.

Decision Making

Edwards, W. The theory of decision making. *Psychological Bulletin*, 1954, *51*, 380–417.

*Edwards, W. Utility, subjective probability, their interaction and variance preference. *Journal of Conflict Resolution*, 1962, *6*, 42–51.

Logan, F. A. Decision making by rats. *Journal of Comparative and Physiological Psychology*, 1965, *59*, 1–12; 246–251.

*Suitable for additional reading by the beginning student. The others are written at a more technical level.

Concluding Remarks

15

To attempt a scientific understanding of behavior is one of the most challenging undertakings in history. This book was written in the belief that the fundamentals of learning and motivation, often revealed most simply in the animal laboratory, provide a useful foundation on which to build. The thesis is that these principles *do* apply, regardless of the context in which behavior is observed. Certainly additional principles may be required to describe the full complexity of human behavior in our various personal, social, and cultural settings. Nevertheless, a reasonable approach is to apply these fundamental principles to their limit and to incorporate new ideas with the same degree of experimental rigor.

Even more important than the principles themselves is an understanding of the philosophy of a scientific approach to the analysis of behavior. The presumption is that behavior is *not* inherently mysterious, magical, or mystical. Recall that primitive people were awed by an eclipse of the sun, but the modern astronomer can predict to the minute the occurrence of an eclipse still years away. Our understanding of behavior is still primitive, but we can be confident that there is an objective explanation for everything we do.

For example, the marvels of hypnotism can be attributed to an extreme degree of susceptibility to suggestion and are thus not so radically different from the everyday influence others exert over us. Those bewildering night dreams can be viewed as meaningful by-products of the brain's restorative processes. And when a husband and wife discover that they are separately reminiscing about the same events, we may well find that unconsciously noticed stimuli in their environment have led to the same associations. We may be tantalized by unexplained phenomena, but this does not mean that they are inexplicable.

The explanation can come from a variety of sources. We are born with an unknown number of behavioral capacities, tendencies, and dispositions. We inherit our parents, our siblings, and our social group and are molded, to a great extent, by them. We live in an environment of physical and chemical substances that affect our bodies and nervous systems and, hence, our behavior. Not only do we develop specific habits for specific situations, but we tend to integrate these habits into a consistent style of life, a personality. We behave not only on the basis of our own personal experiences but also in concert with the behavior of others whose experiences have been different. Learning and motivation are but a part of psychology, which, in turn, is but a part of the total behavioral science enterprise.

Some people view the behavioral sciences as threatening to their sense of personal freedom, dignity, and responsibility. The more they learn about the principles that enable the prediction of behavior, the greater their fear that these same principles might be used to control their behavior. They may envisage an ivory tower staffed with behavioral scientists controlling everyone's destiny. This image becomes even more ominous when such control is assumed to be in the hands of malevolent people. No one likes to view oneself as being simply a puppet in a totally regimented society since such a life would have little meaning and purpose.

However, the first point to make in this context is that behavior *is* inevitably under the control of the types of forces that we have described. That is, the question is not whether our behavior is being controlled or whether we are controlling the behavior of others; the question is whether the control is based on sound scientific knowledge or whether it is haphazard, capricious, or insidious. The advantage of science is that the knowledge is public and subject to independent verification.

It is true that the deterministic thesis of science denies a "free will" with the "power" to violate natural principles. But it does not assert that people are like falling leaves, tossed around at the complete mercy of the forces of wind and gravity. This is because humans can acquire at least some degree of *self-control*. We have alluded to this in earlier chapters, but a few summarizing remarks about this concept may enrich your understanding of it and your ability to use these fundamental principles profitably.

Suppose that you were a complete novice at some activity, such as playing golf, but were motivated to learn and hence went to an instructor for lessons. The instructor begins by telling you how to grip the club, how to address the ball, and how to swing the club. She points out certain important guidelines, such as keeping your left elbow straight during the backswing and keeping your eyes on the ball until after you have hit it. During all this time, your instructor is controlling your behavior simply because you are attempting to follow her instructions, Then, after a while, she leaves you with a bucket of golf balls and tells you to keep on practicing what she has taught you.

You will almost certainly find that you start repeating her instructions to yourself. Your narrative might run something like this: "Let's see now. First, take hold of the club with your left hand so that your thumb points straight down the club shaft; now wrap the little finger of the right hand over the index finger of the left . . ." and so on. What you should realize is that you are now controlling your own behavior by telling yourself what to do. This is the essence of self-control—giving and following your own instructions.

To be sure, this is easier said than done in many situations. First, you have to know what instructions to give yourself and be motivated to give them. Second, you must know how to follow those instructions and expect appropriate reinforcement for doing so. These are all quite simple and obvious in the case of our imaginary golf lesson, and we have used that example to show that there is really nothing magical or supernatural about self-control. The analysis is conceptually the same in all situations.

Suppose there is an interesting program on television and, as you sit down to watch it, you say to yourself, "I really should be doing my homework." Through such a scene, oft repeated in many contexts, you are learning *not* to follow your own instructions. You were not born with weak (or strong) will power but you may have developed, through the fundamentals of learning and motivation, counterproductive tendencies. One superb guiding rule is this: *Never disobey yourself.* A corollary of this rule is never give yourself orders you are unable to follow. Mark Twain once said, "It's easy to quit smoking. I've done it hundreds of times." Mark Twain was admitting that he had not only had a lot of practice quitting, he had an equal amount of practice quitting quitting!

There is no more appropriate way to end this book than to emphasize that these same fundamental principles of learning and motivation that some people fear might be used to deprive them of freedom and dignity are precisely the same principles through which they can gain such freedom and dignity. Self-control is based on the habit, drive, and incentive associated with those internally directed responses by means of which we command our own destiny. Appreciating that fact makes an understanding of these principles all the more important to everyone.

Glossary

Adaptation, sensory A physiological process whereby a stimulus becomes less effective during prolonged stimulation (for example, the decrease in the cold sensation after being in a swimming pool awhile).

Attention A psychological process of selecting from among the available stimuli those to respond to (for example, listening to a lecturer rather than to distracting sounds).

Aversive event A stimulus whose termination leads to an increase in the probability of responses that preceded that termination (that is, any physically or psychologically painful event).

Avoidance learning The acquisition of a response that prevents the occurrence of an aversive event (for example, covering up the evidence of a crime to avoid the consequences).

Avoidance, nondiscriminated Responding that prevents the occurrence of an aversive event that occurs regularly but that is not preceded by a warning signal (for example, checking the water level in your car battery periodically).

Behavior chain A sequence of responses strung together to accomplish a goal (for example, shuffling and dealing cards to engage in a game).

Behavior, covert Behavior that does not qualify as a response because it is not publicly observable (for example, thinking).

Condition of reinforcement The momentary, descriptive properties of a reward, such as its amount, delay, and quality (for example, the flavor of the entrée at dinner).

Conditioning, classical A procedure in which a conditioned stimulus regularly precedes an unconditioned stimulus, the latter eliciting a response that eventually becomes conditioned to the former (for example, darkness regularly follows the sunset, which leads to the response of turning on the lights).

Conditioning, differential classical A procedure in which two similar conditioned stimuli occur in an unpredictable order, but only one is followed by the unconditioned stimulus (for example, learning to like one course in school, but not to like another).

Conditioning, differential instrumental A procedure in which a response is periodically enabled but is rewarded only in the presence of one stimulus and not in the presence of another similar stimulus (for example, learning to accept some invitations but to decline others).

Conditioning, differential operant   A procedure in which a freely available response is rewarded in the presence of one stimulus and not in the presence of another similar stimulus (for example, learning to play practical jokes on some people but not on others).

Conditioning, higher-order   A procedure in which a conditioned stimulus precedes a stimulus that elicits a response because of prior conditioning (for example, judging a person on the basis of the company he or she keeps).

Conditioning, instrumental   A procedure in which a response is periodically enabled, its speed or vigor depending on the condition of reinforcement (for example, a child learning to tie shoes).

Conditioning, operant   A procedure in which a response is freely available and its rate of occurrence depends on the schedule of reinforcement (for example, watching television).

Conditioning, temporal   A procedure in which an unconditioned stimulus occurs at regular intervals but is not preceded by a conditioned stimulus (for example, waking up just prior to the time your alarm clock is set for each morning).

Context   The general environment in which learning occurs (for example, the room, your mood, the atmosphere, and the presence of chaperones at a party).

Decision-making situation   A choice in which the reward is arranged so that each alternative has one aspect that favors it over the other alternative (for example, choosing between possible mates when physical attraction favors one and intellectual attraction favors the other).

Definition, functional   A definition based on how an object or event works (for example, "A reward is something you will work for").

Differentiation learning   Choosing a response or a way of responding based on prior differential reinforcement (for example, adjusting the pressure on the accelerator pedal to control the speed of your car).

Discrimination learning   Choosing a stimulus to respond to based on prior differential reinforcement (for example, selecting a restaurant for dinner).

Disinhibition   The reappearance of an extinguished response in the presence of an unusual context (for example, suddenly being afraid to dance with a new partner after having overcome fears of dancing with familiar partners).

Displacement   The greater tendency to respond to different stimuli than to the original stimulus itself, based on both reward and punishment to the original stimulus (for example, choosing a spouse who is somewhat, but not completely, different from the parent of the opposite sex if you have ambivalent feelings about that parent).

Drive, irrelevant   A drive that is not appropriate to the nature of the reward that has been experienced for making a response (for example, an urge to visit the bathroom while engaged in a card game).

Drive motivation   The internal source of energy driving the organism to do something, often based on biological needs (for example, the feeling of thirst after eating salted foods).

Drive, primary   Conditions that tend to arouse the organism without any special training or experience (for example, a baby crying for food after some period of deprivation).

Drive, secondary   Conditions that were originally neutral but arouse the organism as a result of prior association with aversive events (for example, fear of an examination).

Drive stimulus A distinctive internal cue that arises in conjunction with a drive, (for example, hunger pangs before dinner time).

Escape learning The acquisition of a response that leads to termination of an aversive event (for example, acquiring techniques to deal with attempted crimes such as rape and robbery).

Extinction, experimental The procedure of consistently not reinforcing a learned response, leading to a gradual decrease in response strength (for example, ignoring a child who attempts to get attention by holding his or her breath, after you have previously shown concern about this behavior).

Extinction, resistance to A measure of the number of times that a learned response persists after all reinforcement for the response is stopped (for example, the number of times required for a boy to stop calling a girl he has previously dated but who now turns him down repeatedly).

Feedback Stimuli produced by responses, both in terms of feeling the response occur and in terms of observing its effect on the environment (for example, the feelings involved in a close embrace).

Feedback, negative Feedback that tends to produce responding that will remove the feedback (for example, the feeling of anxiety, if it occurs, upon initiating any sexual activity).

Feedback, positive Feedback that tends to increase the response producing the feedback (for example, the feelings of arousal upon initiating any sexual activity).

Fixation An increase in the persistence of a response produced by punishing it (for example, continuing to dislike a quite palatable food that you were forced to eat as a child).

Forgetting A decrease in the performance of a learned response since the time of learning that is not due to any sensory, motor, or motivational change in the organism (for example, seeing a familiar face but being unable to match a name to it).

Frustration The emotional response experienced when a previously rewarded response is not rewarded (for example, the increase in a child's temper tantrum when a parent no longer responds to a milder attempt to gain attention).

Generalization, gradient of The progressive increase or decrease in the tendency to make a learned response, based on the similarity (or lack of it) between the test stimulus and the original one (for example, the relative attractiveness of women to a man who wants a girl "just like the girl that married dear old dad").

Generalization, response The tendency to make responses similar to the one learned if that one is blocked (for example, switching hands if a jar does not readily open using your preferred hand).

Generalization, semantic The tendency for humans to generalize responses to words with different sounds but similar meanings (for example, the emotions associated with words such as Mom and Mother).

Generalization, stimulus The tendency to make a learned response to stimuli that are similar to the original one (for example, transferring your familiar driving habits to an unfamiliar car).

Goal gradient The tendency for response strength to change progressively as a goal is approached (for example, the feelings you have as a final examination approaches).

Habit The theoretical term for the hypothesized internal process representing a learned association between a stimulus and response (for example, the presumed basis for your standing up and sitting down upon instruction during a ceremony).

Incentive motivation The internal source of energy based on the expectation of reward for making a particular response (for example, the hypothetical basis for deciding whether or not to continue your education in expectation of possible future rewards).

Information value The degree to which a stimulus is differentially associated with the occurrence or nonoccurrence of emotionally significant events (for example, a friend's advice about how good a movie is).

Inhibition The theoretical term for the hypothesized internal process opposing habit as a result of nonreinforcement (for example, the presumed reason you stop watching a TV show that you no longer find entertaining).

Inhibition, external The fact that a learned response is weaker in an unusual context (for example, difficulty in recalling the name of a familiar person in an unfamiliar context).

Inhibition, latent A difficulty in conditioning due to prior exposure to the conditioned stimulus without reinforcement (for example, failure to feel sympathy for a person who always complains).

Instinct A complex chain of behaviors performed without the benefit of learning (for example, feeling fear when starting to fall).

Interference, proactive More rapid forgetting of a recently learned response because of a response learned previously in a similar context (for example, forgetting the name of a recent acquaintance because of a physical resemblance to someone you knew before).

Interference, retroactive More rapid forgetting of a previously learned response because of responses learned more recently in a similar context (for example, forgetting the name of an old acquaintance because of a physical resemblance to someone you recently met).

Interval, interstimulus The interval of time between the conditioned and unconditioned stimuli in classical conditioning (for example, the time between a flash of lightning and a clap of thunder).

Interval, retention The time between the end of learning and the occasion of a test to determine whether the learned response can be performed (for example, the interval between learning this material and taking an exam over it).

Intervening variable Hypothetical events that are not publicly observable but are presumed to intervene between publicly observable events (for example, learning).

Latent learning Learning resulting from practice or experience without reward and hence not evident in performance unless incentive motivation is provided (for example, learning directions while riding in a car).

Learning A relatively permanent process resulting from experience and reflected in a change in performance under appropriate circumstances (for example, learning to introduce people meeting for the first time).

Learning set The fact that organisms can learn a new problem faster if they have had experience with other problems of the same type (for example, learning a second foreign language).

Learning, state-dependent Learning that is most evident under the same conditions that prevailed when it was acquired (for example, poor performance on a test taken when you are anxious after studying while relaxed).

Motivation Relatively temporary and reversible states of the organism that tend to energize or activate the organism.

Neurosis, experimental Maladjustive behavior in animals produced by strong conflict.

Operant level The rate at which a freely available response occurs if the consequences of that response are neutral (neither rewarding nor punishing).

Paradigm A relationship among events that describes an experimental procedure.

Punishment A procedure in which a response is followed by an aversive event.

Punishment, negative Punishment accomplished by removing something emotionally positive (for example, denying access to the family car after a traffic violation).

Punishment, positive Punishment accompanied by applying something emotionally negative (for example, a slap on the wrist—either literally or figuratively).

Receptor-orienting act The response of directing one's receptors toward a source of stimulation (for example, turning to glimpse at what is on television while you are otherwise occupied).

Reflex An automatic response to a stimulus, occurring without prior learning (for example, an eyeblink to a puff of air to the cornea).

Reinforcement Any event that increases the likelihood of the preceding response.

Reinforcement, correlated A procedure in which some quantitative dimension of the reward, such as its amount, depends upon some quantitative dimension of the response, such as its speed (for example, better grades are usually associated with greater effort).

Reinforcement, differential A procedure in which the schedule or condition of reinforcement differs between stimuli or responses.

Reinforcement, negative Reinforcement accomplished by the removal of an emotionally negative event (for example, granting parole to a prisoner for good behavior).

Reinforcement, nondifferential The procedure of giving the same schedule or condition of reinforcement to different stimuli or responses.

Reinforcement, partial The procedure of rewarding a response only occasionally (for example, rewarding oneself with the occasional pleasure of attending plays, lectures, or sports events).

Reinforcement, positive Reinforcement accomplished by giving an emotionally positive event (for example, candy or money).

Reinforcement, primary An event that functions as a reward without any special training (for example, consummation of a sex act).

Reinforcement, secondary An event that functions as a reward by virtue of having been associated with rewarding events (for example, giving praise to another person).

Response Any glandular secretion, muscular action, or other objectively identifiable aspect of the behavior of an organism (for example, laughing at a joke or crying over a misfortune).

Response alternation The tendency not to repeat the same response right away, even if it was rewarded (for example, guessing false on a true-false examination when you have given one or more preceding true answers).

Response, anticipatory   A response that antedates its original time of occurrence as a result of stimuli that precede it (for example, feeling anxious before an exam).

Response, avoidance   A response that prevents the occurrence of an aversive event (for example, any contraceptive precaution).

Response, conditioned   The learned response resulting from pairing a conditioned stimulus with an unconditioned stimulus.

Response, consummatory   An act that reduces a deprivation drive (for example, eating, drinking, or copulating).

Response, escape   A response that terminates an aversive state of affairs (for example, taking aspirin for a headache).

Response, incompatible   A response that physically cannot be performed at the same time as another response (for example, studying rather than going to the movies).

Response, instrumental   An act that is periodically enabled by the environment and that may produce reward or punishment (for example, attending a concert).

Response latency   The amount of time between the occurrence of a stimulus and the occurrence of a response.

Response, learnable   A response that can become associated with originally ineffective stimuli or that can be modified by experience (for example, saying the words "please" and "thank you").

Response, observing   A response that produces an informative stimulus (for example, turning on a television to hear the weather report).

Response, operant   A response that is freely available to the organism and that may produce reward or punishment (for example, stealing or giving at any time).

Response, unconditioned   A response elicited reflexively by an unconditioned stimulus.

Reward   A reinforcer that is emotionally positive.

Satiation, response   The reduced tendency to select a response as a result of repeated performance (for example, the reduced enthusiasm of a teacher who is required to teach the same course several years in succession).

Satiation, stimulus   The tendency to avoid responding to the same stimulus right away even if it was rewarded (for example, boredom may lead you to rearrange your room from time to time).

Schedule of reinforcement   The occasions on which an operant response is reinforced, based either on the passage of time or the counting of responses.

Schedule, continuous reinforcement   A schedule in which every response is reinforced.

Schedule, fixed-interval   A schedule in which the time between reinforcements is a constant, although one response must be made at the end of each interval to receive reward (for example, classes programmed at regular times).

Schedule, fixed-ratio   A schedule in which a constant number of responses is required to obtain reward (for example, the number of stoplights that must be negotiated on your regular route driving home).

Schedule, mixed A schedule in which two (or more) simple schedules are combined so that sometimes one is in effect and sometimes another, without any external signal informing the organism which schedule is in effect.

Schedule, multiple A schedule in which two (or more) simple schedules are combined so that sometimes one is in effect and sometimes another, with distinctive external stimuli signaling which schedule is in effect.

Schedule, variable-interval A schedule in which the time between reinforcements varies, although one response must be made at the end of each interval to receive reward (for example, mealtimes).

Schedule, variable-ratio A schedule in which a variable number of responses is required to obtain reward (for example, turning on the ignition to start a car).

Shaping The procedure of rewarding successive approximations to a desired response (for example, selectively reinforcing vocal behavior in a child learning to talk).

Spontaneous recovery The fact that an extinguished response may reappear on a subsequent presentation of the CS after a lapse of time.

Stimulus Formally, any adequate change in energy falling upon an appropriate sensory receptor. Functionally, any event that functions as such in the principles of behavior.

Stimulus, compound Multiple stimuli presented simultaneously to form a single stimulus event (for example, a person's face).

Stimulus, conditioned A stimulus that initially does not elicit the response in question but that comes to do so as a result of being paired with an unconditioned stimulus.

Stimulus generalization decrement The loss in response strength resulting from a change in the stimulus situation (for example, lower academic performance when first transferring to a new course).

Stimulus-memory trace The hypothesized events in the nervous system that result when an organism is stimulated and that persist for some time after the stimulus is removed.

Stimulus, unconditioned A stimulus that reflexively elicits a response.

Superstition A response learned because it has been adventitiously followed by a reward, even though it did not actually produce the reward.

Theory, scientific A set of hypotheses about the inner workings of a system.

Transposition The tendency to select from among new stimuli on the basis of the relationship previously reinforced (for example, changing keys in music).

Transitivity A property according to which preferences are ranked in a consistent order (for example, if you like steak more than chicken and chicken more than liver, you must like steak more than liver).

Index